Innovative China

Innovative China

New Drivers of Growth

World Bank Group

**Development Research Center of the
State Council, the People's Republic of China**

 Washington, DC

Contents

Boxes

Figures

Tables

Foreword

Four decades ago, Deng Xiaoping initiated the reform and opening-up of China's economy with his famous speech, "Emancipate the mind, seek truth from fact, and unite as one to face the future." Since then, China has witnessed one of the most remarkable periods of sustained growth anywhere in the world, lifting 850 million Chinese people out of poverty. China achieved this growth by investing in its infrastructure and people, expanding the role of markets, and welcoming foreign trade and investments. Reforms were often gradual, pragmatic, and experimental, taking advantage of local pilots before expanding new policies to other regions. Through such reforms, China transformed itself from a predominantly rural, agricultural economy to an industrialized global manufacturing hub and the second-largest economy in the world.

China is now at a crossroads in its development. Rapid industrialization, urbanization, and efficiency gains resulting from four decades of reform and opening-up are no longer sufficient to sustain past growth rates. Declining returns to public investment, a rapidly aging population, and a less favorable international environment add to the urgency of finding new drivers of economic development. China's leadership is fully aware of this challenge. To this end, the Development Research Center (DRC) of the State Council, the Ministry of Finance (MOF), and the World Bank Group (WBG) initiated a joint research program on the new drivers of growth in China's economic transition era. Researchers from the DRC and the WBG worked together for more than two years to analyze China's main development challenges and to propose a new set of policy and institutional reforms. Joint teams were established to work on economic growth and productivity, innovation and technology, human capital development and the labor market, entrepreneurship and competition, industrial upgrading, regional integration and development, global integration and international competitiveness, and governance and institutions.

The teams have held a series of workshops over the past two years, with participation by DRC and WBG experts, as well as domestic and international researchers. Domestic and international study tours were conducted, surveys and focus group discussions with enterprises were carried out, and numerous background papers and case studies were commissioned. Lessons were drawn from China's own experiences, as well as international ones. The focus was on developing pragmatic policy recommendations that could be implemented within China's specific institutional context.

A key conclusion from this report is that boosting productivity will be key to China's future growth prospects and innovation, and that market competition will need to drive productivity-led growth. This effort, in turn, will require addressing three "D's": reducing *Distortions* in the allocation of resources; accelerating *Diffusion* of existing advanced technologies and innovations to take advantage of China's large remaining potential for catch-up growth; and fostering *Discovery* of new technologies, products, and processes to push out China's own production possibility frontier. To promote the three D's, the report identifies six major policy choices and recommends structural and policy reforms in seven key areas. Together they form the proposed "3+6+7" reform agenda.

This report, *Innovative China: New Drivers of Growth,* is the fruit of extensive debate and discussion with the objective of reaching a consensus. The value of a joint study was precisely to foster mutual understanding and a better appreciation of China's institutional realities. The joint study process also informed DRC's internal advice to the government and fed into the preparation of the WBG's new strategy for China.

We hope the report will help guide China's policy makers on the appropriate growth strategy going forward. We also believe that it can provide useful insights to other countries looking to promote innovation and boost productivity in their economies. The success of China's growth strategy, and the policies adopted to achieve it, matter for the international community. We hope that the this report will serve as an evidence-based contribution to an ongoing debate of considerable global significance.

Ma Jiantang
Party Secretary and Vice President
(Minister in charge)
Development Research Center of the
State Council, P. R. China

Victoria Kwakwa
East Asia and Pacific
Regional Vice President
World Bank Group

Acknowledgments

Innovative China is a joint report by China's Development Research Center of the State Council (DRC), China's Ministry of Finance (MOF), and the World Bank and International Finance Corporation (IFC) of the World Bank Group (WBG). A high-level joint steering committee provided the oversight for the report. Members of the Steering Committee were former Minister Jie Xiao, former Minister Jiwei Lou, Minister Kun Liu, former Vice Minister Yaobin Shi, and Vice Minister Jiayi Zhou (all of the MOF for the Government of China), former President Wei Li, Party Secretary and Vice President (Minister in charge) Jiantang Ma, Vice President Junkuo Zhang, and Vice President Guoqiang Long (all of DRC); and former President Jim Yong Kim, Chief Executive Officer Kristalina Georgieva, IFC Chief Executive Officer Philippe H. Le Houerou, East Asia and Pacific (EAP) Regional Vice President Victoria Kwakwa, and East Asia and Pacific (EAP) Vice President Ceyla Pazarbasioglu (all of the WBG).

The chief directors for the report were Party Secretary and Vice President (Minister in charge) Jiantang Ma of DRC, Minister Kun Liu of MOF, former President Jim Yong Kim of the WBG, and IFC Chief Executive Officer Philippe H. Le Houerou. The executive heads of the report were Vice President Junkuo Zhang and Vice President Guoqiang Long of

DRC; Former Vice Minister Yaobin Shi and Vice Minister Jiayi Zhou of MOF; and EAP Regional Vice President Victoria Kwakwa, World Bank China Country Director Martin Raiser, and IFC China Country Manager Randall Riopelle (all of the WBG). Former World Bank China Country Director Bert Hofman and former IFC Chief Economist Ted Haoquan Chu were former executive heads. The main technical coordinators for DRC were Mingjie Ma, Wei Lyu, Changwen Zhao, and Jun Ma. For the World Bank, the Task Team Leader was Hoon Sahib Soh.

Joint DRC and WBG teams were responsible for preparing the main report's eight themes. A series of joint workshops discussed the analytical findings and policy recommendations, with participation from international experts. The teams consulted relevant government agencies, including the Ministry of Foreign Affairs (MFA), Ministry of Finance (MOF), the National Development and Reform Commission (NDRC), the Ministry of Science and Technology (MOST), Ministry of Education (MOE), Ministry of Industry and Information Technology (MIIT), Ministry of Human Resources and Social Security (MHRSS), Ministry of Commerce (MOC), People's Bank of China (PBOC), the State-Owned Assets Supervision and Administration Commission of the State Council

(SASAC), the National Bureau of Statistics (NBS), the State Intellectual Property Office (SIPO), and several nongovernmental organizations, including the Organisation for Economic Co-operation and Development (OECD), World Intellectual Property Organization (WIPO), and McKinsey Global Institute. A study tour of Singapore and the Republic of Korea were conducted to learn about policies to support productivity and innovation. Extensive consultations with private sector representatives included focus group discussions and a new survey of entrepreneurs carried out for the report. A new enterprise survey was also carried out for the report.

The report was prepared by a joint team comprising Mingjie Ma, Changsheng Chen, Yongzhi Hou, Changwen Zhao, Wei Lyu, Qi Zhang, Jun Ma, Shiji Gao, Sen Gong, and Peilin Liu of DRC, and Hoon Sahib Soh, Lin (Amanda) Yang and Jian Chan (consultant) of the World Bank, under the guidance of the executive heads of the report. Eight joint DRC-WBG teams worked on specific research themes.

The team on growth and productivity was composed of Changsheng Chen, Guangpu Yang, Jianwu He, Wei Xu, and Chengjian Li of DRC; and John Litwack, Elitza Mileva, and Luan Zhao of the WBG. Critical contributions were provided by Loren Brandt, Luhang Wang, and Yifan Zhang (all consultants) on firm-level productivity analysis; Richard Herd (consultant) on sectoral capital stock analysis; and Min Zhao (WBG) on subnational government policy. Huitian Bai and Peng Zhou provided excellent research assistance. Lin Yang provided excellent administrative support.

The team on innovation and digital economy was composed of Wei Lyu, Mingjie Ma, Jietang Tian, Jianjun Dai, and Hongru Xiong of DRC; and Denis Medvedev and Marcin Piatkowski of the WBG. Critical contributions were provided by Ge Wang and Baoming Chen (Chinese Academy of Science and Technology for Development); Shahid Yusuf and Philipp Boeing (consultants) each separately on innovation policy; Banning Garrett (consultant), Victor Mulas, and Anastasia Nedayvoda (WBG) on disruptive technologies; Stefan Beisswenger, Xavier Cirera, Marcio Cruz, and Gregor Schueler (WBG) on technology adoption; Ari van Assche and Jo van Biesebroeck (WBG) on importing and productivity; Mingzuo Sun, L. Colin Xu, and Xiaobo Zhang (WBG) on regional patents and growth; Danqing Zhu (WBG) on STI indicators; Justin Hill, Ruimin Pei, Juan Rogers, and Hua Shen (WBG) on the innovation policy mix; Dan Prud'homme and Zhang Taolue (WBG) on intellectual property rights; and Qursum Qasim and Lin Shi (WBG) on firm-level case studies. Yu Shang provided excellent administrative support.

The team on human capital development and the labor market was composed of Seng Gong, Lihui Liu, Bingzi Zhang, Dandan Dong, Weijing Wang, Ruoyun Hua, Fei Teng, Ting Shao, Lu Yu, and Yu Zhouof of DRC, and Omar Arias, Elena Glinskaya, Maheshwor Shrestha, Ning Fu, and Dewen Wang of the WBG. Critical contributions were provided by Yong Guo and Fei Shi (Tsinghua University) and John Giles (WBG) on analysis of the returns to college and turnover; Albert Park (HKUST) and Yang Du (Chinese Academy of Social Sciences) on analysis of the task content of Chinese jobs; Jin Song (Chinese Academy of Social Science) on background research on returns to college; and Samer Al-Samarrai on education spending inputs (WBG). Xichen Li (consultant) provided excellent research assistance. Helpful comments were provided by Harry Patrinos, Philip B. O'Keefe, John Giles, Dandan Chen, Josefina Posadas, Amer Hasan, and Yang Huang (WBG).

The team on entrepreneurship and competition was composed of Jun Ma, Yongwei Zhang, Dongming Yuan, Shuping Ma, Xiaobai Ma, Chenghui Zhang, and Hongming Zhu of DRC, and Chunlin Zhang and Justin Hill of the WBG. Critical contributions were provided by Jianfeng Wu (University of International Business and Economics) on the entrepreneurship survey and the associated discussion; Mariana Iootty De Paiva Dias (WBG) on entrepreneurial support, market competition, and state-owned enterprise reforms; Shanthi Divakaran (WBG) on the venture capital industry; Sylvia Solf and Andres Federico Martinez (WBG) on the business climate; Ana María Avileés, Jeff Chelsky, Sergio Schmukler, and Radu Tatucu (WGB) on the financial sector; and W. Bernard Drum on the case study of U.S. Rust Belt cities. The team is grateful for inputs from Qursum Qasim, Nan Jiang, Facundo Abraham, Jennifer Chien, Lin Huang, Juan Jose Cortina, and Seidu Dauda (all WBG), and from Patrick McGinnis, Qiong Zhang, Jing Zhao, Yi Yan, Yaxin Yan, Anqing Shi, Lin Ma, Yifan Wei, Xinze Yao, and Anne Ong Lopez (all WBG consultants). The survey of entrepreneurs in the five cities was conducted by a team at Beijing Horizonkey Information and Data Co., Ltd., led by Hui Zhang. In the financial market section, comments and suggestions were received from Daofu Chen, Xingchen Zheng, Gang Wang, Junsheng Zhu, and Yang Wang (all DRC), and from John Litwack, Rozani Osman, Ran Tao, and Luan Zhao (WBG). Nan Zhou (WBG) provided valuable statistical support. Jian Chen (consultant) and Changyi Shao (WBG) supported the dialogue with counterparts and relevant stakeholders. Administrative support was provided by Qiujing Yang.

The team on industrial upgrading was composed of Changwen Zhao, Jianlong Yang, Zhaoyuan Xu, Wei Wang, Tao Liu, and Yunhua Zhang of DRC, and Mary Hallward-Driemeier and Gaurav Nayyar of the WBG. Critical inputs were provided by Sebastian Saez and Ruchita Manghnani (WBG) and Erik Van der Marel (consultant) on the services sector and the digital policies; Madhur Gautam, Paavo Eliste, and Jianwen Liu (WBG) on the agriculture sector; Jun Zhao (consultant) on rural surplus labor analysis; Chao Peng (Research Center for Rural Economy, Ministry of Agriculture and Rural Affairs) and Chen Zhang (Renmin University of China) on agriculture analysis; Prof. Binkai Chen (Central University of Finance and Economics) on the upgrading of the manufacturing sector; Jiechang Xia, Yi Liu, and Hongfu Ni (Chinese Academy of Social Science) on services sector analysis and statistical support; and Sugandha Huria and Wei Meng.

The team on regional integration and development was composed of Yongzhi Hou, Peilin Liu, Yunzhong Liu, Zhiyan Sun, and Jianwu He of DRC, and Somik Lall and Joanna Mclean Masic of the WBG. Other authors who provided key inputs to the chapters include Barjor E. Mehta, Binyam Reja, Wanli Fang, Hua Tan, Ted Chu, and Rana Karadsheh (all WBG). Critical contributions came from Uwe Deichmann on the spatial distribution of economic activity; Prof. Vernon Henderson, Prof. Siqi Zhang, and Prof. Qinghua Zheng on the misallocation analytics; Kevin Chen and Xiaobo Zhang (International Food Policy Research Institute, Beijing) on the Yangtze River Economic Belt analytics; Yao Zhao on the regional case studies; Ziming Liu on transport analytics; and Qiliang Mao, Guohua Zhang, Yanming Jin, and Tiezhi Liu on infrastructure analytics. The authors would like to acknowledge Xiao Wu for operational support.

The team on global integration and international competitiveness was composed of Qi Zhang, Jinpin Zhao, Gang Lyu, Yuze Luo, and Fangyu Zong of DRC, and Daria Taglioni (IFC) and Jakob Engel of the WBG. The team acknowledges contributions from Kunfu Zhu and Jianwu He on global value chain (GVC) analysis; Timothy Sturgeon and Eric Thun on the case studies of China's automobile and information and communication technology hardware sectors; Smita Kuriakose, Joanna Lewis, Jeremy Tamanini, and Shahid Yusuf on the case studies of China's solar, wind, and energy sectors; Claire Hollweg on trade vulnerability analysis; Maryla Maliszewska and Fan Zhai on computable general equilibrium analysis; Jose Ramon Perea, Nadia Rocha, Matthew Stephenson, Gonzalo Varela, Alvaro Espitia, and Laura Gomez-Mera on foreign direct investment (FDI) economic analysis; Ramprakash Sethuramasubbu on FDI legal regulatory analysis; Chunlin Zhang on Belt and Road Initiative analysis; Mauricio Monteiro Vieira and Yiren Fund (WBG) on environmental and social safeguards; Bernard Aritua (WBG) on trade logistics; Nicola Spatafora (International Monetary Fund) and José Romero (consultant) on manufacturing export quality; and Masud Cader and Kirstin Roster (International Finance Corporation, IFC), as well as Yi Yao and Edward M. Logan (consultants), on the analysis of export complexity. Administrative support from Cynthia Abidin-Saurman, Jian Chen, and Yu Shang is gratefully acknowledged. The team also thanks Kippy Ye (IFC consultant) for his invaluable support in coordinating industry and policy maker interviews in Beijing, Shanghai, Guangzhou, and Shenzhen in March–April 2017.

The team on governance and institutions was composed of Shiji Gao, Zuojun Li, Jiwen Chang, Xiaowei Xuan, and Haiqin Wang of DRC, and Jurgen Blum and Min Zhao of the WBG. Other authors who provided key inputs to the chapters include Yun Wei (Beijing Urban-Rural Innovation Development Ph.D. Association), Xijun Zhao (Chinese Academy of Sciences), Shunkui Huang (Shenzhen Dapeng New District Management Committee), David Bulman, Mary Gallagher, Andrea Renda, Peter Farup Ladegaard, and Roy Bahl (WBG). Critical contributions were provided by Xun Yan and Qiong Zhang.

On the digital economy, critical contributions were provided by Deepak K. Mishra and Bradley Robert Larson (digital diffusion and adoption), Natasha Beschorner (digital economy and the telecommunications sector); Randeep Sudan (digital economy), Prasanna Lal Das (digital data policy on digital economy), and Erik Van der Marel (digital trade policies).

Peer reviewers of the report were Chong-En Bai, professor of economics and Executive Associate Dean of the School of Economics and Management, Tsinghua University; William Maloney, EFI Chief Economist of the World Bank; Marianne Fay, former Sustainable Development (SD) Chief Economist of the World Bank; and Roberta Gatti, Human Development (HD) Chief Economist of the World Bank.

Overall coordination for the technical work was provided by Mingjie Ma, Wei Lyu, Changwen Zhao, and Jun Ma of DRC, and Hoon Sahib Soh and Jian Chen (consultant) for the World Bank. Support for coordination and management of the work was provided by Hongru Xiong and Minghui Wang of DRC, and Lin Yang and Yu Shang of the WBG. Luan Zhao (WBG) provided overall analytical support in updating estimates and figures. Harold Luis Bedoya and Zoubida Allaoua, World Bank country program coordinator (CPC) and former CPC for China, respectively, provided valuable advice for the report. Tianshu Chen (WBG) provided interpretation support for the project. Zhihong Hao (WBG) managed the World Bank's budget for the report. Kathryn Ann Funk and Yingnan Jia provided coordination support in the Washington, DC, headquarters of the World Bank. Patricia Katayama and Susan Graham managed the publication of the English version of the report.

Executive Summary

The need for new drivers of growth

After nearly four decades of rapid growth, China has entered a new normal of slower growth. China's economy is growing at some 6–7 percent a year, which remains high by the standards of most middle-income economies, and per capita gross domestic product (GDP) stands at nearly US$10,000, about one-fourth of the average for Organisation for Economic Co-operation and Development (OECD) countries. China has considerable room for further catch-up growth. The experience of other countries suggests that the recent slowdown was to be expected at China's current level of income. Only a few economies have maintained growth rates around 7 percent for another decade after reaching China's current per capita income level.

China's next transformation is well under way, and a "new economy" is emerging. China maintains a strong manufacturing base and is the leading global exporter of manufactured goods and one of the central hubs of the global value chain. Its export products are becoming increasingly more sophisticated, and the share of domestic, value-added exports has been rising steadily in the past decade, as domestic supply chains have deepened. The quality of China's manufacturing exports is improving rapidly, and its manufacturing "fitness," a measure of manufacturing capability, is at par with that of high-income economies. Furthermore, services have taken over manufacturing as the largest share of GDP and are now the largest contributor to GDP growth. Meanwhile, domestic consumption, rather than investment, is the main driver of demand, thanks to a growing middle class and rising urbanization.

China's innovation capabilities are growing rapidly, reducing the gap with leading OECD countries. China's ranking on indexes such as the global innovation index has risen steadily and is now the highest among developing countries. The number of domestic patents filed for inventions has increased to an annual 1.56 million (2018), the highest in the world, although the quality of patents remains uneven. China's spending on research and development (R&D) has risen significantly, reaching 2.18 percent of GDP in 2018, compared with the OECD average of 2.4 percent. China's total spending on R&D accounts for around 20 percent of the world's total, second only to the United States. China is among the global leaders in technologies such as e-commerce, artificial intelligence, fintech, high-speed trains, renewable energy, and electric cars. Companies such as Alibaba, Didi Chuxing,

Huawei, and Tencent are operating at the global technology frontier.

China's growing human capital is supporting its innovation capabilities. China runs one of the world's largest education systems, with more than 7 million students graduating from its universities (in 2017), of whom more than 40 percent are in science, technology, engineering, and mathematics. China is second only to the United States in the number of journal publications, and their quality—as measured by the number of citations—continues to improve. China's leading universities are climbing up the global rankings and are producing a growing volume of high-quality research. The country is turning into a research base for global technology companies, such as IBM and Microsoft. China's emergence as an increasingly important innovator is expanding the global stock of knowledge and technologies that can benefit all countries. Despite this progress, China ranks 44th on the World Bank's human capital index (2018), indicating significant potential for improvement. Less than 20 percent (2017) of China's labor force has completed tertiary education, compared with 30–40 percent in OECD countries, and the share of researchers in the labor force is still well below that of OECD countries.

China's productivity challenge

China's productivity growth has been slowing since the global financial crisis and has remained relatively low, despite signs of modest recovery in recent years. Since the crisis, China's growth in total factor productivity (TFP), a broad measure of how productively an economy uses capital and labor, has declined. This decline matters because China's TFP is currently only about half the level of OECD countries, which means that significant potential remains for TFP to be a major driver of future growth. Firm-level data suggest that productivity growth has been slowing due to declining contributions from the entry of new firms and from within-firm productivity increases. The reallocation of resources to more productive firms, including through the exit of less competitive firms,

made a negligible contribution to productivity growth both before and after the global financial crisis. By contrast, the reallocation of resources is typically the main source of productivity growth in high-income economies. China is not alone in the productivity slowdown; the decline in TFP growth following the global financial crisis has been widespread across developed and developing countries alike.

China's old drivers of growth are running out of steam. In the past decades, China benefited from a rapid structural transformation from agriculture to manufacturing and services, high levels of investments, demographic dividends, and rapid rural-urban migration. China can no longer rely on those old drivers of growth. High investment rates have increased China's capital stock, and public sector capital stock per worker has reached OECD levels. Therefore, additional capital investments are likely to add less to growth, and the challenge now is to address sectoral bottlenecks to the effective use of existing infrastructure assets. The allocation of credit appears to have become less efficient since the global financial crisis, because an increasing share of commercial credit has gone to infrastructure and real estate, which has had a declining impact on growth. High investment rates also have resulted in the rapid accumulation of debt, raising financial vulnerabilities in the economy. Demographic dividends are reversing, as China's labor force is set to decline in the coming years and also to age considerably. Employment contributed 2.9 percentage points to GDP growth in the two decades following 1978, almost a third of total GDP growth, but that contribution fell to 0.3 percentage point in the past 10 years and is expected to be negative in the years ahead. The reallocation of labor from agriculture to industry has been a major driving force of China's economic growth, but rural surplus labor has declined considerably and will continue to decline.

China's authorities are fully aware of the need to develop new sources of growth. Innovation and productivity are recognized as important sources of growth in the 5th Plenum of the Central Committee of the 18th

Party Congress, the 13th Five-Year Plan, and the Secretary General's report to the 19th Party Congress. The authorities believe that markets should play a decisive role in allocating resources and that the government's role should be to support the markets. China places a high priority on strengthening domestic capacity for innovation, science and technology, and R&D, and on promoting the transformation and upgrading of its manufacturing industry, particularly by deepening the application of Internet-related technologies and developing smart manufacturing.

A strategic reform agenda for promoting an innovative and productive China

China will need to promote new drivers of growth to address its major challenges to productivity. Sustained growth in the long run will depend on continuous productivity growth. This report proposes the "3+6+7" reform agenda for addressing China's productivity challenges and achieving long-term sustained growth:

- China's future growth will come from **3** D's: removing *distortions*, accelerating *diffusion*, and fostering *discovery*.
- China's authorities are facing **6** strategic choices in furthering productivity and innovation.
- China's authorities will need to address **7** critical areas of structural and institutional reforms.

The three D's

China can pursue more innovative and productivity-led growth by addressing the three D's: removing *distortions*, accelerating *diffusion*, and fostering *discovery* (figure ES.1). The first D, reducing distortions in the allocation of resources, has been a key driver of growth in the past, and continuing reforms would allow China to reach its current maximum potential production frontier. The first D requires land, labor, and financial resources to be allocated competitively and efficiently to their most productive uses in the economy.

FIGURE ES.1   The 3 D's Framework—Reducing Distortions, accelerating Diffusion, fostering Discovery

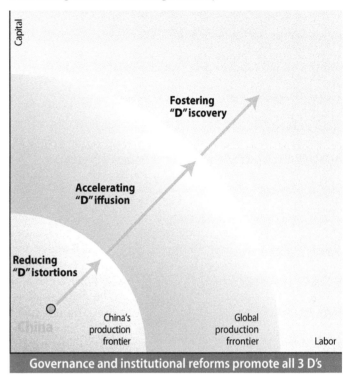

The second D, accelerating the diffusion of advanced technologies and innovations, will help China to extend its current production frontier to the global frontier. Accelerating diffusion would allow China to take advantage of its large remaining potential for catch-up growth by promoting technology diffusion, upgrading the capacity of its workers to adopt and use new technologies, and facilitating access to global technologies and innovations.

The third and last D, fostering the discovery of new innovation and technology, will help China to create new innovations and to push out the global technology frontier. Fostering discovery will become more critical as China becomes richer and edges closer to the global technology frontier.

Governance and institutional reforms underpin the promotion of all three D's. As the economy grows and becomes more complex, the market will assume a greater importance, and the state will acquire a more market-supportive role in promoting market competition and strengthening the business climate.

Six strategic choices

China's policy makers face several strategic choices that will promote the three D's and determine the country's future growth performance. This report identifies six strategic priorities.

Striking the right balance between the three drivers of growth

China's recent policies have emphasized the third D, fostering discovery and new technologies. Investments in new technologies can have a large payoff for the country and contribute to pushing out the global technology frontier. New technology fields are also less crowded than more established ones, providing new opportunities to take a leading position. At the same time, China remains, on average, quite distant from the global technology frontier and thus has substantial remaining potential for catch-up growth. China could double its GDP simply by catching up to OECD countries in its TFP. To take advantage of catch-up growth, China needs to pay sufficient attention to the first and second D's: reducing distortions in the allocation of productive resources and promoting the diffusion and adoption of existing technologies, production processes, and management practices. The first and second D's are likely to produce significant payoffs for China's immediate future and will remain the main drivers of growth for some time to come.

Reshaping industrial policies

Since its early years of reforms and opening up, China has used industrial policies to accelerate its catching up to high-income economies. Those policies often were modeled on examples from other economies, such as Japan and the Republic of Korea, although the outcomes in China, as elsewhere, have been mixed. China is now at a more advanced stage of development and needs to consider a new approach to industrial policies. Within China, industrial policies can undermine market competition when markets are protected, and favored firms benefit from targeted support, contributing to persistent overcapacity. The consensus in developed countries is that, to be effective, industrial policies need to focus on market failures and to be market conforming and enhancing. Industrial policies that leverage and promote market competition are particularly important for China, given its large state presence.

Adjusting the balance between the state and markets

The strategic choice is for the state to be less market interventionist and more market supportive and augmenting. In China, state-owned enterprises (SOEs) are at the core of the coexistence between the state and the market. SOEs will retain an important role in China's economy, but ensuring fair competition between SOEs and non-SOEs would expose firms to competitive pressure and encourage markets to select the most productive enterprises, regardless of their ownership structure.

Attaining mutually beneficial international trade and investment relations with global partners

Global trade tensions have brought uncertainty and downside risks to the global economy. A major risk is the potential weakening of the rules governing global trade and investment and the unraveling of global value chains. As the world's largest trader and second-largest economy, China can play an important role in working with global partners to achieve a common understanding of mutually beneficial global economic relations. China has stated its opposition to protectionism and advocates an open and inclusive global economic system and international partnerships and collaborations. It has taken steps to open up its economy further, such as the recent introduction of the foreign investment negative list, which is the list of sectors in which foreign direct investment (FDI) is restricted or prohibited. With China's rise as a global economic and trading power, its contribution to the multilateral rules for global governance will be critical.

Balancing supply-side reforms with demand-side reforms

China will need to rely less on investments and more on consumption for growth, while maintaining robust overall aggregate demand. Historically, domestic household consumption has played a relatively small role in driving China's growth, reflecting its high savings rate. But China's consumption share in the economy is already growing, and the government can accelerate this growth by encouraging lower household saving through reforms, such as reinforcing the social safety net, pension system, and health insurance and introducing more progressive income taxes to lower the burden on labor. Reforms of the household registration (*hukou*) system would further enhance aggregate demand by further integrating migrants, now some 15 percent of the urban population, into the urban system.

Preparing for the future impact of technological changes

Policy makers need to start preparing China's workers today for the future impact of technology on the workplace. The impact of new technology on jobs, income, and income distribution may be gradual as technologies are developed and diffused, but preparing for the future workplace needs to start now. New technologies and innovations can result in new employment opportunities, but many current jobs may be displaced or require new skills due to automation and artificial intelligence. Technological change has a skills bias, favoring workers with more skills and education, which could lead to rising income inequality. Moreover, recent technological innovations could lead to a "winner takes all" outcome, which further exacerbates inequality. Medium-skill routine jobs, many in manufacturing, are at particular risk of automation. Finally, the share of labor in a broad range of economies has declined in recent decades, part of which can be explained by technological change.

Seven areas of structural and institutional reforms

Addressing China's key strategic challenges to promoting the three D's requires a range of structural, governance, and institutional reforms. The proposed reform agenda is organized into seven major areas.

Reshaping industrial policies and supporting market competition

China could reduce "vertical" industrial policies that target specific sectors and firms, and instead transition to more "horizontal" policies that improve factor markets and the broader business environment and promote market competition. The remaining targeted industrial policies, to be efficient and effective, need to be focused on market failures, such as information asymmetry and externalities. This focus would require using industrial policy more selectively by targeting only a few "strategic" industries. In such industries, support would be made available to all firms rather than to just a few firms. China could further strengthen the discipline of local governments' support for industries—for example, by clearly regulating the limits of local government support and incorporating performance criteria and sunset clauses for discontinuing support. A more active market-led corporate bankruptcy regime would promote the timely discontinuation of government support and facilitate the exit of nonviable firms. Finally, China could systematically expand government-industry dialogue and the monitoring and evaluation of industrial policies to make policy support more transparent and accountable.

Opening more sectors to private and foreign investment would promote greater competition. The government's recent introduction of a negative list for private and foreign investment is a welcome move in this direction. Increasing competition is particularly beneficial for the services sector, where China's market restrictions are greater than those of OECD countries. Further opening the services sector to private and foreign investments also would facilitate the "servicification" of manufacturing (the integration of services and manufacturing), which is currently lower than in higher-income countries, and thereby strengthen China's manufacturing competitiveness.

Reducing market restrictions will be critical to the government's "Mass Entrepreneurship" Initiative, launched in 2015. The enterprise survey carried out for this report indicated that reducing regulations and improving the local business climate would support entrepreneurship more than providing support for firms through government subsidies or financing. China could carry out comprehensive reforms to improve the business climate and the local innovation and entrepreneurship ecosystems. It could develop and publish subnational business climate indicators to support efforts to assess and compare local entrepreneurship ecosystems. A high-level oversight body could coordinate the business climate reforms and institutionalize regular private sector consultations. China also could consider establishing a National Center of Excellence for Entrepreneurship Promotion Policy, dedicated to analyzing, developing, and disseminating entrepreneurship promotion policies.

SOE reforms would complement the improvement of the business climate and the promotion of market competition by helping to ensure fair competition—long advocated in China. China could introduce a formal state ownership policy for SOEs that would articulate the purpose of state ownership and focus the SOEs in strategic sectors. The government could prioritize corporate governance reforms of commercial SOEs and further expose them to market competition. Corporate governance reforms and the "mixed-ownership" reforms initiative, which increases nonstate equity in SOEs, are mutually reinforcing and would promote improved performance of the SOEs.

Competitive neutrality would be supported by full implementation of the government's "fair competition review," launched in 2016. This would help to ensure that competition policy is provided a "fundamental position" in economic policy making. China also could improve the enforcement of competition policies by increasing the capacity of the competition regulatory agency, the State Administration for Market Regulation (SAMR), established in 2018, and providing it with more independent authority.

Promoting innovation and the digital economy

China has built a large and extensive national innovation system, but the system could be improved further in several ways. China's top-down approach to promoting innovation could be complemented with a more bottom-up, market-oriented, and decentralized approach by expanding R&D tax credits and other innovation support programs that are open to all industries. This would help to ensure that the country does not miss out on innovations outside the areas of policy focus or misidentify the industries and technologies of the future. More public R&D support could be reoriented to basic "blue sky" research to complement private R&D and to help address China's relatively low share of R&D devoted to basic research. China also could expand its global innovation partnerships and R&D collaborations to ensure that the government's promotion of "indigenous" innovation does not result in technologies that are only relevant in China.

Strengthening the national innovation system requires not only promoting the discovery of new innovations (the third D) but also supporting the dissemination and adoption of existing innovations and technologies (the second D). Given the importance of management capacity for the adoption and diffusion of technology, the government could expand technology-oriented management extension programs. The programs could provide benchmarking assessments of a firm's managerial performance, given that firms often overestimate their capabilities, and therefore do not invest to improve their managerial capacity. Such programs could be complemented by demand-based instruments, such as matching grants and innovation vouchers, to promote the collaboration of small and medium enterprises (SMEs) and knowledge providers. Recently, high-income countries have used shared technology libraries and collaboration platforms to facilitate technology exchanges and innovative networking.

The government recognizes the importance of protecting intellectual property (IP) rights for promoting innovation. To strengthen IP rights, China could increase the damages and fines for IP infringements; address judicial "local protectionism" (unfair handling of court and administrative enforcement cases to protect local firms) by moving more court cases to out-of-area jurisdictions, including to the specialized IP courts; centrally monitor and limit unfair court rulings and expand the publication of court cases; and strengthen the capacity of the courts and relevant administrative agencies and improve interagency coordination to handle the significant increase in the number of patents.

China's promotion of patents has been quite successful, as China is now the world's largest producer of patents. Rather than focusing on the quantity of patents, China can now focus on improving the uneven quality of its patents by making eligibility for government financial support of patenting more stringent and dependent on the quality of patents. It also could shift the focus of government financial incentives from reducing the costs of patenting to promoting services that make patents commercially valuable, such as services related to patent evaluation and due diligence, marketing and feasibility studies, and proofs of concept. This focus could be part of an overall reorientation of patent promotion policies to broader aspects of investments in innovation. China is currently drafting a new patent law. The draft patent law proposes welcoming provisions that extend the protection for design, increase the damages for infringement, and address indirect infringement. Some of the provisions may need further consultation and piloting before full adoption, including the proposed expansion of the power of local administrative IP enforcement authorities. The government also could consider extending the stronger treatment of patent infringement to trade secrets.

Digital technology is critical to China's developing innovation capacity. China has prioritized digital innovations and aims to become a global leader in key emerging digital technologies, such as artificial intelligence. But China still has significant potential to promote the diffusion of existing digital technologies, as its rate of digital adoption lags that of OECD countries, although it is higher than that of many other upper-middle-income countries. To promote digital innovations, China could facilitate the trade and flow of data by making digital policies more open and less restrictive, including with regard to the requirements for data localization and cybersecurity. More open data policies could facilitate cross-border traffic of innovation and data, which is now a key aspect of global trade. China also could engage more actively in global cooperation and seek a global solution regarding data policies and standards, for example, by working with other countries to develop World Trade Organization (WTO) rules governing data in commerce.

Telecommunications infrastructure provides the infrastructure for digital services. China has made good progress in expanding access to telecommunications services, and now it could focus on improving the quality of services, such as improving access to faster broadband. Quality improvements could be achieved through greater market competition. In this regard, China could accelerate and expand pilots of market liberalization, for instance, in the pilot free trade zones. China also could reorient the regulatory framework for the telecommunications sector toward a greater emphasis on the quality of services and public accountability for performance—for example, by expanding the monitoring and evaluation of sector performance and publicly disclosing data on operational performance. China also could consider enhancing the independence of regulatory authorities, including by further separating the government's regulatory functions from its ownership interests and policy making.

Building human capital

The quality of China's human capital, not the quantity, will increasingly be the cornerstone of its economy. To sustain productivity and innovation-driven growth, China will need to shift investments increasingly from physical capital to human capital. To achieve this, China could develop a new education sector strategy that is focused on developing a workforce for an innovative China that is prepared for the future workplace. The future workplace will be shaped increasingly by technology and will demand nonroutine, cognitive, and interactive social skills. Jobs requiring routine skills will be taken over increasingly by technology. To prepare for this new future, China's new education strategy could highlight the following five major priorities.

First, China could address the remaining regional and socioeconomic disparities in educational attainment to build the universal foundational skills of all its students. This effort is critical because China needs to maximize the productivity of each worker as the size of its workforce declines. It needs to support disadvantaged individuals who fail to acquire critical foundational skills through the basic education system. To achieve this, China would need to close the investment disparities in education and learning for early childhood and compulsory primary education, especially for rural areas, migrants, and "left-behind" children. More than half of China's future labor force is being educated in rural areas and small towns and counties, which significantly lag urban areas in educational performance. China also could focus on providing adequate nutrition and health to disadvantaged children to help ensure their full cognitive development and well-being.

Second, China could consider gradually eliminating tuition fees for upper-secondary education, in accordance with the government's fiscal capacity, for both the vocational and academic streams to help universalize upper-secondary education and reduce disparities in the education system. Whether China can significantly increase the average level of educational attainment will depend on younger cohorts staying longer in school, particularly in upper-secondary schools, where enrollment rates decline sharply. Reducing the cost of tuition and fees for upper-secondary education would encourage the poor and the disadvantaged to remain in school.

Third, China could prepare a comprehensive strategy and policy framework for the balanced and sustainable development of a multitiered tertiary education system. China will need to continue promoting the top tier of world-class universities, but balanced development would ensure that all tiers of the system are resourced adequately and developed. Key reform priorities would include amending the Higher Education Law (1998) to align it with a modern tertiary education system; strengthening the autonomy, accountability, and quality assurance oversight of universities; and developing new regulations to manage the expansion and healthy development of private higher education providers and the new applied universities.

Fourth, China could carry out curriculum and pedagogical reforms to emphasize the promotion of creativity and cognitive and socioemotional skills. These reforms would include experimenting with collaborative classroom approaches that are multidisciplinary and problem and project based and that emphasize teamwork and cooperative learning. Tertiary education can avoid requiring students to specialize too early, which can undermine a broader perspective that is helpful for more creative and cognitive thinking. Also, students could be provided more freedom to devise individual learning goals and educational paths. In this regard, China could harness its burgeoning edtech industry and the associated digital technologies to reorient teaching that would enable more collaborative, personalized, and project-oriented learning.

And fifth, China could strengthen its technical and vocational education and training (TVET) system and develop a comprehensive, lifelong learning system. Increasingly, the acquisition of skills is a continuum throughout one's life that requires a combination of general and technical skills. China could promote a more flexible lifelong training system that fully integrates the technical and academic streams to facilitate transitions between them. It could improve the market relevance of training through closer education–industry collaboration and strengthen the incentives for workplace learning and on-the-job training, such as through "training contracts." In the future, workers are expected to experience more frequent changes of jobs and careers, increasing the importance of lifelong learning. China could expand modular and task-based training that is more suitable for a future workplace characterized by multiple job and career changes. It also could reorient training to fit the needs of a more services-based economy.

These reforms will likely require additional financing. China has more than doubled its public education spending over the last 15 years, but its current public spending on education, at 4.1 percent of GDP (2018), is relatively low for its income level and lower than the average of 5.2 percent for OECD countries (2015). Increased education spending would need to be complemented by a more transparent monitoring system to evaluate the efficiency and impact of the spending, complemented by public access to data on the education sector and school performance to strengthen public transparency and accountability for performance.

Allocating resources efficiently

Improving the allocative efficiency of finance

Efficient allocation of financial and human resources is central to the first of the three D's. More than one in five firms in China rates access to finance as the most significant business constraint, according to the World Bank's enterprise survey. Private firms are almost twice as likely to have been turned down for a loan than state-owned enterprises. SMEs, in particular, face challenges in accessing financing in China. China could promote SME lending by improving market conditions to reduce SMEs' credit risks, by strengthening and expanding the financial infrastructure, and by expanding the use of public and private sector data on SMEs, while adopting appropriate measures to protect data. China could expand dedicated SME lines of credit and the securitization of SME loans to pool SME risks. Consolidating and scaling up the guarantee industry could

help to improve the impact and coverage of credit guarantees for SMEs.

Venture capital and the fintech industry are a growing source of financing in China, including for SMEs. China is now the second-largest venture capital market, after the United States, and the largest fintech market in the world. With the rapid growth of venture capital financing, promoting the quality of fund management will be a priority. In particular, government guidance funds (government investment funds) that target start-ups will need to be market oriented and commercially managed and focused on addressing market failures to avoid crowding out private financing. Capital markets as an exit path for venture firms are more important in China than in other countries, so ensuring that initial public offerings are not unnecessarily administratively delayed would support the growth of venture firms.

With regard to the fintech industry, the major challenge will be to scale up regulatory and supervisory oversight of the industry while still encouraging innovation. Rules regarding disclosure and transparency, sales and marketing, safety of funds, dispute resolution, and data protection and privacy could be expanded. Regulatory authorities could consider a more structured and managed approach to innovation, such as "regulatory sandboxes." Strengthening enforcement capacity, expanding financial education, and improving coordination among the various financial regulatory authorities (People's Bank of China, China Banking Regulatory and Insurance Commission, and China Securities Regulatory Commission) will be critical, given that fintech can have new and innovative features that cut across different markets.

Maintaining sustained growth requires China to not only improve the allocative efficiency of finance, but also to address the significant debt accumulated in the economy. The rapid expansion of China's financial system to support its high investment rates has resulted in significant debt accumulation, raising financial vulnerabilities. Alongside debt accumulation, the expansion of shadow credit has increased the complexity of the financial sector and made bank balance sheets less transparent. The government has taken recent steps to limit shadow credit, but challenges remain in deleveraging an economy that is experiencing decelerating growth.

Improving the allocative efficiency of labor

With its working population expected to age and decline, China will need to access the underutilized labor in agriculture, increase female labor participation, and extend the working lives of its labor force. A key priority is to continue reforms of the *hukou* system, China's household registration system, to promote labor mobility. While important strides are being made on *hukou* reforms, more actions are needed to meet the government's ambitious plan to settle 100 million people in cities, including by further liberalizing *hukou* restrictions in the largest cities, which currently favor highly qualified migrants.

Consolidating the currently fragmented pension and social security system would enhance labor mobility and the allocative efficiency of labor by improving the portability of social insurance entitlements and benefits when workers move across jobs and regions. China could develop a comprehensive pension strategy that provides a road map for transitioning to a system based on pooled pension funds, and that includes a financing strategy for legacy costs. The national strategy also could prioritize the expansion of coverage to the poor. The Chinese authorities have indicated plans to pool pension funds at the national level by following a partial-pooling approach. Similar reforms could be considered for the other social insurance programs. These reforms could be complemented by reforms to strengthen the long-term sustainability of the pension system by gradually increasing the retirement age, establishing pension indexation, and improving the pension benefit adjustment mechanisms. The total social insurance contribution rate in China, over 40 percent, is very high, and lowering it would help to promote domestic consumption.

A priority for China's aging society is to incentivize firms to employ older workers. Policy options include promoting more flexible working arrangements and strengthening lifelong learning and training systems.

Targeted active labor market policies could be expanded for older workers as well as for female workers and workers displaced by technological changes or transitioning out of overcapacity industries. Expanding child and elderly care services could help to keep female workers employed longer.

Leveraging regional development and integration

China has been highly successful in leveraging spatial transformation for its development over the past 40 years. Rapid urbanization supported increased density and proximity. There is still room to increase the pace and efficiency of urbanization, with China still about 8 percentage points less urbanized than is typical for its level of income. Reducing spatial frictions in factor markets—in particular, the rural-urban migration of labor—will be central to enhancing the pace and efficiency of urbanization. Effective national and regional markets for trading land quotas and reducing unnecessarily restrictive land policies are reforms to consider for enhancing the efficiency of the allocation and use of land.

China's regional planning and development have been a key national priority since the start of the reforms and opening up. Four regional strategies—Western Region Development, Northeast Region Revitalization, Rise of the Central Region, and Leading Development in the Coastal Region—aim to optimize spatial development, cultivate new growth poles, and foster territorial cooperation. Regionally coordinated development would be supported by reforms of the government performance appraisal system to incentivize coordination and collaboration, whereas the system traditionally has emphasized competition and local economic development. These reforms could be complemented by reforms of the intergovernmental fiscal and taxation relationship to incentivize cooperation and collaboration further.

Laggard regions often face multiple deprivations of relevance to prospective investors, including human capital, institutional quality, and infrastructure. Therefore, coordinated policy responses, strong skills in planning and execution across a broad range of local government functions, and active collaboration among subnational (provincial and local) and national agencies are critical. The rapid development of Shenzhen, which established a business climate that encouraged entrepreneurship and promoted inward migration, offers valuable lessons for other regions. Finally, the Belt and Road Initiative (BRI), China's ambitious effort to improve regional economic integration and connectivity on a transcontinental scale, could provide new development opportunities for towns and cities in the western region. However, there is a need to ensure that economies of scale and specialization are reaped and that complementary investments and policies are implemented in a coordinated manner.

Infrastructure investment has been an important part of regional development initiatives in China. But given the significant improvements in the country's infrastructure, going forward the priority is not simply to invest more in infrastructure but also to find smarter ways to plan, utilize, and manage infrastructure investments. For example, the priority for the energy sector would be sectoral reforms to ensure that the investments in power generation—in particular, renewable energy—can be used and transmitted efficiently. Similarly, given the rapid expansion of transport connectivity, the priority for the transport sector appears to be reforms to address inefficiencies in logistics chains through more holistic and multimodal networks and improved links between transport networks and selected industries.

Promoting international competitiveness and economic globalization

China's integration into the global economy has been a major driver of its growth and development. China has become the world's largest trader of manufactured goods and a major destination for foreign investments. China has stated that it is committed to building a "community of shared destiny" and promoting an open global economy. Continued reforms to open up its economy will be critical for realizing China's aspiration to become a more productive and innovative economy.

China could pursue "deep" preferential trade agreements to stimulate trade and FDI flows and further integrate with global value chains. Trade and investment agreements with developed countries would require a common understanding of mutually beneficial trade and investment relations. China could further liberalize the imports of intermediate goods and services inputs to its production. China could provide leadership in formulating international rules on FDI and cross-border mergers and acquisitions that a broad cross section of developed and developing economies could support. It could continue to engage in actively strengthening global economic governance, such as to support implementation of the WTO's Trade Facilitation Agreement, and in promoting global goods, including to address climate change. China has stated that it supports reforms of the WTO that reflect the needs of both developing and developed countries.

China has benefited substantially from integration with the global economy through FDI, which has turned the country into a global hub for manufacturing exports and provided access to new technologies and management methods. FDI will remain important for China to catch up to high-income countries. China recently introduced a national foreign investment negative list to liberalize its foreign investment regime further. It could continue to reduce the number of restricted industries on the negative list. China's significant improvements of its business environment, as assessed by the World Bank's Doing Business indicators, benefit foreign as well as domestic investors. China could further promote FDI by ensuring a level playing field between foreign and domestic investors and providing a transparent and predictable policy and regulatory environment.

The new Foreign Investment Law (FIL), which will come into effect on January 1, 2020, is an opportunity to provide a clear and unambiguous legal and regulatory framework by specifying and streamlining associated regulations, administrative reviews, and licensing procedures to protect the rights and interests of foreign investors in China. In this regard, China plans to issue a series of laws and regulations to smooth the implementation of the FIL. The formulation of these laws and regulations would benefit from extensive consultations with both foreign and domestic investors. China could expand regular communication and consultations with foreign firms to help identify investors' concerns and minimize misunderstanding of government policies and regulations.

Foreign investors have raised concerns that they are compelled to transfer technology to gain market access, but China has stated that it has never introduced such policies or practices. It is in China's interests to provide the legal and institutional framework to prevent "forced" technology transfers and to encourage the introduction of foreign technologies in China. The government could introduce a transparent monitoring, verification, and grievance-handling mechanism for technology transfers. The new FIL explicitly prohibits "forced" technology transfers through administrative measures. Specific associated laws, regulations, and guidance are needed to implement and enforce the law. These laws and regulations could aim to ensure fair and equitable treatment of foreign investors, including by specifying an investor dispute settlement mechanism and ensuring coordination and complementarity between the dispute prevention (grievance management) and dispute settlement provisions.

China could expand programs to strengthen the linkages between domestic and foreign enterprises to enhance technology and managerial spillovers and global collaboration. Programs that could be expanded include targeted extension services to upgrade local suppliers and supplier databases, platforms, and matchmaking services to link foreign and local firms. Such programs would benefit from close participation of foreign investors in program design and implementation to ensure that they reflect the needs of the foreign enterprises. China also could continue to expand programs to attract top global managerial talent and help China to access global technologies and connect with the global economy.

China could further improve its outward direct investment (ODI) management system by adopting a more market-oriented approach. It could consolidate and streamline the pre-investment administrative rules, regulations, and approval procedures concerning ODI, and improve the coordination of ODI-related authorities. China could expand and improve the quality of extension services for enterprises engaging in ODI to support risk monitoring of overseas markets and improve firms' understanding of environmental and social safeguards, international rules, and the laws of the host countries.

The BRI provides an opportunity for China to improve its investment in soft infrastructure to complement its investment in hard infrastructure, including the adoption of international standards and rules on trade, foreign investment, and environmental standards. China could introduce a more multilateral approach to BRI through the introduction of institutional mechanisms to coordinate investments, financing, relevant policies and regulations, and platforms for dispute resolution and risk management. BRI investments should aim to be more transparent and environmentally, socially, and fiscally sustainable.

Governing the next transformation

Unlocking the new drivers of growth will require governance reforms to strike a more balanced coexistence between the state and market. As China's economy becomes more complex and innovation driven, the market will need to play a more decisive role and the state to play a more market-supportive role. The role of the state will need to evolve to focus on providing stable market expectations and the rule of law. Priority reforms to support this transition include the following.

First, China can carry out regulatory governance reforms to provide clear, fair, and predictable regulations. China could further streamline policies and regulations affecting businesses to lessen the administrative burden on enterprises and reduce the opportunities for discretionary application and enforcement of regulations. It could strengthen vertical reporting lines of local enforcement agencies, as was done for environmental protection bureaus, to reduce local government discretion. The central government could enhance horizontal coordination among enforcement agencies to achieve more consistent enforcement within a decentralized model. China could make data on regulatory compliance more widely available to the public and improve public communication of regulatory and licensing interpretations and decisions to strengthen transparency and accountability. Finally, China could systematically carry out evidence-based regulatory impact assessments, incorporating them in its policy making.

Second, China can further reform its civil service management system to strengthen incentives to support markets and long-run productivity growth. Local governments in China exercise considerable discretion over implementing policies, enforcing regulations, and supporting local enterprises. China has sought to adjust local incentives by reforming its civil service (cadre) management system to make promotion criteria more comprehensive and less narrowly focused on short-term growth. To further reforms, China could lengthen cadres' terms of office to align incentives better with long-run productivity growth and adopt a "lifetime achievements" approach to performance evaluation by evaluating the long-term impact of reforms. China could strengthen the public accountability of local leaders to help reduce local discretion. Reducing the rigidity of staffing rules and reviewing the competitiveness of public service salaries could ensure that the civil service attracts well-qualified staff. This effort could be complemented by an assessment of the capacity constraints across all levels of government to identify the major bottlenecks in staffing, resources, and skills.

Third, China could reshape and modernize its intergovernmental relations and strengthen fiscal discipline. Reshaping China's intergovernmental relations requires a comprehensive and politically challenging package of complementary reforms. Expenditure responsibilities across different levels of government need to be reviewed, adjusted, clarified, and specified more consistently, addressing issues such as concurrent expenditure responsibilities and substantial discretion by higher levels of government to assign expenditure

responsibilities to lower levels. Reforms are needed to reduce counterproductive interjurisdictional competition for private investments, including by transitioning from a derivation-based to a needs-based tax transfer system, which would reduce the incentives to intervene in markets to support local enterprises.

The hardening of subnational governments' budget constraints is needed to complement the intergovernmental fiscal reforms. The priority is to strictly and fully implement and enforce the 2014 amendments to the budget law that aimed to strengthen fiscal discipline of local governments. A reform road map could include the adoption of capital budgeting, more comprehensive and transparent financial reporting, and stronger management of contingent liability risks associated with public-private partnerships (PPPs) and other off-budget vehicles. The government could develop a comprehensive PPP policy and regulatory framework, drawing lessons learned from the series of regulations issued in recent years. Finally, China could adopt a comprehensive and transparent government financial reporting system to provide the information necessary for monitoring and evaluating the financial sustainability and performance of subnational governments and assessing progress on the fiscal reforms and their impact.

Fourth, China could improve the coverage, quality, and public accessibility of government-related data. China has the potential to be a global leader and to set new international standards in data collection and dissemination. Improved data and greater access to data on government-related operations and basic economic information would help to improve public sector performance by enhancing the transparency and accountability of government operations. China could provide consolidated budget data and fuller public access to household budget survey data, industrial enterprise survey and census data, and improve labor market and education assessment data. Data can be gathered from a variety of new sources, with appropriate arrangements for privacy protection. The government could consider developing an access-to-information policy for the public sector.

Abbreviations

AML	Anti-Monopoly Law
BIT	Bilateral Investment Treaty
BRI	Belt and Road Initiative
CBIRC	China Banking and Insurance Regulatory Commission
CCRC	Credit Reference Center of PBOC
CFIUS	Committee on Foreign Investment in the United States
CPC	Communist Party of China
CSRC	China Securities Regulatory Commission
DARPA	Defense Advanced Research Projects Agency
DVA	domestic value added
ECD	early child development
EU	European Union
FAR	floor area ratio
FDI	foreign direct investment
FIL	Foreign Investment Law
GCI	global competitiveness index
GDP	gross domestic product
GNI	gross national income
GVC	global value chain
ICOR	incremental capital-output ratio
ICT	information and communication technology
IFC	International Finance Corporation
INSEAD	Institut Europeen d'Administration des Affaires
IP	intellectual property
IPO	initial public offering
IT	information technology
ITU	International Telecommunication Union
LGFV	local government financing vehicle
LPI	Logistics Performance Index
MIIT	Ministry of Industry and Information Technology
MIS	management information system

NDRC   National Development and Reform Commission
NEEQ   National Equities Exchange and Quotations
NIS   national innovation system
ODI   outward direct investment
OECD   Organisation for Economic Co-operation and Development
P2P   peer to peer (lending)
PBOC   People's Bank of China
PCT   Patent Cooperation Treaty
PIACC   Program for the International Assessment of Adult Competencies
PISA   Program for International Student Assessment
PPP   public-private partnerships
R&D   research and development
RCA   revealed comparative advantage
SAMR   State Administration for Market Regulation
SIPO   State Intellectual Property Office
SME   small and medium enterprise
SOE   state-owned enterprise
STEM   science, technology, engineering, and mathematics
STRI   Services Trade Restrictiveness Index
TF   Trade Facilities Agreement
TFP   total factor productivity
TVET   technical and vocational education and training
UN   United Nations
WBG   World Bank Group
WIOD   World Input-Output Database
WIPO   World Intellectual Property Organization
WTO   World Trade Organization

Introduction

After nearly four decades of rapid growth, China's economy is transitioning to a "new normal" of slower but more balanced and sustainable growth. Its old drivers of growth—a growing labor force, the expansion of manufacturing, migration from rural areas to cities, the accumulation of capital (thanks to high savings), expanding exports, and opening to foreign investments—are waning or having less impact. China's demographic dividends are reversing, and investment growth—supported by the large domestic economic stimulus that China mobilized after the global financial crisis—is having a declining impact on growth and has resulted in a rapid buildup of debt. The slowdown in global trade after the global financial crisis, China's already large share in global markets, and rising global trade tensions are constraining exports as a driver of growth.

China has two "centenary goals": (1) to become a moderately prosperous society in an all-around manner by 2021, the centennial of the founding of the Communist Party of China (CPC); and (2) to become a great modern socialist country that is prosperous, strong, democratic, culturally advanced, harmonious, and beautiful by 2049, the centennial of the founding of the People's Republic of China. China's policy makers are well aware that the country needs new drivers of growth to achieve its two centenary goals. China's leaders have emphasized that productivity and innovation will be central in the country's next phase of growth. They also have emphasized the market's decisive role in resource allocation, as well as the government's important role in the economy. This guidance has been reflected in numerous policy documents and plans, including the decisions of the 3rd and 5th Plenums of the 18th Central Committee of the CPC, the 13th Five-Year Plan, and the report of General Secretary Xi Jinping to the 19th National Congress of the CPC.

Innovative China: New Drivers of Growth proposes a reform agenda to support policy makers in their efforts to achieve a modern and innovative China. Chinese premier Li Keqiang and former World Bank Group president Jim Yong Kim agreed to study the new drivers of growth, and the result, *Innovative China*, is the product of more than two years of cooperation between the Development Research Center of the

1

State Council, the Ministry of Finance, and the World Bank Group.

Innovative China analyzes productivity and innovation in China's economy, takes stock of China's policy initiatives to promote productivity and innovation, and identifies the key challenges that China faces on its journey to more productivity and innovation-driven growth. It recommends structural, governance, and institutional reforms to promote new drivers of growth, drawn from a review of China's past growth and productivity and its achievements in structural transformation, entrepreneurship, innovation, and technological upgrading. It also compares China's key policies and reforms with international practices, including international and domestic case studies in areas of interest to policy makers.

The main conclusion is that promoting productivity is the key to China's future growth and its ability to become a high-income country. China can achieve higher productivity through a comprehensive program of reforms to address the "three D's":

- Removing *distortions* to strengthen market competition and enhance the efficient allocation of resources in the economy
- Accelerating *diffusion* of advanced technologies and management practices in China's economy, taking advantage of the large remaining potential for catch-up growth
- Fostering *discovery* and nurturing China's innovative capacity as China approaches Organisation for Economic Co-operation and Development (OECD) levels of income in the decades ahead and contributes to extending the global innovation and technology frontier.

The first three chapters of *Innovative China* analyze China's economic growth and productivity. The remaining seven cover the major reform areas: industrial policies and market competition, innovation and technology, human capital and labor, efficient allocation of resources, regional development and integration, international competitiveness and economic globalization, and governance and institutions.

China's Rapid Growth and Evolving Economy

China sustained an annual growth rate of gross domestic product (GDP) that averaged nearly 10 percent for more than three decades (figure 1.1), spurred by reforms that unlocked China's huge growth potential and created conditions for the country to catch up rapidly with higher-income economies. The economy underwent significant structural changes as the labor share of agriculture declined 44 percentage points between 1978 and 2017, according to China's National Bureau of Statistics, and people moved to cities to find more productive employment in the industry and services sectors. A high and rising savings rate financed the investments in infrastructure and production facilities needed for rapid growth and urbanization.

At the outset of reform in 1978, state and collective firms accounted for all of the workforce and investments in the economy. Since then, the state's share has declined to less than 20 percent of the workforce and less than 30 percent of GDP, as market-oriented reforms have allowed the private sector to expand rapidly.[1] Even so, state-owned enterprises continue to play an important role in various areas of the economy.

The reforms associated with China's World Trade Organization (WTO) accession in 2001 accelerated reforms and productivity growth. China is now the world's largest exporting country. It presents a striking example of how opening an economy and integrating in global value chains can boost productivity, competitiveness, and the adaptation of modern technologies. China is increasingly important to global value chains. Its export products have become more sophisticated, with the share of high-technology manufactures in China's exports growing from next to nothing in 1980 to around 30 percent in 2017.

Various international assessments indicate that China has been gradually improving its national innovation capacity, ranking it highest among low- and middle-income countries. But China is still well behind leading Organisation for Economic Co-operation and Development (OECD) countries in innovation capacity. China's spending on research and development (R&D) rose to 2.18 percent of GDP in 2018, up from 1.4 percent in 2007 and near the OECD average. Its spending on R&D accounts for around 20 percent of the world total, second only to the United States. Its number of patents granted annually for

FIGURE 1.1   **Composition of GDP growth in China, 1992–2018**

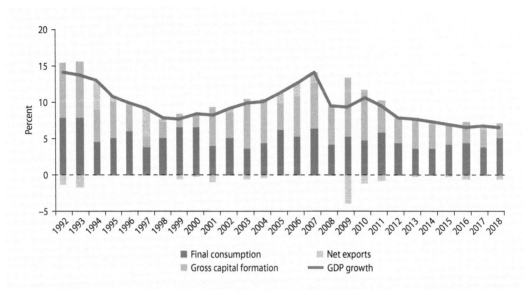

Source: Calculations based on National Bureau of Statistics data.

inventions increased from 68,000 in 2007 to 420,000 in 2017, the highest in the world, although their quality varies, according to China's State Intellectual Property Office. Seventy-six percent of R&D spending is by industries, facilitating commercial applications. China is also a hotbed for venture capital in search of the next technology, raising approximately US$110 billion in the decade, surpassed only by the United States.

China's human capital capabilities are the foundation of its growing innovation capabilities, but it has some way to go to match the OECD countries. Less than 20 percent (2017) of China's labor force has completed tertiary education, much less than the 30 to 40 percent in OECD countries. China has, on average, 2 researchers per 1,000 employed, well below the European Union, which has 10. But capacity is improving rapidly. China's leading universities are climbing the global rankings and producing a growing volume of high-quality research. Each year, 7 million university students graduate, 1.5 million of them in science and engineering, and 30,000 new PhDs in technical disciplines have turned the country into a research base for technology companies such as IBM and Microsoft. China is second only to the United States in the number of publications and the quality of academic papers, as measured by the number of citations. Although overall public spending on education has been increasing rapidly, constituting 4.1 percent of GDP in 2018, China still lags behind the OECD average of 5.2 percent (2015).

China's growth has been slowing to the new normal, but this is not entirely unexpected. History and economics suggest that slowdowns generally occur at about China's current level of income per capita. Some countries remain for extended periods in a "middle-income" trap, and only a select few—such as Israel, Japan, and the Republic of Korea—have maintained growth rates around 7 percent for another decade after reaching China's current income level. China's growth is highly exceptional, as most countries revert to their mean growth after 10 to 15 years of rapid growth.

An economy already transforming

China still has much room to grow to catch up with the high-income economies. Its per capita GDP stands at nearly US$10,000, about a fourth of the average for OECD countries. In many ways, China's next transformation is well under way, and a new economy is emerging rapidly. Chinese firms have developed outstanding manufacturing capabilities, and the value added in high-tech manufacturing is now second only to that of the United States. China is leading or closing the technology gap in e-commerce, fintech, high-speed trains, renewable energy, and electric cars. McKinsey ranks China among the top three investors in fintech, virtual reality, autonomous vehicles, robotics, and big data. Alibaba, Didi Chuxing, Huawei, and Tencent are already operating at the global technology frontier. China's digital services economy has done particularly well. With its large-scale, high penetration of mobile phones and Internet use, China is a major source of innovation and productivity in digital services.

China is a dominant global manufacturer, with a strong and broad manufacturing base offering ample scope for product and process innovations to drive future productivity gains. China's share of global manufacturing value added increased from 7 percent in 2000 to nearly 27 percent in 2015, the largest increase among all countries. China's abundant labor supply, deep economic reforms in the 1980s and 1990s, and accession to the WTO in

2001 all helped to catalyze its development into the "world's factory," with multinational corporations, drawn to its low-cost labor and extensive transportation infrastructure, seeking to set up subsidiaries as export platforms. Economies that continued to grow rapidly beyond China's current income per capita—such as Germany, Japan, Korea, and Singapore—sustained a manufacturing base for much longer than economies that faltered. But although China remains a dominant global manufacturer, the contribution of its manufacturing investment to growth has been falling, along with other key investment sectors of the economy (figure 1.2). Also, manufacturing wages in China have been growing at double digits, much faster than in other economies.

Even as China has continued to expand its share of global manufacturing value added, its industrial structure has been evolving, and the share of manufacturing in GDP has declined from 46 percent in 1994 to 41 percent in 2018 (figure 1.3). The share of services in GDP has been rapidly growing, while the share of agriculture has been declining steeply. Services recently overtook

FIGURE 1.2 **Contribution of fixed-asset investment to growth in China, 2005–18**

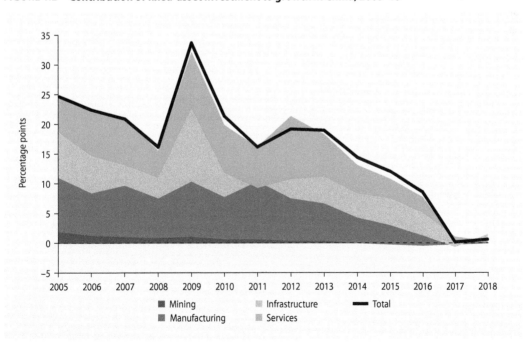

Source: Calculations based on National Bureau of Statistics data.

FIGURE 1.3   **Share of industry in GDP in China, by sector, 1978–2018**

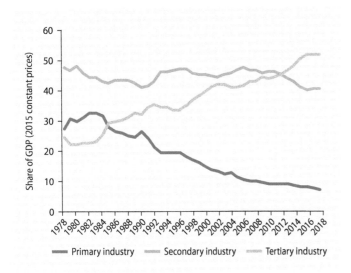

Source: Calculations based on National Bureau of Statistics data.

industry as the largest sector of the economy, and services are now the country's largest employer. Value-added services in China have been growing rapidly, at 11 percent in 2002–13, outpacing the growth in comparator countries, which ranged from 0.73 percent in Japan to 9 percent in India. However, China's

FIGURE 1.4   **Share of services in GDP in China, 2016**

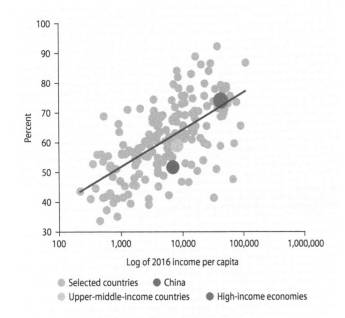

Source: Calculations based on World Development Indicators data.

services sector remains relatively small for its income per capita (figure 1.4), reflecting the continued dominance of export-led manufacturing. Investment in manufacturing is now dominated by private firms (78 percent of total investments, compared with 8 percent for state firms), but investment in services by private firms (37 percent) is less than investment by state firms (44 percent). Therefore, significant potential remains for expanding private services.

Services "embodied" in manufactured goods are an increasingly important determinant of manufacturing competitiveness and are critical for a wide range of economic activities in downstream manufacturing. These services are inputs (design, marketing, and distribution costs included in the value of a good) to trade and enablers (logistics services or e-commerce platforms) of trade. They are important determinants of productivity (Arnold et al. 2011, 2015; Barone et al. 2011) and essential drivers of global value chains (Low and Pasadilla 2016; Sàez et al. 2014). The role of services as inputs to manufacturing can be assessed from the perspective of forward and backward linkages, either for final domestic use or for export.

China's share of value-added services as inputs to manufacturing is relatively small. Based on the OECD's trade in value-added data, the share of value-added inputs from services as part of China's total manufacturing backward linkages is only 26 percent. This is lower than that of Korea (27.5 percent) and India (33.0 percent), and much lower than countries with a larger manufacturing base, such as Japan (35.8 percent) and Germany (41.2 percent). This suggests that services linkages are relatively weak in China's manufacturing sector. Similarly, the share of value-added inputs from services in China's manufacturing exports, at 25 percent, is lower than in most other comparator countries.

Links between manufacturing and modern services—such as R&D, and computer-related services—are relatively weak in China. The share of R&D and business services inputs in manufacturing for both domestic consumption and exports is around 11–12 percent. Although the share has been rising, it is far lower than in many other countries, both high-income and low- and middle-income economies, whose share is 15 to 30 percent. The share of computer and related services inputs to Chinese manufacturing, at around 1.5 percent of total value-added inputs from services, is lower than the 3 to 5 percent in most peer countries.

A corollary to China's rapid industrialization has been the decline in the share of primary agriculture in GDP, from about 31 to 33 percent in the early 1980s to 7 percent in 2018. However, this is a relative trend, and agriculture has continued to grow consistently, at an average annual rate of more than 4 percent since 2004, which is an impressive rate by global standards for agricultural growth. China is now the world's largest agricultural producer, with more than 23 percent of global production, higher than the total of all high-income countries and all other country groups.

The share of agriculture is expected to continue to decline, but agriculture still has potential to contribute to overall growth through industrialization and "servicification" of the sector. This would help expand the agroprocessing and food services (trade, restaurants, prepared foods) segments of the postharvest agricultural value chains. China's agricultural production structure has slowly started to shift, but the country's value added in agroprocessing is only 14 percent of the agriculture sector's total value added, much lower than for high-income countries (90 percent for the United States, 132 percent for Germany) and some low- and middle-income countries (25 percent for the Russian Federation, 29 percent for Brazil). Therefore, China has significant potential to grow by expanding industries associated with agriculture.

Beyond agroprocessing, the "servicification" of agriculture also creates new growth opportunities. The growth of agricultural services, particularly machinery leasing, has accelerated sharply since about 2006–07, driven in part by government subsidies to promote mechanization. With an increasingly "industrialized" structure (capital intensive and mechanized), the use of data-intensive digital technologies and practices will become increasingly important. Farmers

are outsourcing specific production steps, such as land preparation and harvesting, to professional service providers. The emergence of agricultural service providers can provide competitive labor-substituting professional mechanization services. These services help China overcome constraints faced by traditional smallholder agriculture, accelerate productivity growth through greater efficiency, and generate future releases of agricultural labor to other sectors of the economy.

Along with the sectoral transformation of the economy, a gradual transition from an investment-driven economy toward a consumption-driven one has also been taking place in recent years. The final consumption expenditure share of GDP has been volatile and declining since the beginning of the reforms and opening up, falling below 50 percent in the aftermath of the 2008 global financial crisis. But since 2014, consumption has outpaced investment to become the biggest driver of growth, contributing on average 57 percent to overall growth. The final consumption expenditure share of GDP gradually rose to 53.6 percent in 2017. This shift has been supported by a rising share of labor income, reversing a two-decade negative trend, as well as a falling savings rate (figure 1.5).

FIGURE 1.5 Share of labor income and gross savings in GDP in China, 1992–2017

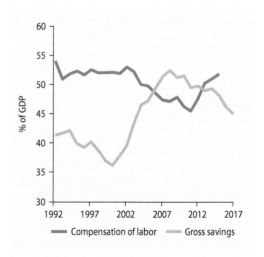

Source: Calculations based on World Development Indicators data.

A rapidly changing and more uncertain global environment

As China's economy transforms, it faces new global challenges and opportunities, shaped by two megatrends: rapid technology advancements and rising protectionist sentiments. Technology-induced disruptions of industries and the workplace are accelerating, becoming more frequent and unpredictable. Many technologists argue that we are at the beginning of a new acceleration in technological change, propelled by digital technologies that enable new products and services. In the United States, it took 39 years for landline telephones to reach 40 percent penetration and another 15 years for them to become ubiquitous. Smartphones, by contrast, reached 40 percent penetration in just 10 years.

The adoption of digital technologies in manufacturing, known as Industry 4.0 or the Fourth Industrial Revolution, is expected to reshape manufacturing. Cloud computing, big data analytics, and the Internet of Things are driving the expansion of the digital services economy and the modernization of business operations and services.[2] Digital platforms such as e-commerce can reduce the cost of entering new markets, thus promoting entrepreneurship and competition. Entrepreneurial start-ups, as agents of disruption propelled by the technology-led economic transformation, leverage technologies to develop new business models and, in some instances, entirely new business categories. Traditional companies, spurred on by the new competition, have come under pressure to adapt their business models or create new products and services. Hotel businesses need to adapt to Airbnb, taxi companies need to cope with Didi Chuxing and Uber, and banks need to react to fintech.

China is already considered a global leader in industries enabled by digital technologies, such as e-commerce and fintech, as well as emerging fields like artificial intelligence. Among the 252 nonlisted start-ups in the world, with a valuation of US$1 billion and above (commonly referred to as unicorns), 98 are from China, surpassed only by the United States, with 106 (PricewaterhouseCoopers

2017). Many of these unicorns are companies that use digital technology to create new innovation in e-commerce, mobile transportation, finance, and education. Digital technologies are central to China's plans for industrial upgrading to improve the productivity and domestic value added of the country's industry supply chains. China has been aware of the importance of deepening the application of Internet-related technologies in manufacturing and of developing smart manufacturing (MIIT 2015). The Internet+ strategy, introduced in 2015, foresees the application of Internet technology to each sector of the economy, as in Internet+finance, Internet+health, and Internet+logistics.[3]

China now has the highest number of Internet users and the largest (and one of the fastest-growing) e-commerce markets in the world. The number of Internet users in China reached 829 million in 2018, and the annual volume of e-commerce trade grew 30-fold from 2004 to 2018 (Ministry of Commerce 2019), reaching RMB 31.6 trillion (figure 1.6). China started from less than 1 percent of the global value of e-commerce transactions a decade ago to reach more than 40 percent, exceeding France, Germany, Japan, the United Kingdom, and the United States combined (Woetzel et al. 2017). E-commerce helps to drive growth by enlarging the market reach of enterprises and helping them to manage their operations efficiently.

Online retail sales have grown particularly rapidly, more than 70 times from 2008 to 2018, to RMB 9 trillion (figure 1.7). In 2008, only 1 percent of retail sales of consumer goods were purchased online in China. In 2018, this share reached 24 percent, making it the highest in the world. However, online retail sales vary across regions. More than 45 percent of online retail sales of consumer goods were conducted in Beijing, followed by nearly 40 percent in Shanghai, compared with less than 2 percent in nine inland provinces.

China also faces a more challenging global environment, with the slowdown in global trade and rising protectionism. China's exports have soared in dollar terms, by 14 percent annually in the past two decades, and the country has become a dominant exporting nation on the world stage. Its integration into the global value chain was marked by huge waves of foreign direct investment, focused on manufacturing for export and, increasingly, for its enormous and rapidly growing domestic market.

The global financial crisis slowed global trade, which contracted by 12.8 percent in 2009, and removed exports as a major of source of growth for China. The volume of world merchandise trade grew by just 2.4 percent a year from 2009 to 2018, which is less than half of the average rate of expansion during 2000–08 (figure 1.8). World merchandise trade continued to experience relatively weak growth into 2019. This weak growth reflects, in part, a slowing demand for capital goods amid elevated trade policy uncertainty, according to the latest edition of the World Bank's *Global Economic Prospects* (June 2019).

There has been some debate about whether the slowdown in global trade reflected a cyclical fluctuation and slow recovery from the global financial crisis or a structural shift away from global value chains. Arguments for the "end of globalization" have rested on various explanations, including rising economic nationalism and protectionism, new manufacturing technologies that reduce the importance of labor costs and enable close-to-market production ("reshoring"), rising labor costs in exporting countries (particularly China), and increased domestic production of intermediate goods in exporting countries (again, particularly China).

China faces external concerns about its "unfair" industrial and trade policies and demands for reciprocity in foreign investments. For the past four decades, China and its major trade partners have embraced globalization. China has gradually opened up its economy and integrated into the global economy. Today, however, tensions between China and other major trading nations are building regarding China's trade and investment policies, intellectual property rights, and overseas investments in critical infrastructure and technologies. A common underlying concern has been fundamental

FIGURE 1.6   **Number of Internet users in China, 2007–18**

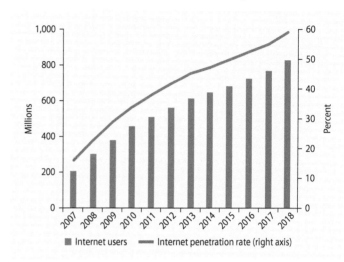

Sources: Calculations based on China Internet Network Information Center, National Bureau of Statistics data; CIECC Research Institute 2016.

FIGURE 1.7   **Value and share of online retail sales in China, 2008–18**

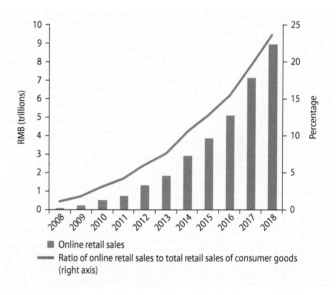

Sources: Calculations based on China Internet Network Information Center, National Bureau of Statistics data; CIECC Research Institute 2016.

differences regarding the role of the state in the economy.

Such tensions can undermine support for the global trading system and constrain China's ability to leverage global trade and investments to promote its growth and development. In response, China's leadership has stated its commitment to supporting

FIGURE 1.8 **Growth in the global trade of goods, 2001–19**

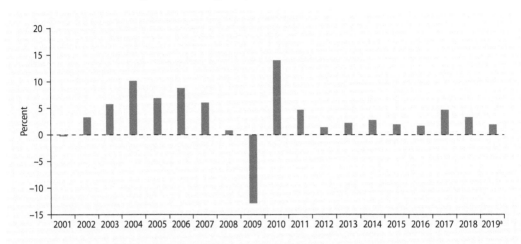

Source: Calculations based on CPB World Trade Monitor data.
a. The 2019 data are for Jan.–April only.

globalization, an open global economy, and a global "Community with a Shared Future for Mankind." It has announced plans to open its domestic markets further to foreign investments and to lower tariffs, and it has launched important major initiatives, such as the Belt and Road Initiative, to promote connectivity.

Notes

1. World Bank estimates based on National Bureau of Statistics data.
2. Cloud computing services use a network of remote servers to store and process data over the Internet. The Internet of Things is the sending and receiving of data through the many digital devices connected through the Internet. Big data analytics reveal patterns, trends, and associations in large sets of data.
3. See "Premier Li on Internet Plus Traditional Industries," *State Council of the People's Republic of China Premier News*, October 5. http://english.gov.cn/premier /news/2016/10/05/content_281475459076998 .htm.

References

Arnold, Jens M., Beata S. Javorcik, and Aaditya Mattoo. 2011. "Does Services Liberalization Benefit Manufacturing Firms? Evidence from the Czech Republic." *Journal of International Economics* 85 (1): 136–46.

Barone, J. Michael, and P. Karen Winterich. 2011. "Warm Glow or Cold, Hard Cash? Social Identity Effects on Consumer Choice for Donation versus Discount Promotions." *Journal of Marketing Research* 48 (5): 855–68.

CIECC (China International Engineering Consulting Corporation) Research Institute. 2016.

Felton, Michael. 2008. "Consumption Spreads Faster Today [Chart]." *New York Times*, February 10.

Low, Patrick, and O. Gloria Pasadilla, eds. 2016. *Services in Global Value Chains: Manufacturing-Related Services*. Singapore: World Scientific.

MIIT (Ministry of Industry and Information Technology). 2015. "Notice of the State Council on Printing and Distributing 'Made in China 2025.'" May 19, MIIT, Beijing.

Ministry of Commerce. 2019. "E-Commerce in China 2018." A report released at the 2019 China E-Commerce Convention in May.

Sàez, Emmanuel, Stefanie Stantcheva, and Thomas Piketty. 2014. "Optimal Taxation of Top Labor Incomes: A Tale of Three Elasticities." *American Economic Journal: Economic Policy* 6 (1): 230–71.

Woetzel, J., et al. 2017. "China's Digital Economy: A Leading Global Force." McKinsey Global Institute, Discussion Paper, August.

The Need for New Drivers of Growth

China's past growth benefited from capital deepening, labor force expansion, and productivity improvements. Decomposing China's economic growth shows that all of these factors played an important role over the past four decades. Almost half of China's gross domestic product (GDP) growth since 1978 was from capital deepening, about a third was from productivity, measured by total factor productivity (TFP), and the rest was from an expanding labor force and investments in human capital (figure 2.1). The structural reforms, initially driven by accession to the World Trade Organization (WTO) in 2001, allowed the country to maintain relatively high TFP growth, but the contribution of TFP has declined sharply since the global financial crisis, from 3.2 percentage points in the years before the crisis to just 1.1 percentage points afterward. Other researchers estimate lower or even negative TFP growth since the global financial crisis.[1]

As a result of the lower contribution of TFP, growth has had to rely to a much greater extent on investments in physical capital (figure 2.2). High investment rates have greatly increased China's capital stock, but additional capital investments are likely to add less to growth in the future. The contribution from labor also has declined sharply,

as China's demographic dividends have reversed, and the working-age population has started to decline. In short, China's previous drivers of growth are losing their impetus.

Investment's diminishing contribution to growth

China made use of its exceptionally high savings rate to mobilize massive resources for investments. The country's rapid accumulation of basic economic infrastructure is the envy of many developing countries. In response to the global financial crisis, China implemented a large public sector stimulus program, which focused on investments in infrastructure and real estate. China's investments now face the challenge of diminishing returns, as measured by the increase in the country's incremental capital-output ratio (ICOR) (figure 2.3). Much of the increase in the economywide ICOR, which represents a declining impact of investments on growth, can be explained by higher ICORs in infrastructure and real estate, reflecting significant investments in those areas (figure 2.4). In contrast to infrastructure and housing, the returns to capital in the business sector deteriorated only marginally after the crisis, which indicates that improving the allocation of capital could enhance

FIGURE 2.1 **Sources of growth in China, 1978–2017**

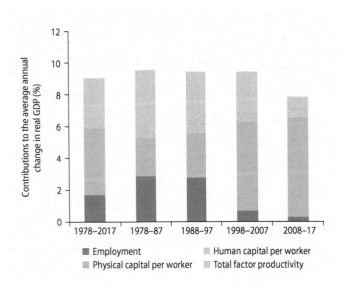

Source: Calculations based on National Bureau of Statistics data.
Note: TFP = total factor productivity.

FIGURE 2.2 **Sectoral gross capital formation as a share of GDP in China, 1990–2016**

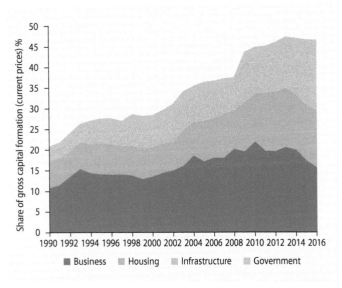

Source: Herd 2017.

FIGURE 2.3 **GDP growth and the incremental capital-output ratio (ICOR) in China, 1995–2018**

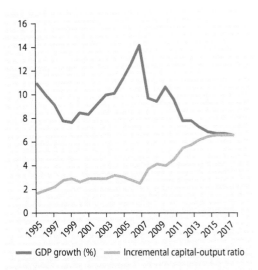

Source: Calculations based on National Bureau of Statistics data.

Private enterprises may have been more pessimistic about market prospects due to the moderation of China's growth, while state-owned enterprises (SOEs) may have increased investments in infrastructure to implement the government's postcrisis stimulus. SOEs have received disproportionately larger shares of credit, with roughly nine-tenths of bonds outstanding issued by state firms.[2] Finally, private firms may already have taken advantage of most of the liberalization of market entry that the state has authorized, and boosting private investments further may require addressing the remaining barriers to market entry.

The investment-oriented stimulus also contributed to the rapid growth of commercial credit to the nonfinancial sector, reaching almost 251 percent of GDP by the end of 2018. The most rapid growth of debt between 2012 and 2015 was for SOEs, and the fastest-growing component of SOE debt during this period was for local government financing vehicles (LGFVs) involved in subnational public investment (figure 2.5). By 2015, infrastructure, construction, and housing accounted for more than half of new debt in the nonfinancial sector. This very rapid expansion in credit to the nonfinancial sector could have hindered China's productivity growth in two important ways. First, as suggested in the decomposition of the ICOR,

productivity and efficiency. With basic public infrastructure now largely in place, the overall returns to public investment for economic growth can be expected to decline.

Rising investments since the global financial crisis have been driven by rising public investment rates, whereas the growth of private investment has been declining. This decline could be due to several factors.

FIGURE 2.4 **Capital-output ratio in China, by economic sector, 1990–2015**

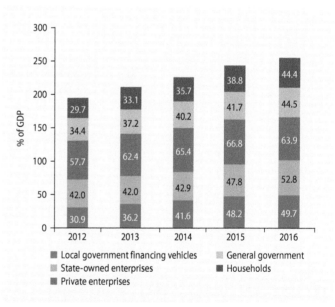

Source: Herd 2017.

the flow of credit to sectors with higher ICORs indicates an inherent inefficiency in the allocation of credit that directly affects productivity. Second, the growing burden of nonfinancial sector debt will itself slow growth in the medium term, when it inevitably will need to be deleveraged.[3] Given such risks, the Government of China has prioritized containing the growth of credit and deleveraging the economy.

Investment growth in China has weakened significantly in recent years, growing at less than half its 2001–10 average pace. Real investment expanded 18 percent a year in the decade before 2011, compared with just 5 percent in 2017 (figure 2.6). The slowdown in investment has occurred in the context of slowing economic growth and rebalancing toward household consumption. Recent efforts to reduce excess industrial capacity and to limit financial risks have also contributed to lower investment. In addition, new economy sectors such as software and information technology as well as consumer services are generally less capital intensive and therefore require less investment.

Despite the recent slowdown, the growth rate and level of investment are still high by international standards. In 2013–17, capital formation in China increased 6.9 percent a year, compared with an average of 4.9

FIGURE 2.5 **Estimated composition of debt accumulation in China, 2012–16**

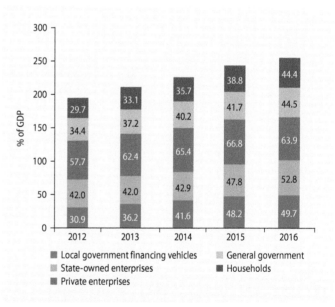

Sources: Calculations based on Bank for International Settlements, People's Bank of China, Wind Information Co., Ltd., and CEIC data.
Note: LGFV = local government financing vehicle. SOE = state-owned enterprise.

percent for upper-middle-income countries. China's gross capital formation—at 44.8 percent of GDP in 2018—remains one of the highest in the world. By comparison, the average investment rate in the Organisation for Economic Co-operation and Development (OECD) is about 22 percent of GDP.

FIGURE 2.6   **Real gross capital formation in China, 2001–18**

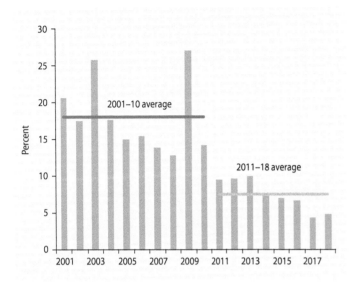

Source: Calculations based on National Bureau of Statistics data.

Although the aggregate impact of investment on growth is declining, capital accumulation can still contribute to future growth, particularly for the business sector, which has not seen a big decline in returns to capital. China's public sector capital stock per worker has already reached OECD levels (figure 2.7). For this reason, more public infrastructure may not address the most critical bottlenecks for China's future growth. By contrast, the nonpublic capital stock of China is only around half that of the OECD, suggesting that capital deepening in the nongovernment sector can still contribute significantly to growth and labor productivity in the coming decades. In this regard, declining private investment rates are an added concern.

All of this points to the importance of setting priorities and being selective in future infrastructure investments. The critical question is what kind of capital—in which industry and in which economic activity—is most productive for China's future growth? Growth can still come from new capital investments if it is in areas that are still lagging, because there are significant differences in the performance of various kinds of infrastructure. China is internationally competitive in transport infrastructure, but it still lags in power and in information and communication infrastructure in remote areas. To make capital investment more productive, China needs to improve its policies and ensure that the market plays a decisive role in the economy.

Labor's diminishing contribution to growth

China's demographic dividends are reversing. While employment contributed almost a third

FIGURE 2.7   **Public and private sector capital stock per worker in China and other countries, 2014**

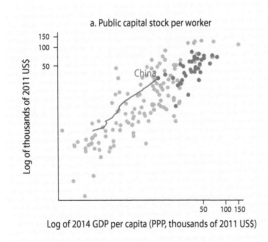
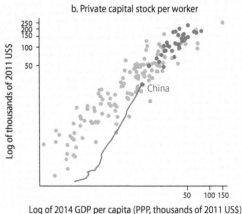

Sources: Calculations based on Penn World Tables 9.0 and International Monetary Fund data.
Note: China's public (panel a) and private (panel b) capital stock per worker at historical levels of income per capita (red line) are compared with 2013 levels in other countries (2011 international US$, thousands, purchasing power parity [PPP], log scale). Organisation for Economic Co-operation (OECD) and Development countries are in purple.

to GDP growth (2.9 percentage points) in the two decades following 1978, its contribution has fallen to 0.3 percentage point in the past 10 years. According to United Nations (UN) estimates, total population growth in the past five years was only 0.5 percent a year, while the growth rate of the working-age population (ages 15–64) began to decline in 2016.

In line with the population decline, China's labor force will also decline in the coming years and age considerably. The labor force is projected to shrink by 47 million, from 793 million in 2010 to 746 million in 2030. UN projections show the labor force declining 1 percent a year in the 2030s, thus contributing negatively to GDP growth. The average age is projected to increase from 38.9 years to 43.3 years. As a result of the aging of the population, the share of people age 60 and above in the labor force is projected to increase from 6.6 percent in 2010 to 13.8 percent in 2030. Hence, it will be increasingly important to keep elderly workers in the labor force. If by 2030 China were to achieve the same labor force participation per age cohort as in Japan today, an additional 38 million workers would join the labor force—almost

5 percent of the labor force. The increases would come almost entirely from people age 50 and above (figure 2.8). The shrinking and aging labor force raises the importance of improving labor productivity by investing in human capital and ensuring that the economy can use workers fully throughout their working lives.

Raising the retirement age can add considerably to the active labor force. In China, the standard old-age dependency ratio, defined as the ratio of the population age 65 and older per 100 persons ages 15–64, was 13.3 in 2015, in line with the average for upper-middle-income countries. The UN projects that the ratio will rise to 32 in 2035. But if the ratio is adjusted to reflect China's current retirement age—60 for men and 55 for women—the ratio would already have been 28 in 2015 and would be expected to reach 59 in 2035. This illustrates the significant impact of China's early retirement age on the structure of its labor force and thus the reduced contribution of labor to the economy. In addition, the retirement age is lower for females than for males, resulting in a faster decline in the female workforce than in the male (figure 2.9). These estimates ignore

FIGURE 2.8 **Projected labor force in China, by age, 2010–30**

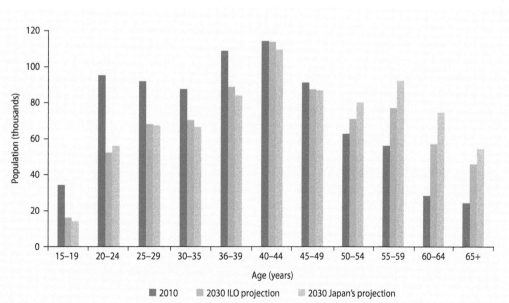

Source: Calculations based on ILOSTAT data.
Note: ILO = International Labour Organization.

FIGURE 2.9   **Population of China, by gender and age group, 1971–2041**

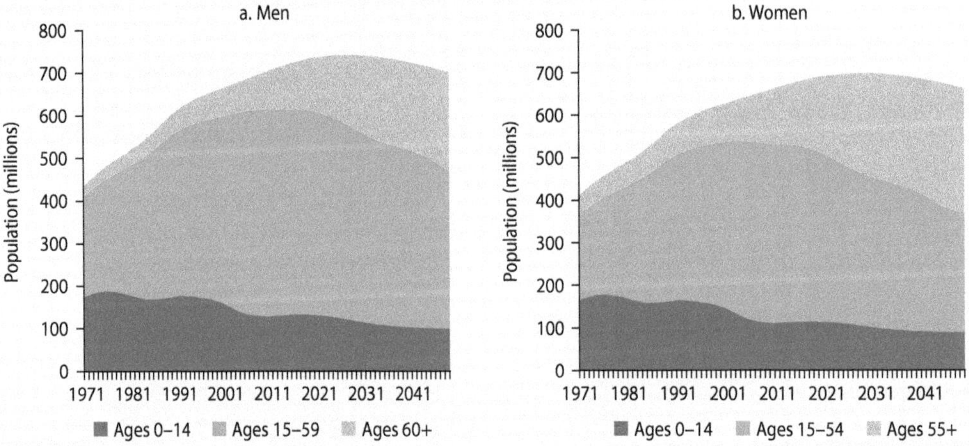

Source: Calculations based on United Nations Population Division data.

the fact that women in blue-collar jobs today often retire at 52, resulting in an even larger gender gap in the retirement age and greater underutilization of the female labor force.

The sectoral reallocation of labor from agriculture to industry has been a major driving force of China's economic growth. As with the declining labor force, the contribution from sectoral labor reallocation is also likely to be more limited in the future. Rural surplus labor was projected up to 2030, using official statistics, based on three scenarios: the business-as-usual baseline scenario of the current technological trajectory, a second scenario reflecting a medium technological trajectory with moderately faster labor productivity growth, and a third scenario representing the fastest technological trajectory and thus the fastest labor productivity growth. Higher levels of technology and labor productivity in agriculture would imply greater rural surplus labor, which in turn would indicate greater potential for labor reallocation to other sectors of the economy.

The estimated labor surplus ranged from approximately 165 million to 230 million in the early 2000s but has since declined steadily. The rural labor surplus in 2018 is estimated to range from 20 million under scenario one to 95 million under scenario

three. Under scenario one, based on the current technological trajectory, very little rural labor surplus remains, and the economic contribution of labor through its reallocation from agriculture is expected to be fairly negligible. The much larger estimated rural surplus labor under scenario three indicates that technological advancement can significantly raise the potential for sectoral reallocations of agricultural labor.

Under all three scenarios, rural surplus labor is projected to decline continuously. It is projected to disappear by 2023 under scenario one. Hence, the small remaining labor surplus is projected to disappear completely within four years. With faster technological trajectories, rural surplus labor is projected to remain up to 2030, ranging from 24 million in scenario two to 48 million in scenario three.

These estimates of rural surplus labor are based on official aggregate statistics, which indicate that a large share of labor remains in agriculture—almost 43 percent, according to rural *hukou* status in 2016. But household data indicate that rural households devote, on average, only about one-third of their time to farming.[4] If the estimated rural labor supply is adjusted according to the actual time spent farming, no rural surplus labor would remain in 2018 under all three scenarios.

Notes

1. This report's estimates of TFP growth are similar to results from Bosworth and Collins (2008) and Perkins and Rawski (2008) and are somewhat higher than results from Chow and Lin (2002), Feenstra, Inklar, and Timmer (2015), Wei, Xie, and Zhang (2017), Woo (1997), Wu (2011), Wu (2017), and Young (2003). The more recent papers (Wei, Xie, and Zhang 2017; Wu 2017) found that aggregate TFP actually declined after the global financial crisis. Although this report's estimates of recent TFP growth are higher, the overall trend and hence the associated qualitative interpretation are similar to the other estimates.
2. Data are from the Wind Information Co., Ltd. The exact shares were 90 percent in 2015 and 86 percent in 2016.
3. See, for example, Reinhart, Reinhart, and Rogoff (2012).
4. See the Research Center for the Rural Economy's nationally representative panel surveys from 2003 to 2013.

Bibliography

Aghion, P., and P. Howitt. 1992. "A Model of Growth through Creative Destruction," *Econometrica* (60) 323–51.

Bai, C.-E., C.-T. Hsieh, and Z. M. Song. 2016. "The Long Shadow of a Fiscal Expansion", Brookings Papers on Economic Activity, Fall 2016, pp. 129-181.

Barro, R. J., and X. Sala-i-Martin. 2004. *Economic Growth*. Cambridge, MA: MIT Press.

Bosworth, B., and S. M. Collins. 2008. "Accounting for Growth: Comparing China and India." *Journal of Economic Perspectives* 22 (1): 45–66.

Cecchetti, S. G., M. S. Mohanty, and F. Zampolli. 2011. "The Real Effects of Debt," BIS Working Paper No. 352, Bank for International Settlements.

Checherita, C., and P. Rother. 2010. "The Impact of High and Growing Government Debt on Economic Growth: An Empirical Investigation for the Euro Area," ECB Working Paper 1237, European Central Bank.

Chow, G., and A. Lin. 2002. "Accounting for Economic Growth in Taiwan and Mainland China: A Comparative Analysis." *Journal of Comparative Economics* 30 (3): 507–30.

Dollar, D., and S.-J. Wei. 2007. "Das (Wasted) Kapital: Firm Ownership and Investment Efficiency in China," IMF Working Paper 07/09, International Monetary Fund, Washington, DC.

Feenstra, R. C., R. Inklaar, and M. P. Timmer. 2015. "The Next Generation of the Penn World Table." *American Economic Review* 105 (10): 3150–82; data available at http://www.ggdc.net/pwt"www.ggdc.net/pwt.

Haltiwanger, J., R. Kulick, and C. Syverson. 2018. "Misallocation Measures: The Distortion That Ate the Residual," NBER Working Paper 24199, National Bureau of Economic Research.

Herd, R. 2017. "Estimating Capital Formation and Capital Stock by Economic Sector in China." Background paper for this report, World Bank, Washington, DC.

Hofman, B., and J. Wu. 2009. "Explaining China's Development and Reforms: Commission on Growth and Development," Working Paper 50, World Bank, Washington, DC.

Hsieh, C.-T., and Z. Song. 2015. "Grasp the Large, Let Go of the Small: The Transformation of the State Sector in China," NBER Working Paper 21006, National Bureau of Economic Research.

Lardy, Nicholas R. 2014. *Markets over Mao: The Rise of Private Business in China*. Washington, DC: Peterson Institute for International Economics.

———. 2016. "State Firms: A Growing Drag on China's Economic Growth?" Background paper for this report, World Bank, Washington, DC.

Perkins, D., and T. Rawski. 2008. "Forecasting China's Economic Growth to 2025," In *China's Great Economic Transformation*, edited by L. Brandt and T. Rawski. Cambridge: Cambridge University Press.

Reinhart, C. M., V. Reinhart, and K. S. Rogoff. 2012. "Public Debt Overhangs: Advanced Economy Episodes since 1800." *Journal of Economic Perspectives* 26 (3): 69–86.

Research Center for the Rural Economy's nationally representative panel surveys from 2003 to 2013.

Seck, A. 2012. "International Technology Diffusion and Economic Growth: Explaining the Spillover Benefits to Developing Countries," *Structural Change and Economic Dynamics,* (23) 437– 51.

Timmer, M. P., G. J. de Vries, and K. de Vries. 2015. "Patterns of Structural Change in Developing countries." In *Routledge Handbook of Industry and Development,* J. Weiss and M.

Tribe, eds., pp. 65-83. Data available http://www.rug.nl/ggdc/productivity/10-sector/.

Wei, Shang-Jin, X. Xie, and X. Zhang. 2017. "From 'Made in China' to 'Innovated in China': Necessity, Prospects, and Challenges." *Journal of Economic Perspectives* 31 (1): 49–70.

Woo, W. T. 1997. "Chinese Economic Growth: Sources and Prospects." Working paper, Department of Economics, University of California, Davis.

Wu, H. X. 2011. "Accounting for China's Growth in 1952–2008: China's Growth Performance Debate Revisited with a Newly Constructed Data Set." RIETI Discussion Paper 11-E-003, Research Institute of Economy, Trade, and Industry, Tokyo.

———. 2017. "China's Institutional Impediment to Productivity Growth: An Industry-Origin Growth Accounting Approach." Unpublished paper.

Young, A. 2003. "Gold into Base Metals: Productivity Growth in the People's Republic of China during the Reform Period." *Journal of Political Economy* 111 (1): 1220–61.

3

The Productivity Challenge

The recent slowdown of China's economic growth results in large part from declining productivity growth. Macroeconomic estimates of total factor productivity (TFP)—a measure of economic efficiency and innovation, including technological innovation—experienced a significant slowdown in growth, from about 3.51 percent in the 10 years before the global financial crisis to 1.55 percent in 2008–17. Nascent signs of improvement have emerged in recent years, but TFP growth remains significantly lower than its precrisis levels (figure 3.1).

The estimated slowdown in TFP growth based on macroeconomic data is consistent with estimates based on industrial manufacturing enterprise data (figure 3.2). Enterprise TFP growth can be decomposed into the entry of new firms, exit of firms, improvements among incumbents (within-firm TFP growth), and reallocations of resources to more productive firms. The entry of new firms would contribute positively if they are more productive than incumbents. The exit of poorly performing firms also would raise productivity, as would reallocating resources among existing firms toward more productive firms. Liberalizing markets can expand the potential contribution through each of these channels.

Enterprise data indicate that average manufacturing TFP growth in China essentially halved after the global financial crisis. This decline can be attributed almost entirely to the falling contribution of firm entries. Before the global financial crisis, new firm entries were the largest contributor to productivity growth. After 2007, the contribution of firm entries to TFP growth was lower by nearly a full percentage point, matching the estimated decline in overall average TFP growth. The rate of entry of new industrial firms[1] had increased to more than 12 percent annually in 2004 but subsequently declined by 3.5 to 4 percent by 2013. This contributed to the declining impact of new entries on overall TFP growth. The lower rate of entry could have been due to a combination of factors, including overcapacity in certain sectors and entry barriers in others. Industries suffering from overcapacity would discourage new entries due to low profit margins. High entry barriers to otherwise profitable industries would prevent new entries.

There is evidence that the rate of firm entry increased after 2013, perhaps reflecting the government's "Mass Entrepreneurship" Initiative, and this could have contributed to improved enterprise TFP growth. The TFP

FIGURE 3.1 **Aggregate growth of total factor productivity (TFP) in China, 1978–2017**

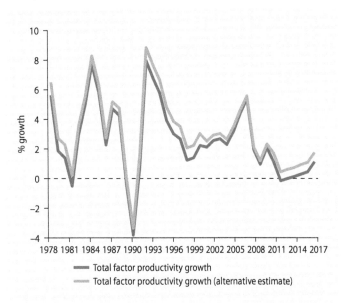

Total factor productivity growth

Total factor productivity growth (alternative estimate)

Source: Calculations based on National Bureau of Statistics data and authors' calculations.
Note: TFP growth is based on a production function that includes separate estimates of human capital. TFP growth (alternative estimate) does not include separate estimates of human capital.

FIGURE 3.2 **Growth of total factor productivity (TFP) in industry in China before and after the global financial crisis, 1998–2013**

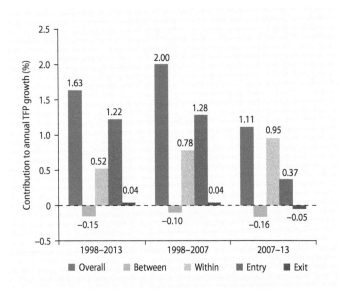

■ Overall ■ Between ■ Within ■ Entry ■ Exit

Sources: Brandt, Wang, and Zhang 2017, based on National Bureau of Statistics enterprise survey data.

analysis of the enterprise data in this report extends only up to 2013, based on data availability,[2] but macroeconomic estimates of TFP growth show a modest recovery in the most recent years (figure 3.1). The recent incipient recovery of TFP growth coincides with a decline in investment rates and government reforms to reduce the growth of credit, address overcapacity in industries, and tighten local government budget constraints. Government promotion of innovation and new technologies may also be starting to have an impact. More recent data and analysis are needed to assess the underlying drivers of recent improvements in TFP growth.

Given the declining contribution of firm entry since the global financial crisis, the higher productivity of incumbent firms has become the main contributor to TFP growth in China. Both before and since the global financial crisis, there have been few or no gains in TFP growth from firm exits or reallocation of productive resources among firms. This indicates that poorly performing firms are not exiting sufficiently to contribute to overall TFP growth, and more productive firms are not receiving sufficient productive resources (labor, capital, and intermediate inputs). Chapter 2 provides evidence of rising inefficiency in the allocation of resources to infrastructure and housing, as evidenced by rising incremental capital-output ratios. The minimal contribution of resource allocation may be due to a variety of reasons, including "zombie" firms that should exit the market, but instead remain to capture resources and productive small and medium enterprises that are having difficulty accessing financial and other resources.

Consistent with the recent slowdown of TFP growth, China's labor productivity growth has also been declining. The slowdown in labor productivity growth has been due to lower contributions from both the services and industry sectors (figure 3.3). The declining contribution of services has been due to a large decline in productivity growth within the sector, from an average of 9.3 percent a year in 2006–10 to 3.6 percent in 2011–15. Industry's contribution has declined because the reallocation of labor has increasingly been to services rather than to industry. Given that the labor productivity of services is lower than that of industry, China's aggregate labor productivity growth has slowed.

FIGURE 3.3 **Contribution of labor productivity to growth in China, by sector, 2003–17**

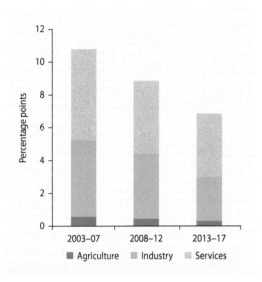

Source: Calculations based on World Development Indicators data.

The slowdown in labor productivity growth may indicate that China is beginning to enter the next stages of its economic development. Typically, countries grow richer by accumulating physical and human capital and experiencing structural transformation of their economies, as reflected in agriculture's declining share of the economy and industry's rising share. As economies develop further, growth decelerates due to diminishing returns to capital accumulation and declining gains from structural transformation of the economy.

The recent slowdown in the growth of China's labor productivity and TFP has coincided with a decline in productivity growth across many other countries. An aging workforce, slower growth of human capital, weakening momentum of global trade integration, and the waning effect of the information and communication technology (ICT) boom are among the possible longer-term structural causes. Excessive investments before the global financial crisis also could have contributed to the subsequent decline in productivity growth, as economies adjusted to the overcapacity by reducing outputs and investments and deleveraging. Therefore, the slowdown could be viewed as a combination of long-term structural and shorter-term

cyclical factors. Finally, the beneficial effects of widespread structural reforms in emerging economies during the 1990s and early 2000s may have petered out, and the global financial crisis may have postponed new reforms (World Bank 2018).

Promoting new drivers of growth through the "3+6+7" reform agenda

China will need to promote new drivers of growth to address its major productivity challenges. Sustained growth in the long run will depend on continuous productivity growth. This report proposes the "3+6+7" reform agenda to address China's productivity challenges and achieve long-term sustained growth:

- "3" refers to the three D's that are the keys to promoting productivity-driven growth: removing *distortions*, accelerating *diffusion*, and fostering *discovery*.
- "6" refers to the six strategic choices for promoting the three D's.
- "7" refers to the seven critical areas of structural and institutional reform.

The three D's

To promote continuous productivity growth and cultivate new drivers of growth, China could pursue policies to deepen the structural and institutional reforms that promote the three D's: removing *distortions*, accelerating *diffusion*, and fostering *discovery* (figure 3.4). The first D, reducing distortions in the allocation of resources, has been a key driver of growth in the past, and continuing reforms would allow China to reach its maximum potential production frontier. The first D requires reforms of financial, labor, and land markets to ensure that resources are allocated competitively and efficiently to their most productive uses in the economy.

The second D—accelerating diffusion of more advanced existing technologies, products, and management techniques—will help China extend its current production frontier to the global frontier. By taking advantage of China's large remaining

FIGURE 3.4   **The three D's: reducing distortions, accelerating diffusion, and fostering discovery**

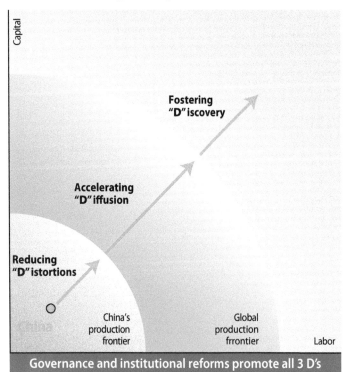

potential for catching up to the global production frontier, the second D would have a significant payoff for China in the immediate future. Accelerating diffusion requires innovation and science and technology policies that promote the diffusion of technology; an upgraded education and training system that prepares workers to adopt and use new technologies; and an economy that is more open and integrated with the rest of the world to facilitate access to global technologies and innovations.

The third and last D, fostering discovery of new innovation and technology, will help China to extend the global production frontier. The third D will become more critical as China becomes richer and edges closer to the global frontier. It requires a more open, bottom-up, and collaborative national innovation system based on modern world-class universities, stronger intellectual property rights, and a greater emphasis on basic "blue sky" research.

Governance and institutional reforms underpin the promotion of all three D's.

As the economy approaches the global production frontier, the state will need to assume a more market-supportive role, to promote market competition, and to strengthen the business climate. Market participants will need to have a stable and predictable market and fair competition.

China is now pursuing all three drivers of growth simultaneously. The three D's are interrelated and interconnected. The returns (in productivity gains) to existing technologies and new discoveries will be higher if productive resources can flow to a more productive use in the economy. The country could save resources by addressing existing inefficiencies in resource allocation more forcefully, which would benefit both diffusion and discovery. Policies and institutional reforms that promote market competition and a state that is more supportive of markets would support all three D's. Greater market competition would allow more competitive firms to access resources and encourage firms to invest in innovation and research and development (R&D). When the state focuses on promoting market competition, a conducive business environment and level playing field, firms have the confidence to invest long term in truly innovative R&D.

Six strategic choices
Striking the right balance between the three drivers of growth

China's recent policies have focused on the third D, fostering discovery and new technologies. Investments in new technologies can have a large payoff for the country and contribute to pushing out the global technology frontier. New technology fields are also less crowded than more established ones, providing new opportunities to take a leading position. At the same time, China remains, on average, quite distant from the global technology frontier and thus has substantial remaining potential for catch-up growth (figure 3.5). China could double its GDP simply by catching up to Organisation for Economic Co-operation and Development (OECD) countries in its TFP. To take advantage of catch-up growth, China needs to pay sufficient attention to the first and second D's,

FIGURE 3.5 **Total factor productivity (TFP) relative to the global technology frontier, 2014**

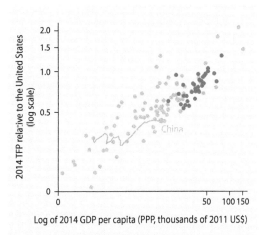

Source: Calculations based on Penn World Tables 9.0 data.
Note: Red line is China's TFP relative to the United States at similar levels of income per capita. PPP = purchasing power parity.

reducing distortions in the allocation of productive resources and promoting the diffusion and adoption of existing technologies, production processes, and management practices. The first and second D's are likely to produce significant payoffs for China's immediate future and remain the main drivers of growth for some time to come.

Ensuring that industrial policies support market competition rather than supplanting it

Since the early years of reform and opening-up, China has used industrial policies to accelerate its catching up to the high-income economies. Those policies were often modeled on examples from other economies, such as Japan and the Republic of Korea, although their outcomes in China, as elsewhere, have been mixed. China is now at a more advanced stage of development, and a new approach to industrial policies needs to be considered. Within China, industrial policies can undermine market competition when markets are protected, and favored firms benefit from targeted support, contributing to persistent overcapacity. The consensus in high-income countries is that industrial policies, to be effective, need to focus on market failures and be market conforming and

enhancing. Industrial policies that leverage and promote market competition are particularly important for China, given its unique context and large state presence.

Adjusting the balance between the state and markets

The strategic choice is for the state to be less market interventionist and more market supportive and market augmenting. In China, state-owned enterprises (SOEs) are at the core of the coexistence between the state and the market. SOEs will retain an important role in China's economy. Fair competition between SOEs and non-SOEs ensures that the markets will select the most productive enterprises, regardless of their ownership structure.

Reaching a consensus with global partners on mutually beneficial international trade and investment relations

Global trade tensions have brought uncertainty and downside risks to the world economy. A major risk for the world economy is the potential weakening of the rules governing global trade and investment and the unraveling of global value chains. As the world's largest trader and second-largest economy, China can play an important role in working with global partners to achieve a common understanding on mutually beneficial global economic relations. China has stated its opposition to protectionism and advocates an open and inclusive global economic system and global partnership and collaboration. It has taken steps to open up its economy further, such as the recent introduction of the national foreign investment negative list, which is the list of industries that restrict or prohibit foreign direct investment (FDI). With China's rise as a global economic and trading power, its contribution to the multilateral rules for global governance will be critical. China could provide leadership in formulating international rules on FDI and cross-border mergers and acquisitions that a broad cross section of both high-income and low- and middle-income economies could support.

Balancing supply-side reforms with demand-side reforms

China will need to rely less on investments and more on consumption for growth, while maintaining robust aggregate demand. Historically, domestic household consumption has played a relatively small role in driving China's growth, reflecting its high savings rate (figure 3.6). But China's share of consumption in the economy is already growing, and the government can accelerate this growth by encouraging a lower household savings rate through policies that would reinforce the social safety net, the pension system, and health insurance. Reforms of the household registration (*hukou*) system would further enhance demand by bringing migrants, now some 15 percent of the urban population, into the urban system.

Starting to prepare now for the future impact of technological changes

Policy makers need to start preparing China's workers today for the impact of technology on the future workplace. New technologies and innovations can result in new employment opportunities, but many current jobs may be displaced or require new skills, due to automation and artificial intelligence. Historical experience suggests that employment can expand with technology-induced productivity gains, but not necessarily in the industries experiencing the technological changes. Medium-skill routine jobs, many in manufacturing, seem to be at particular risk of automation. Technological change also has a skills bias, favoring those with more skills and education, which could lead to rising income inequality. Moreover, recent technological innovations tend to lead to a "winner takes all" outcome, which further contributes to inequality. Finally, the share of labor in a broad range of economies has declined in recent decades, part of which can be explained by technological change. The impact of new technology on jobs, income, and income distribution can be gradual as technologies are developed and adopted, but preparing for the future workplace needs to start now.

Seven critical reform areas

Addressing China's key strategic challenges to promoting the three D's requires a range of structural, governance, and institutional reforms. This report organizes the proposed reform agenda into seven areas:

- Reshaping industrial polices and supporting market competition (chapter 4)
- Promoting innovation and the digital economy (chapter 5)
- Building human capital (chapter 6)
- Allocating resources efficiently (chapter 7)
- Leveraging regional development and integration (chapter 8)
- Promoting international competitiveness and economic globalization (chapter 9)
- Governing the next transformation (chapter 10).

Although the reform areas contribute to all three D's, they differ in their impact on them. Many reforms reduce distortion in the economy by strengthening market competition and improving factor allocation. Reforming innovation policies and building human capital would benefit both the diffusion of existing innovations and the discovery of new ones. Regional and global

FIGURE 3.6   **Share of income and consumption in GDP in selected countries, 2016**

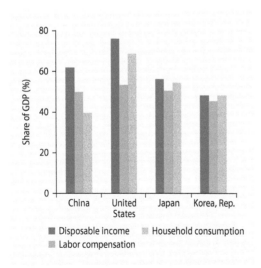

Sources: World Development Indicators and National Bureau of Statistics.

integration also would benefit diffusion of existing innovations, while greater market competition and the promotion of entrepreneurship would strengthen China's capacity for generating new innovations.

The impact of reforms on future growth

Reforms to promote the three D's are expected to have a significant impact on China's future growth. For this report, China's growth prospects were estimated using a long-term growth-forecasting model, based on the conditional convergence literature.[3] No single model can capture a country's full spectrum of growth opportunities and challenges or the interactions between them, but the projections here provide a coherent and transparent illustration of China's plausible future growth trajectories. The forecasting model assumes that a country's long-run (steady-state) productivity depends on the quality of its policies, institutions, and other specific factors. The model therefore approximates the impact of policy and institutional reforms proposed in this report. The World Economic Forum's global competitiveness index (GCI) is used as a measure of the quality of institutions and policies.

The GCI, a comprehensive set of indicators capturing the determinants of growth and competitiveness that have emerged from the literature, is strongly and positively correlated with the level and growth of productivity (World Economic Forum 2014). The *2017–18 Global Competitiveness Report* ranks China as the 27th-most competitive country in the world (World Economic Forum 2017). The growth-forecasting model assumes that, once a country has reached its steady-state productivity, its labor productivity will grow at the rate of technological progress at the global technology frontier. If a country is below its steady-state labor productivity, its productivity will grow faster than technological progress until it "catches up" to its long-run level.

The long-term projections are based on three scenarios (table 3.1). Scenario 1 represents "comprehensive reforms," in which China's GCI (and long-run

productivity) significantly improves. Scenario 2 represents "moderate reforms" and assumes no significant changes in the quality of China's institutions, policies, and other competitiveness factors (that is, no changes in the country's relative long-term productivity). Scenario 3 is a "limited reforms" scenario, in which a high level of accumulated debt further slows growth. It captures the risk of a substantial and long-lasting slowdown in growth stemming from China's debt overhang and assumes that the negative impact of a high debt burden on growth can be considerable, even in the absence of a financial crisis, consistent with empirical evidence.

The comprehensive reforms scenario assumes that China will improve its GCI score to the average of countries ranked in the top 10 in the quality (not quantity) of its infrastructure; tertiary education enrollment rate; domestic and foreign competition (goods market efficiency); and pace of technology adoption, including the use of ICTs. As expected for an upper-middle-income country, China also has significant opportunities for further improving its ranking in business sophistication and innovation. Scenario 1 assumes that China will successfully implement reforms to close the remaining gaps in the GCI with the top 10 performers by 2030.

Under scenario 1, China's GDP growth with comprehensive reforms is projected to slow from an average of 7.2 percent in

TABLE 3.1 **Projected growth of GDP and labor productivity in China under three scenarios, 2001–50**
Percent

Scenario	2001–10	2011–20	2021–30	2031–40	2041–50
Working-age population	0.5	0.1	−0.1	−0.4	−0.9
1. Comprehensive reforms					
GDP growth	10.6	7.2	5.1	4.1	3.0
Labor productivity	10.0	7.1	5.4	5.0	3.8
2. Moderate reforms					
GDP growth			5.1	2.9	2.2
Labor productivity			5.4	3.9	3.0
3. Limited reforms					
GDP growth			4.0	1.7	2.3
Labor productivity			4.3	2.7	3.0

Sources: Calculations based on National Bureau of Statistics data and United Nations Population Division 2017.

FIGURE 3.7   **Projected gross national income (GNI) per capita in China, 2011–46**

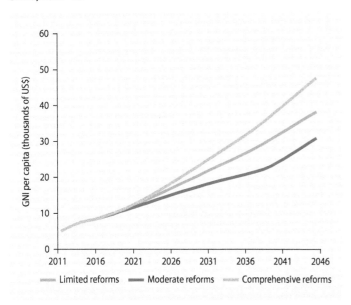

Limited reforms   ▬ Moderate reforms   Comprehensive reforms

Sources: Hubbard and Sharma 2016; calculations based on United Nations and World Development Indicators data.
Note: GNI per capita uses the Atlas method.

2011–20 to an average of 5.1 percent in 2021–30 and 4.1 percent in 2031–40. By contrast, GDP growth would be 2.9 percent in 2031–40 with moderate reforms under scenario 2, and it would decline further to 1.7 percent with only limited reforms under scenario 3. Similar differences can be expected for labor productivity growth.

High-income levels are within China's reach in the not-too-distant future in all three scenarios. Based on the projections, China is expected to attain high income status around 2023 under both the comprehensive and moderate reform scenarios (figure 3.7).[4] China's gross national income (GNI) per capita, US$8,690 in 2017, is projected to double by around 2030 under both the comprehensive reforms scenario and the moderate reforms scenario.

A significant income gap opens up over the long term in the three scenarios. By 2050, under the scenario with moderate reforms, income per capita could be about 25 percent greater than under the scenario with limited reforms, and it could be an additional 25 percent higher with comprehensive reforms. This means that by 2050, GNI per capita

could potentially be as high as US$41,000 with comprehensive reforms or as low as US$27,000 with limited reforms.

Notes

1. The National Bureau of Statistics data used are for industrial firms with sales greater than RMB 20 million.
2. The National Bureau of Statistics industrial enterprise survey data are currently available to researchers only up to 2013.
3. Barro and Sala-i-Martin (2004) provide an extensive overview of the theoretical and empirical literature on growth convergence.
4. The World Bank's high-income threshold for fiscal 2018 is set at US$12,236 GNI per capita. GNI measures the value added produced by a country's citizens plus the income of the country's nationals earned abroad. The projections assume that the threshold will grow at the rate of long-term inflation of the special drawing rights basket.

Bibliography

Adler, G., R. Duval, D. Furceri, S. K. Çelik, K. Koloskova, and M. Poplawski-Ribeiro. 2017. "Gone with the Headwinds: Global Productivity" IMF Staff Discussion Note SDN/17/04, International Monetary Fund, Washington, DC.

Au-Yeung, W., M. Kouparitsas, N. Luu, and D. Sharma. 2013. "Long-Term International GDP Projections," Australian Treasury Working Paper 2013-02.

Ball, L. 2014. "Long-Term Damage from the Great Recession in OECD countries," *European Journal of Economics and Economic Policies: Intervention.* Edward Elgar, 11(2) 149–60.

Barro, R. J., and X. Sala-i-Martin. 2004. *Economic Growth.* Cambridge, MA: MIT Press.

Brandt, L., K. Storesletten, and G. Kambourov. 2016. "Firm Entry and Regional Growth Disparities: The Effect of SOEs in China." 2016 Meeting Papers 182, Society for Economic Dynamics.

Brandt, L., J. Van Biesebroeck, and Y. Zhang. 2012. "Creative Accounting or Creative Destruction." *Journal of Development Economics* 97(2) 339-51.

Brandt, L., L. Wang, and Y. Zhang. 2017. "Productivity in Chinese Industry: 1998–2013." Background paper for this report, World Bank, Washington, DC.

Cai, Y., and Y. Fu. 2017. "The Technical and Structural Effects of TFP Growth: Measurement and Decomposition Based on China's Macro and Sector Data." *Economic Research Journal* 52 (1), 72–88.

Conference Board. 2018. "Global Productivity on Upward Trajectory." Conference Board (press release), March 26. https://www.conference -board.org/press/pressdetail.cfm?pressid=7372.

Foda, K. 2016. "The Productivity Slump: A Summary of the Evidence, Global Economy and Development at Brookings." Retrieved from https://www.brookings.edu/wp-content /uploads/2016/08/productivity-evidence.pdf.

Hsieh, C.-T., and P. J. Klenow. 2009. "Misallocation and Manufacturing TFP in China and India" *Quarterly Journal of Economics*, Vol. CXXIV, Issue 4.

Hubbard, P., and D. Sharma. 2016. "Understanding and Applying Long-Term GDP Projections." East Asia Bureau of Economic Research Working Paper No 119.

National Bureau of Statistics. Enterprise survey data.

Tian, X., and X. Yu. 2012. "The Enigmas of TFP in China: A Meta-Analysis." *China Economic Review* 23 (2) 396–14.

United Nations Population Division. 2017. *2017 Revision of World Population Prospects*. New York: United Nations.

World Bank. 2018. *Global Economic Prospects: Broad-Based Upturn, But for How Long?* Washington, DC: World Bank.

World Economic Forum. 2014. *2014–15 Global Competitiveness Report*. Geneva: World Economic Forum.

———. 2017. *2017–18 Global Competitiveness Report*. Geneva: World Economic Forum.

Wu, H. X. 2011 "Accounting for China's Growth in 1952–2008: China's Growth Performance Debate Revisited with a Newly Constructed Data Set," RIETI Discussion Paper 11-E-003.

———. 2017. "China's Institutional Impediment to Productivity Growth: An Industry-Origin Growth Accounting Approach." Informal.

Young, A. 1995. "The Tyranny of Numbers: Confronting the Statistical Realities of the East Asian Growth Experience." *Quarterly Journal of Economics* (110) 641–80.

———. 2003. "Gold into Base Metals: Productivity Growth in the People's Republic of China during the Reform Period." *Journal of Political Economy* 111(1) 1220–261.

4

Reshaping Industrial Policies and Supporting Market Competition

Industrial upgrading was an important driver of growth in China in past decades. During this period, China experienced a significant structural transformation. The share of agriculture sector value added in gross domestic product (GDP) declined from 27.7 percent in 1978 to 7.2 percent in 2018. In the same period, the share of industry declined from 47.7 percent to 40.7 percent, and the share of services rose from 24.6 percent to 52.2 percent. China also experienced industrial upgrading within sectors. The share of low-technology manufacturing to total manufacturing declined from 29.4 percent in 1999 to 24.6 percent in 2017, and the share of medium-technology manufacturing industry rose correspondingly.

China still has a high potential for industrial upgrading. Industry competitiveness can be enhanced through greater "servicification" of manufacturing and the application of new technologies. The government sees considerable scope for China to leverage product quality as a new driver of manufacturing growth. For services, "modern" services are increasingly traded internationally, facilitating scale economies and technology diffusion and creating new opportunities for growth. The digital economy offers significant potential to boost productivity by improving manufacturing processes as well as enhancing the agriculture and services sectors. Although the share of agriculture can be expected to continue to decline, the industrialization and servicification of agriculture can be an important source of productivity growth in the future by expanding agricultural value chains to agroprocessing and food services.

To promote industrialization, many countries have used industrial policies throughout their history. Market failures, coordination externalities, technology spillovers, and dynamic productivity gains have been the main justifications for targeted industrial policies. However, researchers have expressed doubts about the effectiveness of industrial policies. To implement targeted industrial policies effectively, policy makers need to be able to identify the market or government failures that have held back an industry from developing. Often, this identification requires some judgment on the degree of hard evidence required to justify supporting a specific industry.

Even if justified, targeted industrial support does not guarantee success. For industries to become internationally competitive, policy makers need to identify the country's comparative advantages correctly and to develop and implement a credible support plan effectively. Doing so is becoming increasingly difficult in light of the rapidly changing landscape of technology and globalization, heightening the risks of betting on the wrong industry or technology. For example, new labor-saving technologies in a more integrated global environment can rapidly weaken the competitiveness of a country's labor-intensive industry.

East Asian economies that succeeded in becoming high income, such as Japan and the Republic of Korea, used targeted industrial policies widely and actively, at least in the early stages of their development. They combined greater integration with the international economy and heavy government involvement in nurturing industries and companies. However, there is skepticism about the effectiveness of selective interventions to promote specific industrial sectors, and many observers note the widespread failure of interventionist industrial policies across other countries and regions. Some observers attribute the successful development of East Asian countries more to good fundamental macroeconomic policies, competent governments with good capacity, and high investment rates in physical and human capital and less to targeted industrial policies.

East Asian economies also modified their policies as they became larger and more complex and transitioned to a more knowledge- and technology-intensive economy. They realized that heavily interventionist industrial policies had to be modified at later stages of development. This approach typically involved reducing "vertical" industrial policies that target specific sectors and firms and instead transitioning to more "horizontal" policies that improve factor markets and the broader business environment. Some observers credit the success of East Asian countries more to horizontal learning strategies and less to sector targeting (Cirera and Maloney 2017). This evolution of industrial policies indicates that it is important for countries to know when to phase out previously successful industrial policies. The challenge is that once

industrial policies are in place, incentives and the political economy can make it difficult to adjust or abandon them.

Governments in other high-income countries have supported specific technologies and industries, particularly by targeting research and development (R&D). In the United States, government agencies such as the Defense Department's Defense Advanced Research Projects Agency (DARPA) and the National Institutes of Health provided critical financing for key technologies that contributed to the growth of the biotechnology industry, the Internet, and the Apple iPhone.[1] The European Commission's Industry Policy Strategy emphasizes horizontal policies, such as improving the information and communication technology (ICT) infrastructure, intellectual property rights, and upgrading of workforce skills. These policies are complemented by support for key enabling technologies and industries—such as the space, defense, automotive, and steel industries—including through various funds, such as the European Structural and Investment Funds (five funds worth more than €450 billion) and Horizon 2020 (€77 billion for 2014–20). Some European Union (EU) countries also have national industry promotion strategies, most notably Germany's Industry 4.0, that promote manufacturing upgrading by increasing the digitization and interconnection of products, value chains, and business models.

Promoting industrial development has been a major priority for China, with an emphasis on promoting science, technology, and innovation. The outline of the National Medium- and Long-Term Science and Technology Development Plan (2006–2020) provides a blueprint for strengthening the country's scientific, technological, and innovation capabilities. It emphasizes the promotion of indigenous or independent innovation, through the absorption and "re-innovation" of foreign technology and the nurturing of the national innovation system to produce original innovation. Manufacturing 2025 outlines an ambitious plan for "techno-industrial" policies to promote a multitude of advanced industries and technologies, such as information technology, new energy, and new materials for China to modernize its industries and become a leading manufacturing power. The plan calls for market-oriented and government-led development that gives markets a decisive role in allocating resources, creates a stable environment for business, and actively transforms government functions.

Industrial policies to support market competition

China is evolving as its economy grows beyond middle income and increasingly approaches the global technology frontier. Industrial policies can continue to play an important role as China becomes a high-income country, but the policies will need to evolve to deal with expanded and more complex markets and increasing technological uncertainty and unpredictability.

To analyze industrial policies in China, case studies were conducted of automobiles, mobile phones, semiconductors, and renewable energy (solar and wind), with a focus on policies to promote technology and innovation (Sturgeon and Thun 2018; Kuriakose et al. 2017). These industries benefited from significant growth of domestic demand and targeted state support over the years, and they embody the global technology and innovation upgrading long sought by the government. Each industry differs in the type of technology used and market structure, but cross-cutting themes emerged from the analysis.

The key message is that industrial policies, to be effective, have to be less distortionary and support and complement market competition. Industrial policies are less effective when they undermine open and fair market competition. They can lead to too little competition when markets are protected and favored firms benefit from targeted support and can lead to "too much" competition when support for industries and firms produces persistent overcapacity. By constraining market mechanisms, both outcomes hinder efforts to promote technology and transition to innovation-led growth.

With too little competition, firms can enjoy profits by capturing the rents from protected markets, which can contribute to overinvestment and excess industrial capacity, as experienced by some of the

heavy industry sectors in China (box 4.1). Without competitive pressure, firms have little incentive to invest in innovation and technological upgrades or to differentiate themselves from their competitors. Industries such as the automobile and wind turbine sectors could benefit from more open competition.

This chapter proposes reforms specific to industrial policies. The main proposals are to (a) focus and streamline industrial policies; (b) improve government-industry dialogue and the monitoring and evaluation of industrial policies; (c) instill greater discipline in local governments' support for industries; and (d) ensure timely exits of nonviable firms. Industrial policies, however, need to be considered in the context of the broader set of complementary reforms.

The broader reform agenda encompasses a wide array of reforms: reforms of innovation promotion that target support for specific technologies; reforms of the services sector to remove barriers to entry; reforms to improve the business climate by shifting the policy focus from vertical to horizontal interventions; reforms to promote market competition and antimonopoly policy to ensure fair competition; and reforms of foreign direct investment (FDI) policy to address the requirements for joint ventures and technology transfer policies. These reforms are discussed throughout the report, but at the core is the need to promote market competition. State-owned enterprise (SOE) reforms are particularly critical for China, given the importance of SOEs in its economy.

Focusing and streamlining industrial policies

Industrial policies need to be selective, focused, and streamlined. In China, the central authorities formulate policies, but local governments implement them, since much of government spending is local. Local officials are, in theory, agents of the central government, making them highly responsive to central policies and objectives, and they try to demonstrate that they are actively implementing central policies. But they also enjoy some degree of autonomy and discretion, so

BOX 4.1   **Industrial excess capacity in China**

China has experienced chronic excess capacity in its industry sector. Industrial capacity utilization rates in China have been consistently below 80 percent since the global financial crisis (figure B4.1.1). Although excess capacity usually occurs during an economic downturn due to weak demand, the persistence of excess capacity in China cannot be fully explained by demand-side factors. Rather, overinvestment appears to be the fundamental problem that led to excess capacity in China, which was exacerbated by a massive fiscal stimulus carried out in response to the global financial crisis. Excess capacity affected the heavy industries, such as ferrous and nonferrous metals, chemicals, and transport equipment manufacturing. The government understands that it needs to deal with excess capacity to enhance the efficiency of the industry sector and to improve the quality of economic growth.

In 2015, China's authorities introduced a comprehensive program aimed at reducing excess capacity, which included reducing 150 million tons of crude steel capacity and 800 million tons of coal capacity over 2016–20. Measures included setting targets for capacity reduction of central state-owned enterprises (SOEs), strengthening environmental and energy efficiency standards, suspending production in mining and raw materials sectors during peak heating seasons, limiting financial supply to overcapacity sectors, and restructuring or liquidating inefficient enterprises. Strong government actions during 2016–17 appears to have had a significant impact on curbing excess capacity. As a result, industrial capacity utilization rates recovered, rising to 78 percent in 2017, the highest rate since 2013. These actions, together with ongoing efforts to restrict industrial production in polluted sectors, helped to lift prices and contributed to the growth of corporate profits in China in 2017.

However, challenges remain to reduce excessive capacity further. While the focus has been on eliminating existing capacity, some firms have been building new capacity. Policies have so far focused mainly on reducing the capacity of large SOEs through administrative measures, but such measures are less binding on private producers. Finally, reducing excess capacity requires winding down inefficient enterprises through bankruptcy and closure and resolving the corresponding increase in bad debts, as well as removing market-distorting policies, such as subsidies that promote the emergence of new capacity. However, the number of bankruptcies tends to be comparatively low in China.

With too much competition, an industry suffers from persistent overcapacity, and firms compete on low price and low quality. The resulting lower profitability reduces incentives to innovate by eroding payoffs to new technology and reducing the amount of resources available to invest in R&D. If the sectors are exporting, persistent overcapacity can also lead to international trade disputes and accusations of "dumping," as with photovoltaics.

FIGURE B4.1.1   **Industrial capacity utilization rates in China, 2013–19**

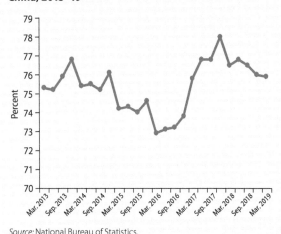

Source: National Bureau of Statistics.

policy implementation can be uncoordinated and have consequences unintended by central authorities. Streamlining and focusing industrial policies would reduce unintended and uncoordinated local responses and facilitate central government monitoring and management of local policy implementation. It would also help make policy interventions more coherent, transparent, and predictable.

What are some general criteria for streamlining industrial policies? The typical arguments are to focus on market failures and externalities—which would generally favor promoting innovation and technologies that are new and have significant potential for information and technology spillovers—rather than to focus on specific industries or firms. For industrial policies that focus on particular industries, the government could be more disciplined and selective in identifying the targeted industries to support. It could ensure that the support is not concentrated on a few firms in any sector, emphasize new firm entry, encourage younger enterprises, and phase out support for noncompetitive firms in a timely manner by ensuring that the support has clear sunset clauses and performance criteria (see also Aghion et al. 2012). These clauses and criteria would help to ensure that the benefits of policy support are justified by the costs of the support. Even where industries have been promoted successfully in technological upgrading, the costs may have been too large and spending too inefficient. Rigorous evaluations of industrial policies are needed that compare benefits with the costs of providing support, including all direct and indirect support provided to specific industries and firms.

Improving government-industry dialogue and monitoring and evaluation of industrial policies

An institutional framework that improves the flow of government-industry information in an inclusive and transparent way is important to identify key market constraints and failures and to monitor the impact of industrial policies. This public-private dialogue is important because the private sector is likely to have better access to policy-relevant market information, and therefore a wide range of private sector actors helps to make the process effective. Such dialogues were considered a key factor in the success of industrial policies in Japan and Korea. The dialogues can be used to seek out new investment ideas, achieve coordination among different state agencies, and push for necessary regulatory changes.

An institutionalized process for government-industry dialogue has to ensure that the risks of corruption and state capture by industries are adequately managed. Public transparency of information and regular evaluation of the effectiveness and efficiency of industrial policies can be helpful in this regard. New types of ICT and web-based platforms can improve the transparency and inclusivity of the dialogue as well as facilitate the collection and dissemination of information.

Instilling greater discipline in local governments' industrial policies and ensuring that all types of businesses can enjoy equal support

Reform of industrial policies requires addressing the role of local governments and central-local dynamics. To carry out industrial policies, local governments have provided support to local firms through financial subsidies, tax deductions, subsidized interest, and public venture capital. They have provided land at a discount and helped local firms deal with permits and approvals. They also have established high-technology development zones, science parks, and, more recently, technology incubators (Breznitz and Murphree 2011; Heilmann, Shih, and Hofem 2013; Zhou 2008). It is generally acknowledged that competition among local governments and their experimentation and initiatives have contributed to the country's rapid growth, complementing and compensating for the underdeveloped private sector in the earlier stages of development. But with the expansion of the private sector and the need to transition to more innovation-intensive growth, local governments need to evolve along with industrial policies.

Efforts to reform local government incentives and behaviors need to preserve the positive elements of local initiatives while tempering the excesses. Local government support for local industries has at times resulted in excessive entries of new firms and inadequate exits of failing firms due to continued support and protection provided by local governments. This situation has contributed to persistent overcapacity and oversupply in various industries. This excessive supply has also been accompanied by local protectionism and the fragmentation of industries, at times hindering the formation of national markets, standards, and new technologies, and resulting in considerable waste. Market fragmentation also has led to rent dissipation and suboptimal scale, reducing the resources for R&D and the incentives to innovate because local firms are protected from competition.

The incentives of local governments contribute to market fragmentation. China has a centralized cadre management system, through which individual positions and careers of government officials are managed. The cadre management system has traditionally evaluated the performance of local officials based largely on local economic growth. Thus, local officials have had strong incentives to promote local economic growth, which has led at times to local protectionism and reluctance to allow local firms to fail, hindering market adjustment to industrial oversupply. In response, the government has broadened the performance evaluation criteria of local officials beyond the growth of local GDP, in an effort to reflect "high-quality" growth.[2] With the expansion of the criteria, the challenge is to ensure that local officials do not continue to perceive targets for local growth as being the most important.

The disparities between local revenues and expenditures create further incentives for local governments to hold onto local enterprises. Subnational governments are typically responsible for about 85 percent of public expenditures, but central transfer payments account for less than 50 percent of local expenditures. Most of the remaining gap is financed by other local revenues, such as local shared tax and debt finance (China Ministry of Finance). For the major taxes shared between the central and local governments (value-added tax and corporate and personal income taxes), the portion allotted to local governments is based on the location of tax collection (derivation-based revenue sharing). This incentivizes local governments to promote local enterprises. Reforms of the tax rules could help address the disparities in local budgetary revenue and expenditures, accelerate reforms of intergovernmental fiscal relations, and also encourage local governments to compete based on the provision of quality public services, rather than by supporting local enterprises.

On the expenditure side, limits to the type and extent of support that local governments can provide to local enterprises could be specified more clearly and concretely—and could be better regulated, perhaps modeled on EU restrictions regarding support for local enterprises. The new regulations should address the need to discourage local protectionism, such as for electric vehicles, which dampens competition and fragments the national market, and hinders national standardization and diffusion of technology. To facilitate enforcement, industrial policy needs to be transparent and relevant information made publicly available. Performance criteria and clear sunset clauses would help ensure that those industries and firms that are unable to improve their competitiveness lose access to support.

Government guidance funds have become an important source of local government support for local enterprises. Professionally managing and operating the funds in a market-oriented way would help to ensure that the funds support market competition and innovation. At an estimated RMB 5.3 trillion (early 2017), the funds dwarf government appropriations for science and technology and for nationwide spending on R&D (Divakaran and others 2017). With the sizable mobilization of funds, the challenge is to ensure an adequate number of good investment opportunities. With regard to high-technology investments, the scarcity of engineering and managerial skills may be a more binding constraint than financing.

Ensuring the timely exit of nonviable firms

China has a comparatively low rate of firm exits (figure 4.1). Ensuring that noncompetitive firms exit markets is necessary for market-supportive industrial policies to work. A more active market-led bankruptcy and corporate restructuring regime is needed that would distinguish viable and nonviable companies and address them accordingly, by reorganizing the former and liquidating the latter, including zombie firms. Lenders and firms need to recognize a firm's insolvent state early. The regulatory and supervisory framework needs to ensure timely recognition, since banks are often reluctant to resolve overindebted borrowers and to dispose of distressed loans. Otherwise, the banks' capacity to provide fresh loans to the economy remains locked in nonviable, loss-making firms at the expense

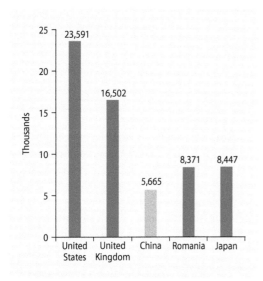

FIGURE 4.1 **Annual number of insolvency cases in selected countries, 2017**

Source: Online official statistics for each country, available as of November 2017.

of new, more vibrant ones. Once banks recognize problem loans, they need to distinguish viable and nonviable debtors, based on financial strength and prospects. A standard methodology, such as that used by European countries after the global financial crisis, provides a good basis for such assessments. But qualitative judgments are also important.

China's Enterprise Insolvency Law largely adheres to international good practices, but it has several drawbacks. Procedures are quite costly. Creditors are excluded from participating in making important decisions during insolvency proceedings. And the law does not contemplate priority for fresh financing, cross-border provisions, or prepackaged (hybrid) restructurings. Nor does the law have specific provisions for the insolvency of corporate groups. The number of cases for insolvency and for business restructuring and reorganization is relatively small in China, and a majority of bankruptcy proceedings end in liquidation (85 percent of resolved insolvency cases).[3] The insolvencies are often initiated as a last resort, when the companies are already in an untenable financial state, and it is too late to consider restructuring.

One way to promote the restructuring of viable firms is to take fuller advantage of informal workout procedures. To help

debtors and creditors negotiate settlements, local governments could promulgate nonbinding guidelines that draw on international examples, such as the London Approach popular in the United Kingdom in the 1970s and 1980s and, more recently, the International Association of Restructuring, Insolvency, and Bankruptcy Professionals (INSOL) Principles for Multi-Creditor Workouts (International Federation of Insolvency Professionals 2000). For out-of-court workouts, some countries have prepackaged reorganizations, "prepacks," to grant an accelerated channel for reorganization and to prevent very few creditors from withholding support in an attempt to extract exorbitant terms.

The China Banking Regulatory Commission issued notices in 2016 and 2017 (the Creditor Committee Guidelines) that require lenders of a distressed borrower to form creditor committees.[4] The guidelines regulate the operation of such committees and the types of enterprises to restructure. They also recommend intercreditor agreements to document terms agreed on as part of a workout. But they fall short of encouraging restructurings.

Multicreditor workouts seem comparatively rare, for various reasons. The Creditor Committee Guidelines appear to be purely voluntary, and creditors may have incentives to dispose of their distressed loans rapidly, which would be quicker than engaging in lengthy restructurings. The guidelines do not seem to be accompanied by legal or regulatory incentives for banks to engage in workouts, and they do not seem to encourage workouts to happen organically within a predictable general framework. Instead, they are considered on a case-by-case basis. A general framework could be introduced for restructuring distressed loans, with interbank agreements that bind dissenting creditors in the workout. Such a framework could be accompanied by temporary tax breaks and other provisions to encourage banks to engage in such restructurings, as provided in Korea, the Philippines, and Turkey.

When informal or hybrid proceedings fail, debtors and creditors have recourse to a formal, court-driven reorganization, the type of proceeding envisaged under China's Enterprise Insolvency Law. When a firm is fundamentally nonviable, the objective should be to convert the assets of the firm to cash as quickly as possible through a collective proceeding (rather than individual debt enforcement). Countries with systems that do this effectively have several common features. First, the test for when a company can be put into such a procedure is clearly laid out, most often based on the firm's cash flow. Second, creditors are given a large say in who administers the process and how they do so, which helps to maximize value since their economic interests are at stake. Third, the court can reverse transactions that are on noncommercial terms (such as asset sales to related parties at less than market value) or that unfairly favor one creditor. Ensuring speedy access to a court, promoting a culture of restructuring in the business and legal communities, and expanding the number of regulated restructuring professionals and specialized courts would also support market-led bankruptcies and corporate restructuring.

Promoting greater competition in the services sector

A more vibrant and competitive services sector can contribute significantly to productivity growth. Although the share of services in

China's economy has been increasing recently, reaching 52.2 percent in 2018, a large part of this rise has been due to the growth of financial services and real estate. There is still potential for further development of the services sector, particularly higher value-added services—such as R&D, ICT-related services, and consumer services—which will be increasingly demanded by a growing and more consumption-driven economy.

Internationally, the integration of services with manufacturing and agriculture is increasingly viewed as a key contributor to economic growth and development. High-income countries tend to use more inputs from the services sector, which can help to promote greater specialization within industry sectors by outsourcing services and focusing on core competencies.

In China, the contribution of service inputs to productive sectors is low relative to that in other countries (figure 4.2). The contribution of traditional services, such as distribution and transport, to manufacturing is relatively higher than more modern services. Taking further advantage of some of the more modern services—such as R&D, business, and digital services—could help to upgrade China's manufacturing even further. These modern services have a high impact on economic development because they have a high value-added and are easily tradable, such as through the Internet, which considerably reduces trade costs. In particular, new digital technologies—such as the Internet of Things, cloud computing, and Big Data—are driving new innovations in China's services sector. China now has the largest e-commerce market in the world, providing new opportunities for suppliers and consumers to connect to markets. But although digital services have been growing in China, unlocking their potential requires strengthening their linkages with manufacturing.

Reducing restrictions in the services sector would help to promote greater competition and growth of services. The globalization of services also enables China to tap into services as a source of growth. The Services Trade Restrictiveness Index (STRI) of the Organisation for Economic Co-operation and Development (OECD) indicates that market

FIGURE 4.2   **Inputs into productive sectors in selected countries, 2011**

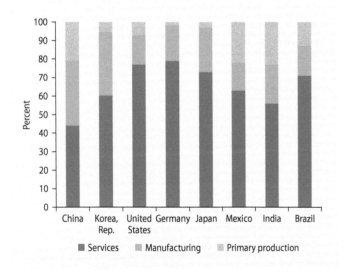

Source: Calculations based on Organisation for Economic Co-operation and Development (OECD) Trade in Value Added (TiVA) data.

restrictions on the services sector in China are in line with those in some of the other major upper-middle-income countries—such as Brazil, India, Indonesia, the Russian Federation, and Turkey—but are more restrictive than those in OECD countries (figure 4.3). The difference with OECD countries is mostly due to higher restrictions on foreign entry. Other types of restrictions are aligned more closely with those in OECD countries, although a gap remains between China and the better-performing countries. FDI restrictions affecting firm entry in China are mainly those that limit foreign equity holdings, followed by screening and approval restrictions. OECD's product market regulation indicators for China are also relatively high for barriers to trade and investment, barriers to entrepreneurship, and the degree of state control.

China could open more services to private investment, to expand opportunities for competitive and innovative private companies. Opening up the services sector further, by reducing market barriers to FDI, would promote a more attractive domestic environment for investment. Recent announcements of the opening of financial

services to majority foreign ownership are welcome, but more could be done. Reform measures would need to be designed according to the type of market restrictions affecting each subsector, because the types of restrictions vary significantly across the services sector. Market restrictions can target either firm entry or firm operations. STRI indicates that in China entry barriers seem to matter more for business, telecommunications, and ICT-related services, while operations barriers appear to be more important for transport and logistics services.

Reducing restrictive barriers in services would need to be complemented by regulatory governance reforms to sustain the impact of the reforms and address regulatory uncertainty identified by both foreign and domestic investors as critical for doing business in China. An improved regulatory governance framework would allow for continuous revisions and systematic fine-tuning of regulations after the initial reforms. Chapter 10 discusses regulatory governance reforms overall. Regulations for the services sector would need to account for fundamental market failures specific to each subsector,

FIGURE 4.3   Services Trade Restrictiveness Index in selected countries, 2017

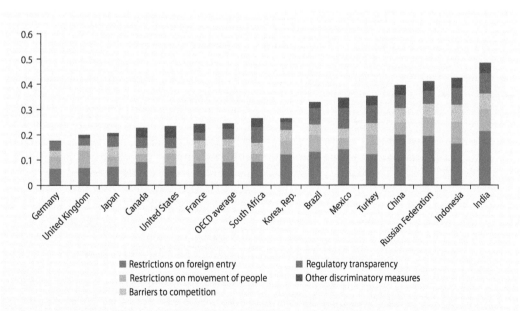

Source: Organisation for Economic Co-operation and Development (OECD) Services Trade Restrictiveness Index.
Note: Higher scores indicate that services trade is more restrictive.

such as asymmetric information in finance, natural monopolies in network industries, such as telecommunications and digital platforms, and public good characteristics in education and health services. Strong and effective institutions and regulatory bodies would be required to address such market failures.

Promoting entrepreneurship and improving the business climate

Entrepreneurship has been a key driver of China's economic growth since the 1980s. New firms have been a source of improved products and services and competitive pressure on incumbents, thus contributing to higher productivity. The first major wave of entrepreneurial activity occurred in the 1980s, when reform in agriculture led to the emergence of township and village enterprises, created by entrepreneurial farmers in the legal form of collective ownership. The second major wave crested after the late 1990s, when domestic private enterprises emerged, fundamentally reshaping the structure of the Chinese economy.

The third, and current, major wave is being propelled by the Mass Entrepreneurship Initiative, launched in 2015 (box 4.2). The initiative aims to remove institutional barriers to mobilizing and realizing the entrepreneurial spirit of the Chinese people. A wide range of national and subnational policies has been put in place to promote entrepreneurship, notably in supporting targeted groups of the population (such as university graduates, staff of R&D institutions, and migrant workers); promoting venture capital, microlending, guarantees, and leasing; providing support infrastructure such as incubators, coworking spaces, and accelerators; supporting entrepreneurial training and advocating an entrepreneurial culture; providing tax exemptions to micro and small enterprises; helping these enterprises access government procurement; and implementing business regulatory reforms.

The Mass Entrepreneurship Initiative has seen a surge in business creation. In 2014–16, the average annual growth in the number of

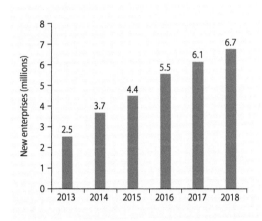

FIGURE 4.4 **Number of new enterprises registered annually in China, 2013–18**

Source: State Administration for Industry and Commerce.

enterprises accelerated to 19.3 percent, from 9.5 percent in 2008–13. In 2016, 15,100 enterprises were registering daily, up from 2,376 in 2013. The number of "market participants," including all enterprises as well as business individuals (*getihu*) and farmers associations, increased 44 percent between 2013 and 2016 (State Administration of Industry and Commerce 2017).

With the surge in business creation, more systematic collection and analysis of relevant data would allow the government to assess the impact of the initiative on new firm entries as well as exits and the contribution to economic growth. For example, part of the increase in the registration of private enterprises may stem from a change in the registration category of private businesses, from informal *getihus* to private enterprises (box 4.2). If confirmed, the surge in business registration may be overestimating the creation of new private enterprises, particularly those with potential for further growth and expansion. Addressing such questions would allow policy makers to understand which policy measures worked and to what extent.

Roughly 500 entrepreneurs in five Chinese cities surveyed for this report indicated that the most effective elements of the Mass Entrepreneurship Initiative are those that improve the overall local business environment and promote competition

---

BOX 4.2   **Impact of the Mass Entrepreneurship Program in Guangdong Province**

This report carried out a preliminary assessment of firm entry and exit in Guangdong Province using the business registry. There has been significant growth in the establishment of new firms over time, primarily in the private sector and in services. This growth could reflect various elements of the Mass Entrepreneurship Initiative, particularly reforms of the business registry, which have lowered the costs of setting up new firms.

There has been a marked reduction in the size of new start-ups, particularly in services. Data on the establishment of *getihu* (small, individual-run enterprises in the informal sector) show a pronounced increase in their absolute number through 2017, but then a leveling off. As a result, their share of new establishments (firms plus *getihu*) fell after 2017. One possible explanation is that new business owners may

have decided to register as firms rather than as *getihu,* a result of business registry reforms that lowered registration costs. This could explain some of the acceleration in the number of new firms in labor-intensive services such as wholesale and retail trade and the secular decline in average firm size in the sector.

After initially rising, exit rates for firms recently declined sharply. But falling exit rates could also reflect reforms of the business registry that may have increased the cost of exit. A rising number and percentage of firms with zero sales ("zombie" firms) also indicate that the cost of exit may have been a factor. The extent to which declining exit rates reflect a real decline could have implications for productivity if resources are tied up in less productive firms that require government and bank support to remain in operation.

Source: Brandt and Zhang 2017.

and talent migration, rather than direct government subsidies or financing. In China, enterprises in provinces with faster diffusion of technology benefited from fundamental reforms of the enabling business environment, a good education system, and effective governance. By contrast, the level, composition, and source of R&D investments had quite modest effects on enterprise technology adoption. Provinces getting basic policies right also do well in exploiting the benefits of technology. Case studies of old industrial regions in the United States, carried out for this report, concluded that an enabling environment was more important for economic revival than subsidies or tax incentives to companies. Also, strong public-private partnerships were important for designing, financing, and implementing regional revitalization programs, including programs to develop entrepreneurship and to provide higher education, research, and vocational training, backed by public investments.

China improved its business climate as measured by the World Bank's Doing Business indicators.[5] China was recognized in *Doing Business 2013* as the top improver

in its region, and again in 2019 for making the greatest improvement in its "distance to frontier" score between 2002 and 2015. As a result of these reform efforts, China is now ranked 46th globally. But Doing Business indicators also show that administrative and regulatory burdens remain high—and that reforms to deal with permits, get credit (secured transactions), pay taxes, and resolve insolvency could all improve the business climate (figure 4.5).

China could consider carrying out comprehensive reforms to improve the business climate. Reform programs would need to define clear objectives related to the long-term strategic vision of the country. Successful governments generally follow a longer-term agenda that aims to increase the competitiveness of the economy. Adopting a more comprehensive approach increases the chances of success and impact, given that reforms in different areas tend to be complementary. Colombia, India, Mexico, Russia, and the United Kingdom all incorporated business regulation reforms into a broader competitiveness agenda. Clear, evidence-based frameworks for prioritization are critical to translating the long-term vision into a

FIGURE 4.5   **Doing Business's distance to frontier and the rankings for China and comparators, 2019**

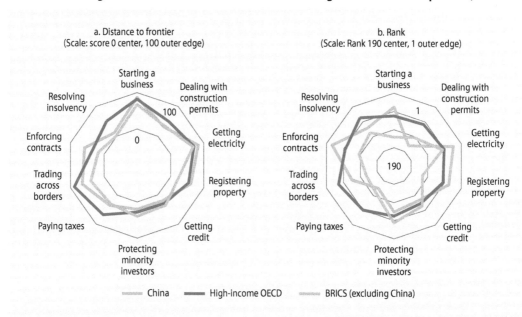

Source: World Bank Doing Business database.
Note: BRICS = Brazil, Russia, India, China, and South Africa.

reform program with specific objectives and activities.

Successful countries establish reform structures, with various degrees of institutionalization. Effective structures involve relevant public agencies and private representatives and create clear mechanisms to ensure coordination and information flows among all parties. Many countries establish high-level oversight committees or public-private councils that prioritize the reform agenda and maintain the momentum of reforms. Technical working groups then lead implementation at the agency level, with representatives from all key agencies as well as knowledgeable members of the private sector. Of the seven countries analyzed for this report that carried out comprehensive business climate reforms, all established high-level oversight mechanisms, technical working groups, and a coordinating unit.[6] Some created new institutions and public-private bodies to anchor the agenda for business environment reform, usually within a broader mandate to promote competitiveness. In 2008, Korea established the Presidential Council on Competitiveness to advise the government on regulatory

reforms, innovation, and other policy matters affecting the private sector. The council included ministers and heads of government research agencies, private sector representatives, academics, and members of civil society, such as labor representatives. Its responsibilities include identifying reform priorities, preparing an implementation road map, and helping to coordinate implementation.

Consultations with private firms have been used widely to identify reform priorities. Korea, Russia, and the United Kingdom have used a bottom-up approach involving private sector stakeholders. Korea established the Public-Private Regulatory Reform Task Force to strengthen the interaction between the Presidential Council on Competitiveness and the private sector and to accelerate reforms. The task force identifies burdensome regulations through consultations with businesses and formulates concrete reform proposals in collaboration with relevant government entities. It also monitors monthly progress on the issues raised by businesses and identifies bottlenecks in implementation. In the United Kingdom, the Business Reference Board systematically consults with the private sector. This public-private mechanism involves triannual meetings with 97 business organizations representing more than 750,000 members. It seeks a frank dialogue on regulation and enforcement issues with sector business associations. In addition, the United Kingdom uses the Business Perceptions Survey as a key source of data on business views regarding the U.K. regulatory environment. In 2011, the U.K. government also launched the Red Tape Challenge, an effort to review the country's stock of more than 21,000 active statutory rules and regulations. Using a public website, the government gathered the views of the business community and the public from April 2011 to April 2013, reaching its goal of identifying 3,000 pieces of regulation to be scrapped or improved (World Bank 2012).

Given the significant increase in new firm entries in China, business climate reforms can now focus on improving the quality and efficiency of local innovation and entrepreneurship ecosystems to support the new firms. The ecosystem would cover seven dimensions: the policy and regulatory environment; the cultural environment; access to finance; access to R&D and skills; availability and quality of supporting services; access to markets for inputs and outputs; and large established companies as connectors in the ecosystem network. Taking lessons from the revival of old industrial cities in the United States, local governments could focus on investing in education and training and on partnering with private stakeholders and civic organizations in designing, financing, and implementing programs to promote the local economy. Also, government support for local entrepreneurship could be subjected to more rigorous monitoring and evaluation.

China has identified improving its business climate as a high priority. Premier Li Keqiang has called for efforts to remove barriers to market access, to lower transaction costs, and for local governments to explore ways to create a healthy business environment for fair competition. In 2018, the State Council announced that the time required to start a business in municipalities, subprovincial cities, and provincial capitals would be reduced from an average of more than 20 workdays to 8.5. The government plans to introduce this reform in five cities—Dalian, Ningbo, Qingdao, Shenzhen, and Xiamen—to be followed by a national rollout. Measures to reduce the time required for government approval of construction projects from the current average level of more than 200 workdays to 120 workdays will be piloted in 15 cities, including Beijing, Shanghai, and Tianjin, as well as in Zhejiang Province.[7] In February 2019, a state council executive meeting, chaired by Premier Li Keqiang, announced that China's central government would eliminate, or delegate to lower-level authorities, more items that require government approval and also implement nationwide the reform of the construction-project-reviewing system.

China could introduce subnational business climate indicators, made publicly available to induce competition among local governments for attracting enterprises. These indicators could be developed from a range of sources, including the Doing Business database. By combining the Doing Business approach with a strong local engagement strategy, subnational assessments could increase ownership of the reform agenda at all levels of government. Subnational Doing Business assessments in Mexico strongly encouraged local regulatory reforms. During the six subnational Doing Business benchmarking rounds in Mexico, the number of reforming states increased considerably. The subnational assessments encouraged competition for reform and inspired peer-to-peer learning.

China could also consider setting up a new National Center of Excellence for Entrepreneurship Promotion Policy. This could be either a new agency or an existing agency tasked with the new role and responsibilities. The center's main objective would be to analyze and develop entrepreneurship promotion policies and disseminate relevant knowledge and experience. It would focus on the "how to" of policy design and delivery, including providing best-practice advice and knowledge, identifying good examples, learning from failed approaches, disseminating best practices, and developing knowledge networks and monitoring and evaluation frameworks. The proposed center would not be a government department or office that holds the power to issue or implement policies. Instead, it would help local policy makers design and deliver best-practice policies, drawing on national and international research and findings.

The center would develop national learning networks that diffuse local and international knowledge. It would link training and mentoring with best-practice "linkage organizations," such as incubators. It would support cities to develop customized policy packages tailored to local contexts. It would facilitate competition between subnational governments to improve the business environment. The center could also support second-tier cities in developing a "buddy system" with more advanced cities in the country and with market leaders globally, facilitating learning networks in China and internationally. For second-tier cities, the center would facilitate the transfer of best practices to initiate integration with more advanced regions. For example, Shenyang is looking to Germany's Industry 4.0 for best practices. Sharing best practices and potentially bringing in international service providers to partner with local service providers and boost standards would support further market development.

Ensuring fair competition and reforming state-owned enterprises

China recognizes that different types of businesses need to enjoy equal government support, regardless of ownership or scale, and that foreign-funded enterprises, private enterprises, and state-owned enterprises (SOEs) must all enjoy a level playing field. There were 167,000 nonfinancial SOEs in China in 2015, with RMB 37.8 trillion (US\$5.6 trillion) in state-owned equity capital, equivalent to 52 percent of GDP that year. From 2008 to 2015, the number of nonfinancial SOEs increased 52 percent, and their state owner's equity increased 180 percent. In this context, SOE reforms have been critical, and China's unprecedented development success would have been inconceivable without its SOE reform efforts. The reforms in the 1980s and 1990s fundamentally transformed the SOE sector, allowing it to contribute to economic growth and develop in line with its role in the national economy. The radical market-oriented reform and restructuring in the late 1990s were followed by a decade of improving SOE financial performance, which narrowed the gap with non-SOEs. The average return on equity of industrial SOEs rose from 2.0 percent in 1998 to 14.4 percent in 2006 and 15.7 percent in 2007. The gap with non-SOEs narrowed from 5.4 percentage points in 1998 to 2.7 percentage points in 2006 before falling back to 4.4 percentage points in 2007.

As early as 1993, a Communist Party of China (CPC) decision to establish a socialist market economy affirmed that the state must create the conditions to allow enterprises of all ownership types to compete equally and for the government to treat them on equal terms (CPC 1993). A 2013 CPC decision on deepening reforms reiterated the position by requiring the state to ensure that enterprises of all ownership types use factors of production on equal terms and participate in market competition in an open, fair, and equal manner (CPC 2013). Greater competition, including reforms of SOEs, is now vital for China's search for new drivers of growth. After departing from the traditional Soviet model, in which state ownership dominated the urban sector, China has chosen to move to a "basic economic system," characterized by the coexistence of multiple types of ownership, including public and private, and domestic and foreign. Policy makers can work toward clarifying the boundaries between competition and industrial policies to ensure that industrial policies support market competition.

Continuing reform in the direction set by the 2013 CPC decision and the 19th National Congress can generate new momentum for China's economic growth (CPC 2013). The key is to ensure that SOE reforms enable enterprises of multiple types of ownership to coexist and compete in the market. This requires that the SOE reforms not only improve the performance of SOEs but also

FIGURE 4.6   **Entrepreneurs' perceptions of fair competition in the market in China, 2017**

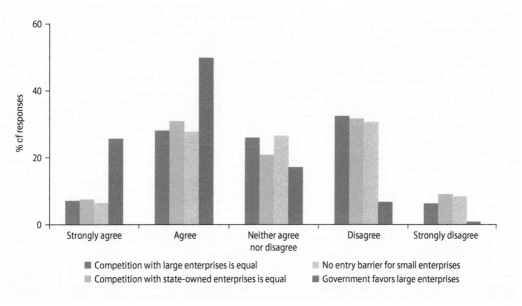

Source: World Bank survey of entrepreneurs in five Chinese cities.
Note: SOE = state-owned enterprise.

ensure that competition between SOEs and non-SOEs is on equal terms.

In a survey of entrepreneurs in five cities conducted for this report, approximately 41 percent of respondents disagreed that competition between small private enterprises and SOEs is on an equal basis in their city (figure 4.6). There were also concerns regarding market entry for smaller firms, where many entrepreneurs (39 percent) disagreed with the statement that small domestic private enterprises face no barriers to entry into most sectors. The majority of entrepreneurs (75 percent) indicated that government favors large domestic enterprises over young entrepreneurial businesses. Overall, entrepreneurs in the five cities said that they do not feel that they operate in an environment of equal competition or equal treatment.

Articulating a policy regarding state ownership

Accelerating China's SOE reforms and ensuring fair competition first require clearly articulating the purpose of state ownership.

This articulation could be conveyed by introducing a formal and explicit state-ownership policy for SOEs, in line with the recommendations of a government study (DRC 2014). Establishing a stand-alone state-ownership policy to codify national strategy in one formal document of the State Council would introduce strategic clarity to the role and management of SOEs, including the overarching objectives for managing state capital in business enterprises.

It is crucial for the state-ownership policy to articulate different objectives for different types of SOEs, depending on the degree of their commercial orientation. China has categorized SOEs into commerical SOEs and public-interest SOEs. The former is further divided into two subcategories: SOEs whose main business is in competitive industries or fields (commercial-competitive SOEs), and those that undertake special projects in industries or fields that are crucial to China's national security and national economy (commercial-strategic SOEs).

The priority for the commercial-competitive SOEs is to strengthen their commercial orientation and expose them to market competition by introducing three reforms. The first is to ensure managerial autonomy by reducing government interference that goes beyond its shareholder role, by deepening the reform of the state capital management system.[8] The second is to strengthen corporate governance by expanding the "mixed-ownership" reforms, to further increase nonstate equity in SOEs. This would convert the SOEs into state-participated enterprises with a more balanced equity structure, in which no single shareholder holds an ownership stake large enough to enable single-shareholder dominance. The third is to ensure that commercial-competitive SOEs are fully exposed to market competition.

Due to their contribution to the public good, commercial-strategic and public-benefit SOEs would need to be treated differently from commercial-competitive SOEs. These two types of SOEs should be reasonably compensated for the costs of providing public goods and undertaking noncommercial strategic projects, to ensure their financial sustainability and to allow for an accurate assessment of their performance.

The proposed state ownership policy could selectively identify sectors in which commercial-strategic and public-benefit SOEs would not have a significant presence, as part of an overall process of determining the strategic allocation of state capital. The desirable allocation of state capital across economic activities has been an objective of China's SOE reform since the mid-1990s. Across the world, selectivity is also a common practice in allocating state capital to economic activities (OECD 2015). China could consider several options for accelerating reform in this area; for example, it could transform commercial-competitive SOEs from wholly state-owned to state-controlled or state-participated enterprises through "mixed ownership" reforms; it could withdraw capital from some nonstrategic, non-public-interest SOEs, especially those financially distressed and nonviable; and it could improve the allocative efficiency of financial resources channeled to those SOEs by further reforming the financial sector and strengthening the commercial orientation of financial institutions.

The proposed state-ownership policy could define how Chinese citizens—the ultimate owners of state capital—benefit from the operations of SOEs. The main channels for Chinese citizens to directly receive financial benefits from SOEs include the transfer of SOE dividends to the public finance budget to fund social expenditures, and the transfer of some state ownership stakes in SOEs to social security funds to strengthen their financial position.[9]

Implementing competition policy more effectively

Competition policy in China is embodied in the 2008 Anti-Monopoly Law (AML). Strengthening this law's enforcement would help to level the playing field and ensure that different types of businesses receive equal treatment, regardless of ownership or scale. International experience indicates that competition policy requires regular reviews and updating. After almost a decade of implementation, this would be a good time to assess the law's track record and make necessary amendments. To gather feedback, the national government could consult with lower governments and the private sector.

The enforcement of China's AML had been the responsibility of the Anti-Monopoly Commission of the State Council, established in 2008. The commission's most visible contributions have included the drafting of various policy documents, including guidelines for the definition of relevant markets under the AML. Under the commission, three agencies had shared responsibility for enforcing the law: the National Development and Reform Commission (NDRC), the Ministry of Commerce, and the State Administration of Industry and Commerce.

In line with the global trend to unify enforcement responsibilities, China announced plans to establish a stand-alone independent regulatory agency for competition. The 13th National People's Congress, held in March 2018, decided to consolidate the AML enforcement responsibilities of the three agencies into the newly established State Administration for Market Regulation (SAMR), which would also act as the Office of the Anti-Monopoly Commission of the State Council.

This latest reform would help to address the long-standing fragmentation of AML enforcement caused by the division of responsibilities among the three previous authorities and increase the independence of the AML enforcement function from other government functions, such as industrial, trade, and FDI policies. Nonetheless, AML enforcement remains only part of the scope of work of SAMR, which has a lower status than a ministry in the Chinese government system. In order to give competition policy a more fundamental role, it will be crucial for the government to ensure the authority of the AML enforcement unit of SAMR to enable it to deal effectively with inevitable conflicts between competition policy and other government policies, including industrial policy. It will also be critical to ensure that SAMR is well staffed and resourced and to expand the disclosure of enforcement guidelines and other information to enhance credibility and predictability. In many countries, competition authorities have a semi-independent or independent status to help them enforce competition laws and regulations.

As a major step in strengthening the role of competition policy, the State Council launched a "fair competition review" in 2016 (State Council 2016), and five ministries, led by NDRC, enacted an implementation plan. The fair competition review is intended to ensure that no directive, instructive document, or ministerial policy measure is enacted, and that no draft law, regulation, or State Council policy measure is submitted to the State Council for enactment when it has the effect of excluding or restricting market competition. The review is to be conducted by the policy-making and -drafting body that proposes the legal, regulatory, or policy rules. The State Council has codified 18 criteria under three broad categories for the fair competition review: market entry and exit; free flow of products and production factors; and regulatory and policy measures that have an impact on either the cost of production and operation or the behavior of producers and market participants.

Full implementation of the fair competition review will go a long way toward implementing the government's 2013 decision to give competition policy a "fundamental position" in economic policy making. Seen as a first step, the review will need to be extended, when conditions are ready, to cover not only the "flow" but also the "stock" of competition policy—that is, the laws, regulations, documents, and policies enacted before the reform. This is important because the implementation plan will not stop the enactment of new anticompetitive regulatory and policy measures as long as they are based on relevant laws, regulations, and rules set by the State Council. It may also be necessary to elaborate and develop further the 18 criteria to ensure fuller coverage of anticompetitive government actions. The goal could be a national "fair competition standard" to define in specific and enforceable terms exactly what government actions can be regarded as aligned with the principle of fair competition among all enterprises. The standard should be applicable to domestic market competition and be aligned with China's role in and commitments to the global economy.

Making mixed-ownership reforms effective

Mixed ownership is a key component of China's SOE reform strategy, as put in place by the CPC and the State Council in 2015. Bringing nonstate equity capital into SOEs is intended to improve their corporate governance and performance. China United Network Communications Group Co. (Unicom Group), one of the six SOEs picked by the NDRC in 2016 for a pilot in mixed ownership, completed the reform transactions in 2017, shortly before the 19th CPC National Congress, in which almost RMB 78 billion (US$11.7 billion) of shares, representing a 35 percent stake in the group's Shanghai-listed subsidiary, were sold to more than a dozen investors, including technology giants Alibaba Group Holding Ltd. and Tencent Holdings Ltd.[10] Unicom Group will remain the biggest shareholder, with 37 percent, but it will give up the majority stake.

China Eastern Air Holding, China Nuclear Engineering and Construction Group, China State Shipbuilding, China Southern Power Grid, and Harbin Electric are the five other companies initially selected for the pilot mixed-ownership program.

In their equity structure, most SOEs are no longer wholly state-owned enterprises. A review of 2013 firm-level data for 16,499 state-owned and -controlled industrial enterprises (accounting for 89 percent of the assets of state-owned and -controlled industrial enterprises) showed that only 38.3 percent of their sales revenue was produced by wholly state-owned enterprises. In contrast, 55.2 percent was accounted for by "state-controlled enterprises," mostly domestic limited-liability companies and joint stock companies that are not wholly state owned. This situation is a result of reforms since the 1990s that encouraged such diversification through initial public offerings, employee shareholding programs, and the sale of additional shares to nonstate investors. But some of these efforts have not been fully realized because some enterprises still have a dominant state majority shareholder.

Improving corporate governance is the key to making mixed ownership effective. It is particularly critical that shareholder institutions have well-defined mandates and carry out their ownership responsibilities with the requisite autonomy and in a professional manner with high levels of transparency and accountability. International best practices for SOE corporate governance point to five key priorities for the state as owner.

One, clearly define the mandate of key stakeholders, to define accountability and provide the basis for determining objectives and targets. This would provide conceptual clarity for the roles and responsibilities of the board, management, and employees, and help with decision-making and measuring performance.

Two, have the state, as owner, focus on the exercise of core ownership rights without infringing on the day-to-day management of SOEs. While shareholder rights are usually defined in laws, more important is how such rights are exercised in practice. As owner and shareholder, the state may feel justified establishing policy or standard operational procedures, and even intervening directly in operational matters. But this can lead to interference in management matters, with suboptimal results.

Three, build professional boards of directors. The board's composition and functioning have a sizable impact on the governance of the company, on its operational and financial performance, and thus on its ability to maximize returns to state capital. Boards following good practices require members who act in the interest of the company, who face no conflicts of interest, and who have the competence and experience, including in the private sector, to lead the company.

Four, professionalize SOE management. Good practices increasingly call for empowering the board to appoint and, subject to clear terms, remove the chief executive officer when necessary. In countries with highly developed SOE frameworks, boards may also be empowered to oversee executive pay. Some countries require setting executive remuneration within the confines of broader public sector pay policy, but the policy should allow for flexibility and not limit the ability of the SOE to hire competitively.

Five, adhere to high standards of transparency, disclosure, and financial discipline. Transparency and disclosure are vital to holding shareholder institutions and SOE managers accountable for their performance. Good practice requires annual financial statements prepared in accordance with accounting standards and other requirements for listed companies, and audited by the statutory auditor (if required) and an independent external audit firm. Dividend policies can strengthen financial discipline and improve capital allocation.

Notes

1. According to Mazzucato (2015), the Internet was initially funded by DARPA, the global positioning system was funded by the U.S. Navy, touchscreen display was funded by the Central Intelligence Agency, and the voice-activated personal assistant Siri was funded by DARPA.

2. Chapter 10 of this report discusses the reform agenda for the cadre management system.

3. *Financial Times,* 2017.

4. China Banking Regulatory Commission, "Notice on the Banking Sector Financial Institutions—Notice of the Work of the Creditors' Committee—1196 of 2016," July 6, 2016; China Banking Regulatory Commission,"Notice Regarding Furthering Work on Banking Financial Institutions Creditor Committees," May 10, 2017.

5. Doing Business indicators measure the "ease of doing business," covering rules and regulatory processes relating to 10 stages of a firm's life cycle, from starting a business through to operations and insolvency. The indicators are applicable to local small to medium domestic firms across 190 economies. In China the assessments have been carried out for Beijing and Shanghai.

6. Colombia, Republic of Korea, Malaysia, Mauritius, Russia, Rwanda, and Turkey.

7. See http://www.xinhuanet.com/english/2018 -05/02/c_137151807.htm.

8. This reform has already started, following guidelines of the State Council.

9. A reform whose implementation has been accelerated recently.

10. "China Unicom Officially Announces Mixed Change Plan," *China Securities Journal,* August 21, 2017. http://news.xinhuanet.com /fortune/2017-08/21/c_1121513237.htm.

Bibliography

Aghion, P., J. Boulanger, and E. Cohen. 2011. "Rethinking Industrial Policy." Bruegel Policy Brief, volume 4.

Aghion P., M. Dewatripont, L. Du, A, Harrison, Jing Cai, and P. Legros. 2015. "Industrial Policy and Competition." *American Economic Journal: Macroeconomics* 7(4) 1–32.

Ahmad, N., and A. Hoffman. 2007. "A Framework for Addressing and Measuring Entrepreneurship." OECD, Paris.

Brandt, Loren, and Thomas Rawski, eds. 2019. *Policy, Regulation, and Innovation in China's Electricity and Telecom Industries.* New York: Cambridge University Press.

Brandt, Loren, and Xiaobo Zhang. 2017. "Firm Dynamics in Guangdong." Background paper for this report, World Bank, Washington, DC.

Breznitz, Dan, and Michael Murphree. 2011. *The Run of the Red Queen: Government, Innovation, Globalization, and Economic Growth in China.* New Haven, CT: Yale University Press.

Cirera, Xavier, and William F. Maloney. 2017. *The Innovation Paradox: Developing-Country Capabilities and the Unrealized Promise of Technological Catch-Up.* Washington, DC: World Bank.

CPC (Communist Party of China). 1993. "Decisions on Some Issues of Establishing a Socialist Market Economic System." Retrieved from http://cpc.people.com.cn/GB/64162 /134902/8092314.html.

———. 2013. "Decisions on Some Important Issues of Comprehensively Deepening Reform." Retrieved from http://news.xinhuanet.com /politics/2013-11/15/c_118164235.htm.

Divakaran, Shanthi, Patrick McGinnis, Jing Zhao, and Yi Yan. 2017. "Government and Venture Capital in China: The Role of Government Guidance Funds." Background paper for this report, World Bank, Washington, DC.

DRC (Development Research Center of the State Council). 2014. "Study on State Assets Management Reform."

Drum, B. 2017. "Lessons from the Revival of US Rustbelt Cities." Background paper for this report, World Bank, Washington, DC.

Financial Times. 2017. "China Bankruptcy Cases Surge as Economy Slows." February 27.

Hallward-Driemeier, M., and G. Nayyar. 2017. *Trouble in the Making? The Future of Manufacturing-Led Development.* Washington, DC: The World Bank.

Heilmann, Sebastian, Lea Shih, and Andreas Hofem. 2013. "National Planning and Local Technology Zones: Experimental Governance in China's Torch Programme." China Quarterly 216: 896–919.

International Federation of Insolvency Professionals. 2000. *Statement of Principles for a Global Approach to Multi-Creditor Workouts.* London: INSOL International. https://www.insol .org/pdf/Lenders.pdf.

Iootty, Mariana, and Seidu Dauda. 2017. "Assessing Firm Markup in China: First Insights into the Manufacturing Industry." Background paper for this report, World Bank, Washington, DC.

Klapper, L., and I. Love. 2011. "The Impact of Business Environment Reforms on New Firm Registration." Policy Research Working Paper 5493, World Bank, Washington, DC.

Kovacic, William, Cyril Lin, and Derek Morris. 2017. *Accelerating China's Growth by Strengthening Competition: Some International Perspectives.* Beijing: Cairncross Foundation.

Kuriakose, Smita, Joanna Lewis, Jeremy Tamanini, and Shahid Yusuf. 2017. "Accelerating Innovation in China's Solar, Wind and Energy Storage Sectors." Background paper for the this report, World Bank, Washington, DC.

Lin, L. 2015. "Re-Engineering a Venture Capital Market: The Case of China. NUS Centre for Law and Business Working Paper 15/04," National University of Singapore, Faculty of Law, Singapore.

Mason, Colin and Ross Brown. 2014. "Entrepreneurial Ecosystems and Growth Oriented Entrepreneurship." Background paper for OECD LEED Programme and Dutch Ministry of Economic Affairs workshop. January. https://www.oecd.org/cfe/leed/Entrepreneurial-ecosystems.pdf.

Mazucato, M. 2013. *The Entrepreneurial State: Debunking Public vs. Private Sector Myths.* London: Anthem Press.

Mazzucato, M. 2015. *The Entrepreneurial State: Debunking Public vs. Private Sector Myths.* New York: PublicAffairs.

Motta, M., A. M. Oviedo, and M. Santini. 2010. "An Open Door for Firms: The Impact of Business Entry Reforms." Viewpoint 323, World Bank Group, Washington, DC.

National Policy Statement on Entrepreneurship in Ireland. 2014. Retrieved from https://www.localenterprise.ie/Documents-and-Publications/Entrepreneurship-in-Ireland-2014.pdf.

NDRC (National Development and Reform Commission) and four other ministries. 2017. "Tentative Implementation Plan for the Fair Competition Review Mechanism." Retrieved from http://www.ndrc.gov.cn/gzdt/201710/W020171026610334156557.pdf.

OECD (Organisation of Economic Co-operation and Development). 2015. *OECD Guidelines on Corporate Governance of State-Owned Enterprises.* Paris: OECD Publishing.

Piketty, T., Y. Li, and G. Zucman. 2017. "Capital Accumulation, Private Property and Rising Inequality in China, 1978-2015." NBER Working Paper No. 23368, National Bureau of Economic Research.

Rodrik, D. 2008. "Normalizing Industrial Policy. Commission on Growth and Development." Working Paper, volume 3.

State Administration of Industry and Commerce. 2017.

State Council. 2015. "Opinions of the State Council on Several Policy Measures for Vigorously Promoting the Public Innovation of the Masses." Retrieved from http://www.gov.cn/zhengce/content/2015-06/16/content_9855.htm.

———. 2016. "State Council Opinion on Establishing Fair Competition Review Mechanism in Building Market System." Retrieved from http://www.gov.cn/zhengce/content/2016-06/14/content_5082066.htm.

Sturgeon, Timothy, and Eric Thun. 2018. "China New Drivers of Growth: Case studies of China's automotive and ICT hardware sectors." Background paper for this report, World Bank, Washington, DC.

World Bank. 2013. *Doing Business 2013.* Washington, DC: World Bank.

World Bank and DRC. 2012. *China 2030: Building a Modern, Harmonious, and Creative Society.* Washington, DC: World Bank. http://documents.worldbank.org/curated/en/781101468239669951/pdf/China-2030-building-a-modern-harmonious-and-creative-society.pdf.

Xinhua News Agency. 2015. "The Opinions of the CPC Central Committee and State Council on Deepening the Reform of the System and Mechanism to Accelerate the Implementation of the Innovation-Driven Development Strategy." Retrieved from http://www.gov.cn/xinwen/2015-03/23/content_2837629.htm.

Zhang, Q. 2016. "Un-level Playing Ground between SOEs and Non-SOEs in China: Micro-Data Evidence." Background paper for this report, World Bank, Washington, DC.

Zhou, Yu. 2008. *The Inside Story of China's High-Tech Industry: Making Silicon Valley in Beijing.* Lanham, MD, and Paris: Rowman & Littlefield and OECD Publishing.

5

Promoting Innovation and the Digital Economy

Broadly conceived, a national innovation system (NIS) covers the supply of innovation generated by research and development (R&D) institutions and enterprises, the demand for innovation by enterprises, and the accumulation and allocation of resources that enable both the supply of and demand for innovation (figure 5.1). This chapter focuses on policies and institutions relevant to the supply of innovation, but such policies are only one of many components of the NIS that have strong complementarities and synergy. Therefore, understanding the policy priorities for China's NIS necessitates taking a holistic approach that considers the findings in this chapter together with those in other chapters that cover industrial policies and market competition, the business climate, the financing of innovation, trade and foreign direct investment (FDI) regimes, and investments in human capital.

China is already well advanced in building an NIS capable of supplying the innovation and technologies needed for productivity-led growth. The challenge now is to refine an already large, existing system. Currently, the country's innovation system focuses on promoting the third D, fostering *discoveries* of new innovations and technologies. To complement the third D, refining the current

system entails placing greater emphasis on the second D, accelerating *diffusion*, so that the country's R&D policies and institutions could be reoriented to increase the emphasis on promoting the diffusion of technology and innovation.

China's rapidly increasing innovation capacity

China has built a large and extensive NIS to supply the innovation and technologies required for productivity growth. Evaluations of China's innovation capacity differ across various international assessments, but they all indicate that gaps remain between China and high-income countries. The global innovation index—developed by the World Intellectual Property Organization (WIPO), INSEAD, and Cornell University—is the most positive, indicating that China's innovation capacity has been improving steadily. China is moving up in cross-country rankings, from 29 in 2011 to 17 in 2018, and it is the highest-ranking middle-income country and the first middle-income country to join the 20 most innovative countries (Cornell University, INSEAD, and WIPO 2016). China's improvements stand out among

FIGURE 5.1   **National innovation system**

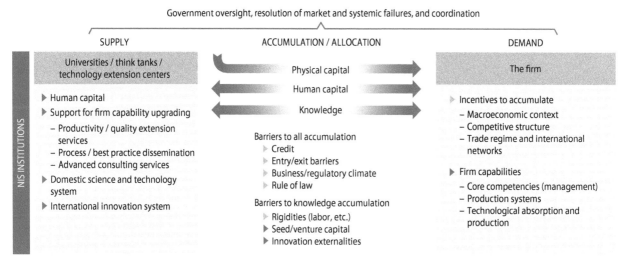

Source: Cicera and Maloney 2017.
Note: NIS = national innovation system.

comparable countries, which have experienced few improvements or a decline in their ranking (figure 5.2). China also has improved its innovation quality and now is ranked 17 in the relevant indicator.

In contrast to improvements in the global innovation index, China's innovation assessment by the World Economic Forum has improved little over the years. In 2016/17, China ranked 28 out of 144 countries on overall competitiveness and 74 on technological readiness, compared with 27 and 78, respectively, in 2010/11. According to the information and communication technology

FIGURE 5.2   **Ranking on the global innovation index of select countries, 2007–18**

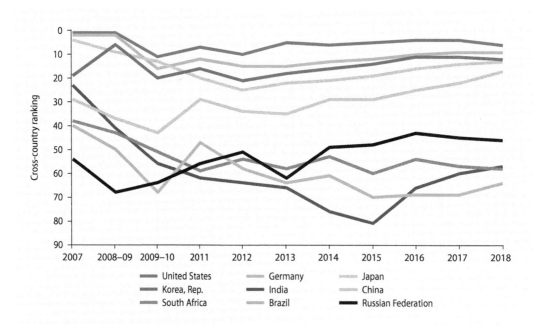

Source: Global innovation index by WIPO, INSEAD, Cornell University.

(ICT) development index for 2016, China was ranked 81, behind the República Bolivariana de Venezuela and Bosnia and Herzegovina, although this was an improvement over its ranking of 84 in 2015 (ITU 2016). The Bloomberg index of innovative economies ranks China 20, between Canada and Poland. China scores high on patent density (7) and high technology density (9) and is in the middle of the range on R&D intensity (15) and manufacturing value added (19); however, it is near the bottom (43) on tertiary efficiency, productivity, and researcher concentration (Jamrisko and Lu 2017).

R&D investments and number of patents have risen rapidly in recent years. China spent 2.18 percent of gross domestic product (GDP) on R&D in 2018, compared with the Organisation for Economic Co-operation and Development (OECD) average of 2.4 percent (figure 5.3). In 2013, China's aggregate spending on R&D became the second highest in the world, after the United States, and accounted for around 20 percent of global spending on R&D. R&D expenditures as a share of GDP are multiples above what is common for a country at China's level of development. Unlike in other middle-income countries, where the public sector is responsible for a large share of R&D expenditures, in China R&D spending by enterprises accounts for three-fourths of total spending.

In line with higher spending on R&D, China's domestic patenting has increased dramatically over the last half decade (figure 5.4, panel a). It has the world's largest number of domestic patents, with more than 1.7 million domestic patents granted in 2016. In 2016, China filed the world's third-highest number of applications under the Patent Cooperation Treaty (PCT),[1] with ZTE the most frequent, and Huawei the second-most frequent PCT filers in the world (figure 5.4, panel b). Due to such companies, China became the third-largest applicant for international patents in 2016 and is likely to overtake second-place Japan soon. China is also second only to the United States in the number of scientific publications. The quality of China's research papers is also improving. According to Nature Index's weighted fractional count of the quality of global research

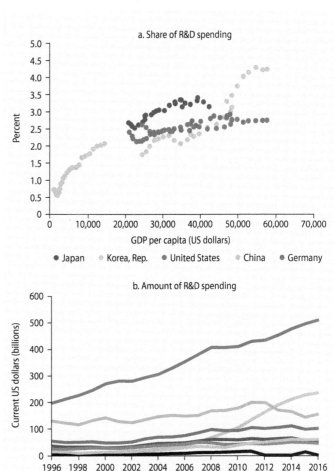

FIGURE 5.3 **R&D spending in selected countries, 1996–2014**

a. Share of R&D spending

Japan • Korea, Rep. • United States • China • Germany

b. Amount of R&D spending

China • United States • Japan • Germany
France • United Kingdom • India • Korea, Rep.

Source: For panel a, calculations based on Organisation for Economic Co-operation and Development (OECD) data. For panel b, calculations based on National Science Board 2018.
Note: R&D = research and development.

outputs, China is now second only to that of the United States.[2]

China's enterprise sector accounts for approximately three-fourths of total R&D spending, above the OECD average of two-thirds and also that of most middle-income countries. Enterprise sector spending includes R&D outlays of state-owned enterprises (SOEs), which in 2015 amounted to about one-third of the total, down from 55 percent in 2005 (Molnar 2017). ICT producers accounted for about one-third of total R&D spending in China, followed by automobiles and transport and ICT services. The contribution of Chinese ICT to global innovation is

FIGURE 5.4 **Number of domestic and international patents, 1990–2016**

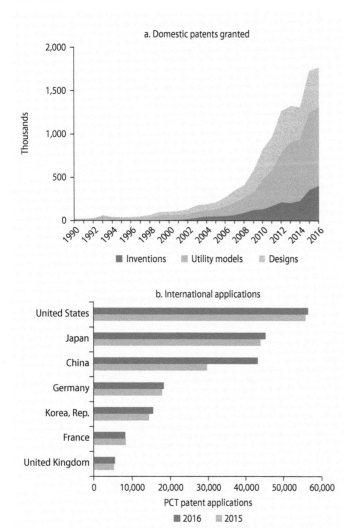

a. Domestic patents granted

Thousands

■ Inventions   ■ Utility models   ■ Designs

b. International applications

United States
Japan
China
Germany
Korea, Rep.
France
United Kingdom

0   10,000   20,000   30,000   40,000   50,000   60,000

PCT patent applications
■ 2016   ■ 2015

Sources: For panel a, State Intellectual Property Office (SIPO) data; for panel b, World Intellectual Property Organization (WIPO) data.
Note: Panel b refers to applications under the Patent Cooperation Treaty.

growing; Huawei is the third-largest corporate R&D spender in the global ICT industry (and the only Chinese company on the list of the world's largest R&D companies).

The top five Chinese companies accounted for almost 30 percent of total R&D spending in China, a higher proportion than among the top five companies in the United States and the European Union (EU), where they represented less than 20 percent of total spending. This indicates that, in China, enterprise research is more concentrated in the largest firms, and the majority of enterprises

may be investing relatively little in R&D. The average R&D intensity (defined as the ratio of R&D investment to total revenue) of all Chinese companies (among companies with at least €24 million in annual R&D spending) was only 2.8 percent, less than half of average spending in the United States (6.2 percent), indicating a sizable gap between many Chinese companies and their global counterparts, regarding investments in innovation and technology. However, among the world's 2,500 most-R&D-intensive companies, R&D spending by Chinese companies grew 18.8 percent in 2017, compared with 7.2 percent in the United States and a 3 percent decline in Japan, suggesting that Chinese companies are catching up rapidly (European Commission 2017).

Multinationals have played a significant role in China's international patenting, reflecting the increasing globalization of R&D. Multinational enterprises based in China helped to drive the rapid growth in U.S. patents through imported innovation platforms, including management, networks, and corporate structures that provide the necessary complementary factors within multinational corporations (Branstetter 2012). This pattern is distinct from the pattern seen in the Republic of Korea, where the vast majority of international patents are registered by indigenous enterprises. The foreign share of domestic invention patents in China—patents granted by the State Intellectual Property Office (SIPO)—is sizable but declining, from 44 percent in 2001 to 25 percent in 2016. Given the significant share of domestic innovation carried out by foreign firms, it will be important to enhance local knowledge, product, and entrepreneurial spillovers. Countries like Korea that have traditionally been less dependent on FDI, as well as countries like Singapore that have had much higher levels of FDI, have taken steps to enhance the capacity of indigenous firms to absorb technology spillovers, providing important lessons for China.[3]

China's patents still lag those of frontier countries on a variety of measurements of quality, such as patent citations, retention rates, patent commercialization (as measured by patent out-licensing), and average number of claims. A key aspect of quality is China's reliance on "utility" patents, which are less costly, easier, and faster to obtain but have a shorter duration of protection than invention patents. Although other countries also offer utility patents, the vast majority of the world's utility patents are filed in China (WIPO 2018). Utility patents granted in China have skyrocketed in recent years (figure 5.4, panel a), accounting for 43 percent of the stock of patent applications in 2016.

Utility models are useful instruments supporting latecomers' catch-up process. Because of their relatively low eligibility requirements, they have provided learning opportunities to latecomer firms in East Asia. But precisely for the same reason, they may not be as useful in China today as they were at earlier stages of development, as they tend to have less technological intellectual value. Utility patents, as well as design patents, have relatively low retention rates, indicating that they often do not hold sufficient economic value to justify paying the retention fees. For utility patents granted in 2013, 61 percent were abandoned within five years, as the patent holders stopped paying the retention fees.[4] The equivalent share was even higher for design patents (91 percent).

The huge increase in the number of patents may reflect policy incentives. More patents reflect greater investment in R&D and possibly improved protection of intellectual property rights. But government policies to encourage patenting also have played a significant role in increasing the number of patents. Different layers of the government have set ambitious patenting targets and rolled out intellectual property (IP)–conditioned state financial incentives. However, due to insufficient quality-related requirements for patents, these programs may have contributed to the rising quantity of patents at the expense of quality, particularly for utility patents. Many patents may not be economically, technologically, or commercially viable.

Having largely achieved the original objective of increasing the quantity of patents, the government could now shift its focus to promoting the quality of patents by reorienting support to broader aspects of investment in innovation that would produce patents of higher quality and greater commercial viability. The government has recognized the need to adjust incentives for patenting. It could shift the focus of government financial incentives from reducing the costs of patenting to promoting services that make patents commercially valuable, such as services related to patent evaluation and due diligence, marketing and feasibility studies, and proofs of concept. This focus could be part of an overall reorientation of patent promotion policies to broader aspects of investments in innovation.

Improving the managerial capacity of Chinese firms will also be critical for enhancing the quality of patents, innovation, and technological upgrading. Such capacity is vital in harnessing higher technological capabilities, through process and product innovation, R&D, and patenting, and ultimately firm competitiveness and productivity. Some even argue that, in East Asia's newly industrialized economies, the organizational and managerial capacity of firms to acquire, learn, and apply technology has been more important than conventional R&D, and that at least 30 percent of the differences in total factor productivity (TFP) among countries stems from variations in management quality. Despite China's impressive growth of industrial production, the quality of management at firms is far behind the frontier (figure 5.5, panel a).[5] Chinese managers may be quite good at running short-run assembly lines but compare relatively poorly in just-in-time management, long-run strategic planning, and human resources management, all critical for innovation.

China's top firms, which would be expected to contribute the most to innovation, appear to have managerial qualities that lag those of U.S. firms, more than for firms in the bottom or middle of the firm distribution (figure 5.5, panel b). While Chinese firms are among the biggest in the world, none made the list of Thomson Reuter's Top 100 Global Innovators, which was led by U.S. and Japanese firms.

In recognition of the need to strengthen the innovation capacity of firms, China has extensive innovation support policies that span the gamut of economic objectives (productivity, diversification, human capital,

FIGURE 5.5   **Managerial capabilities of Chinese firms and their competitors**

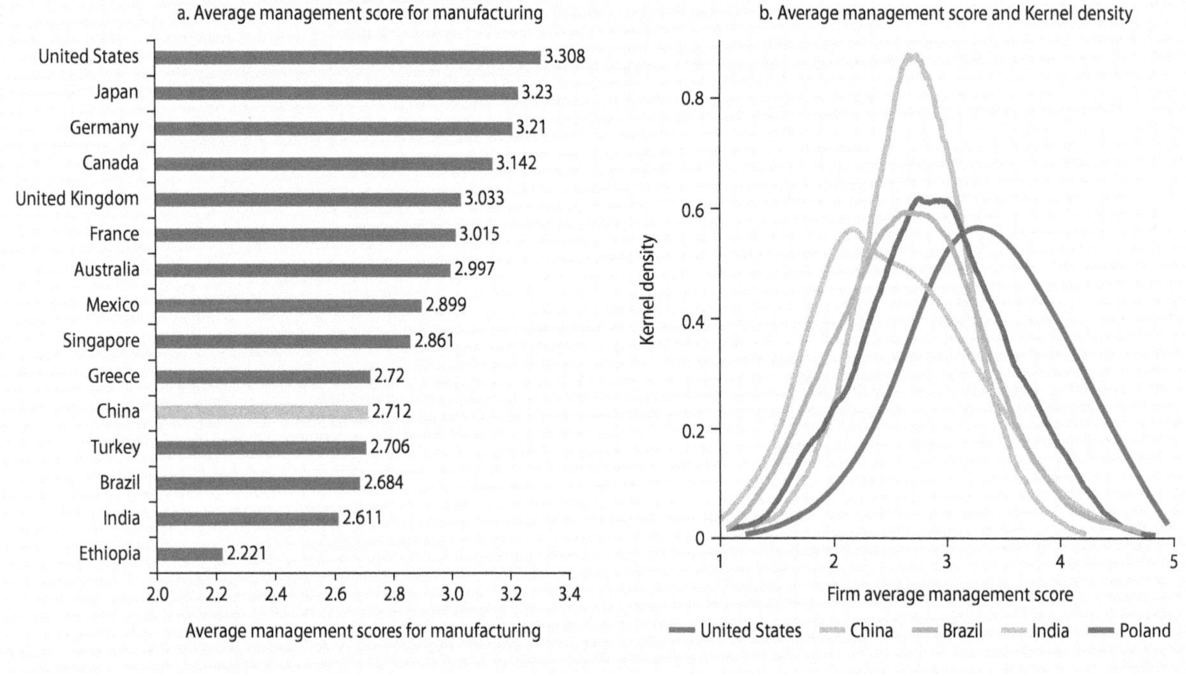

a. Average management score for manufacturing

United States	3.308
Japan	3.23
Germany	3.21
Canada	3.142
United Kingdom	3.033
France	3.015
Australia	2.997
Mexico	2.899
Singapore	2.861
Greece	2.72
China	2.712
Turkey	2.706
Brazil	2.684
India	2.611
Ethiopia	2.221

Average management scores for manufacturing

b. Average management score and Kernel density

Firm average management score

United States   China   Brazil   India   Poland

Source: Cirera and Maloney 2017.

entrepreneurship, and inclusion) and science, technology, and innovation objectives (research excellence, technology transfer, and R&D and non-R&D innovation) that are commonly seen in other countries. The policies employ a wide range of instruments to support innovation, such as fiscal incentives, grants, loan guarantees, vouchers, equity, public procurement, technology extension services, incubators, accelerators, competitive grants and prizes, science and technology parks, collaboration, and networks.

It is critical to ensure that innovation policy instruments are aligned with firms' needs. In China, supply-side policies are emphasized more than demand-side policies, and instruments aiding applied research outnumber those supporting basic research. These instruments tend to favor financial mechanisms over regulatory, advisory, and collaborative support. This indicates that the main market failure that the authorities seek to address is funding and access to finance. However, evidence on managerial capabilities of Chinese firms suggests that other critical nonfinancial gaps are present

as well. Finally, most policies are targeted at younger firms (start-ups and seed and pre-seed entities) and micro and small firms. Although these policies may help to address the sharp decline in the contribution of new entrants to firm-level productivity growth in China, more analysis is needed to assess whether they are easing the constraints on high-productivity entrants.

Promoting the diffusion of innovation and technology

As a developing country, China has much to gain from catch-up growth by promoting the diffusion and adoption of existing innovations and technologies. It will need to prepare for growing technological disruptions through a combination of policies promoting technology transfer, science-industry collaboration, and R&D-based and non-R&D-based innovation, and upgrading of the skills and managerial capacity of firms to innovate and absorb technology. The majority of potential productivity gains, even in developed countries (55 percent), appear to result from adopting best practices and technologies

TABLE 5.1   Mechanisms to facilitate technology diffusion

Diffusion mechanism	Operational mode (primary)	Example
Dedicated field services	Diagnostics, guidance, and mentoring	Manufacturing Extension Partnership (United States)
Technology-oriented business services	Advice linked with finance; capacity development	Industrial Research Assistance Program (Canada); I-Corps (United States)
Applied technology centers	Contract research, collaborative applied research, prototyping, and standards	Fraunhofer Institutes (Germany); Manufacturing USA (United States); Kohsetshushi Public Technology Centers (Japan)
Targeted R&D centers	Advanced research on emerging technologies intertwined with commercialization missions	Campus for Research Excellence and Technological Enterprise (Singapore)
Knowledge exchange and demand-based instruments	Technology community networking; knowledge transfer incentives	Knowledge Transfer Networks (United Kingdom); Innovation Vouchers (multiple countries)
Open-technology mechanisms	Shared technology library; virtual networking	BioBricks/Registry of Standard Biological Parts (United States)

Source: Shapira and Youtie 2017.
Note: R&D = research and development.

rather than developing new ones (Manyika et al. 2015). Mechanisms to support the diffusion of new and existing technologies range from broad management extension services to more sophisticated R&D institutions, and more recently, technology information and collaboration platforms (table 5.1).

Manufacturing extension activities have been widely adopted. The broader management and field extension services tend to follow a model similar to traditional agricultural extension services and to emphasize supporting small and medium enterprises (SMEs) to absorb existing technologies. In Germany, Mittelstand-Digital helps SMEs to understand the advantages of digital applications and to take concrete steps toward Industry 4.0. It does so primarily through "SME 4.0 competence centers" that demonstrate how digitization, innovative networking, and Industry 4.0 can be used in business practices. In Japan, Kohsetshushi Public Technology Centers provide free advisory services to SMEs as well as access to laboratories on a cost-sharing basis (Ezell and Atkinson 2011). The United States supports technology diffusion through the Manufacturing Extension Partnership, a network of local centers in all U.S. states at 400 locations and with a staff of 1,600 funded from federal, state, and industry sources.

Technology extension programs can be narrowly focused on specific technologies, such as specific digital technologies. Many countries have used matching grants and technical assistance to facilitate the digitization of SMEs, sometimes by partnering SMEs with large ICT companies. Similarly, vouchers can incentivize the collaboration of SMEs and knowledge providers in developing and adopting Industry 4.0 processes. Grants have financed the collaboration of SMEs with local consultants or universities to support the technological needs of SMEs.

For more specialized technologies, OECD countries have used technology and R&D centers. Some technology centers, such as those in Catalonia, Spain, arose from public-private partnerships (PPPs) to solve technological problems and develop solutions for specific sectors or clusters. The centers tend to be very specialized in specific technologies and are managed as a network, as with the Fraunhofer Institutes in Germany—a network of 60 private nonprofit research institutes that undertake contract research for the government and for business organizations (Shapira and Youtie 2017). But the capabilities of the Fraunhofer Institutes are inseparable from the strength of Germany's engineering sector. Without strong capabilities in the private sector, implementing these models may be difficult in other contexts.

Today, France, Germany, Japan, and the United States are leading the efforts to deploy existing and new policy instruments to facilitate the adoption and diffusion of advanced technologies, although Brazil and China are also making deep inroads

(Staufen AG 2015). The first steps in these efforts are to set up a central secretariat or platform that orchestrates all efforts around Industry 4.0, to conduct foresight studies, and to create national plans involving multistakeholder working groups. Germany and the United States provide leading examples of creating integrated approaches to deploying policy instruments (BMBF 2017; GTAI 2018). The United States, for example, launched the Advanced Manufacturing Partnership 2.0 (AMP 2.0) in 2011, a "national effort bringing together industry, universities, and the federal government" (White House 2011). Made up of 19 industries, academia, and labor representatives, the AMP Steering Committee published a report in 2014 titled "Accelerating U.S. Advanced Manufacturing," which provides policy recommendations on skill building, research, and technology adoption (AMP Steering Committee 2014). Overseeing the implementation of these recommendations is the Advanced Manufacturing National Program Office, as part of the National Institute for Science and Technology, with its manufacturing.gov platform. It coordinates multistakeholder PPP initiatives.

Given the importance of management capacity for technology adoption and diffusion, strengthening managerial capacity needs to be at the core of SME extension programs. The government of China could consider introducing a package of measures and management extension programs, titled perhaps the Mass Initiative for World-Class Enterprises. This initiative would highlight the importance of high-quality management for productivity through awareness and best-practice campaigns. It could provide detailed benchmarking information for firms to assess their managerial performance against local and international peers. It could support training and advisory services on management upgrading against these benchmarks. It could provide specialized support in designing, building, and using brands, and in developing and integrating servicification and technology use. And it could promote business services that SMEs can outsource, particularly in lagging regions, so that SMEs can focus on their core capabilities.

Improving research and development

Moving from top-down to more bottom-up and open innovation

Because new technologies expand and mature faster than before, the pace of technology adoption has accelerated globally, such that predicting technology trends is increasingly challenging. Consider former market leaders, such as Kodak and Nokia, which missed the digital and smartphone revolutions and lost most of their market shares. The same applies to governments, which run an ever-larger risk of misidentifying industries and technologies of the future, especially in countries like China that are moving closer to the global technology frontier. The disruptive and unpredictable nature of technology development implies that governments can no longer take all of the risk or internalize the process of generating innovation by directing top-down technological change.

To manage risks better, China's top-down approach to promoting innovation could be complemented with a more market-oriented, private-sector, bottom-up approach. China could derive lessons learned from the EU's "smart specialization" concept. Smart specialization is about prioritizing public support for innovation in economic activities that may not yet be fully "visible" but that have the largest developmental potential based on an economy's current comparative advantages. Smart specialization is underpinned by an entrepreneurial discovery process, which helps to identify, select, modify, and eliminate (as necessary) innovation policy priorities—smart specializations—to support promising new industries and economic activities and to ensure that they reach a critical mass of development. Bottom-up innovation policy could be invigorated by expanded R&D tax credits and stronger innovation support programs open to all industries.

Strengthening basic research

As China shifts from catch-up growth to the forefront of innovation, it could increase the relatively low share of R&D devoted to basic research. Reorienting public R&D more to basic and "blue sky" research would complement private R&D. China could also strengthen research project management and reform its research funding system so that funding is allocated more competitively, and is less dependent on personal networks, to ensure equal access. Research evaluation should be bolstered, including through greater use of peer reviews.

The multiplicity of national and local agencies responsible for financing and overseeing science and technology programs engenders coordination problems and leads to considerable duplication and waste of research funding. For example, biotech research has no less than nine ministerial-level agencies sharing responsibilities under the State Council Leading Group. Better coordination mechanisms could help reduce the fragmentation and duplication of research, but this will take time, and some waste is inevitable without streamlining programs and oversight agencies.

To support basic research and innovation, a major priority is to move to a more bottom-up system and to nurture the underlying learning and creative culture that supports basic research. Grassroots initiatives and the freedom for young researchers to pursue fresh research ideas are hampered not only by the bureaucratic structure but also by research hierarchies that concentrate decision-making authority and resources in the hands of senior researchers and their bureaucratic allies. And evaluating research is linked primarily to the quantity of publications and patents, inducing—even compelling—researchers to focus on publication and downstream contract work for firms. Recognizing such challenges, the Chinese Academy of Social Sciences and other agencies are attempting to revamp the approach to evaluating researchers in order to make it more qualitative and more focused on outcomes.

Promoting research collaboration

A key challenge is to ensure that promoting "indigenous" innovation does not undermine China's ability to benefit from open and collaborative innovation. In the modern era, open and collaborative research and innovation, through both domestic and international collaborations, is the surest way to invigorate China's innovation capacity. Indeed, an open and globally integrated innovation system is critical to strengthening domestic innovation capacity and avoiding technologies that are only relevant in China.

Chinese scientists are engaged in collaborative research in more than 94 countries. The close to 100,000 doctoral degree scientists of Chinese origin in science, technology, engineering, and mathematics in the United States facilitate research collaboration. China has programs to encourage returnees in the science, technology, and innovation community to play a catalytic role in transforming China's research environment. Such programs could be reviewed to identify and address the obstacles to working with returnees more efficiently and to enhance the environment for attracting researchers from abroad.

The relatively underdeveloped R&D capacity of Chinese enterprises could be addressed by paying greater attention to university-research linkages and research and innovation networks, modeled on successful programs in high-income countries. China could establish a network of incubators centered on existing science and technology parks, with links to business and professional networks, to build ecosystems to incubate new technologies and connect market leaders with start-ups. Having already reaped huge benefits from expanding its international R&D cooperation, China should consider being even more active in global research initiatives, such as the Human Frontier Science Program. Its involvement in the Human Genome Project has already resulted in Chinese enterprises and academics collaborating with the world's leading geneticists, moving the country to prominence in the global genomics research community.

Improving intellectual property policies

China's intellectual property laws and regulations have improved over the years and have made significant progress in adopting international standards. In the past, part of the motivation for these reforms was to comply with international IP treaties and respond to foreign concerns. More recent reforms of IP law are motivated by the need to provide a stronger appropriability environment for domestic Chinese firms that now have greater technological capabilities for innovation. This orientation aligns with the government's interest in encouraging domestic enterprises to invest in innovation and R&D. A major priority for improving the IP legal framework is to strengthen appropriability further by increasing damages for IP infringement and to clarify or remove ambiguous provisions on relevant laws that can limit appropriability, such as those for licensing IP from state-funded research.

Despite the significant progress in establishing a modern IP rights system, China recognizes that more could be done to strengthen the protection of intellectual property in the country. According to a 2016 countrywide representative survey of patent holders by SIPO, 70 percent of respondents said that patent protection in China needs to be reinforced. A further 59 percent said that their patents could be easily circumvented. Such concerns with China's IP protection could discourage investment in innovation and R&D, and thereby reduce knowledge, product, and entrepreneurial spillovers and ultimately economic growth. Foreign firms still indicate difficulties in protecting and enforcing intellectual property rights in China, which may discourage them from developing frontier technology in the country or transferring such technology to China-based entities. Strengthening the IP regime and enforcing intellectual property rights are particularly important for start-ups and SMEs, which have fewer resources and limited experience to deal with intellectual property theft.

Generally, judicial IP enforcement has become more efficient and effective, although IP litigation cases can still be lengthy. Damages awarded for IP infringement help ensure that judicial IP enforcement is effective. China's newly revised trademark law has punitive damages that increase the consequences for trademark infringement, and the patent law is being revised by significantly raising the degree of punishment and compensation. A major deterrent to the effectiveness of judicial IP enforcement is the low amount of actual damages awarded in IP cases, which can be attributed to the fact that judges tend to rely on statutory damages[6] rather than the full damages afforded by the law. Understanding and addressing the reasons that judges behave this way could help to improve IP enforcement.

The government has made progress in strengthening IP enforcement through the launch of specialized IP courts in recent years. Stronger enforcement now entails an array of adjustments to IP court procedures, such as strengthening specialized enforcement units, applying more significant fines and sanctions for noncompliance, improving acquisition and admissibility of evidence, and encouraging judges to impose higher damages on those who infringe intellectual property rights. Better coordination of administrative IP enforcement among the relevant bodies and among civil, administrative, and criminal procedures in IP cases would also be beneficial.

Judicial "local protectionism" (unfair handling of court and administrative enforcement cases to protect local firms) undermines the perceived fairness of IP court enforcement. In China, plaintiffs have a better chance of winning IP disputes in their local area jurisdictions (China IP Index Report 2016; Judicial Big Data Research Institute 2017). In general, local protectionism can lead to discrepancies in the outcomes of trials of IP cases, potentially undermining trust in the system. Reform measures are needed to deter local protection further, possibly by moving more court cases to out-of-area jurisdictions, and additional central initiatives are needed to monitor and limit unfair court rulings as well as to expand IP courts across the provinces or nationwide.

Over the past decades, China has gradually established a complex and relatively unique government system for administering IP rights. In addition to the standard enforcement agencies used in other countries, such as the judiciary and customs, local government administrative agencies also enforce IP rights in China. It can be challenging to coordinate across such a large and complex system and to ensure consistent IP enforcement for all regions. IP administration officials have been facing a significant challenge as the number of IP disputes handled by local IP enforcement authorities has risen rapidly in recent years.

Despite such challenges, China's government institutions for administering IP rights have generally become better managed. As part of the institutional reforms announced by the State Council in March 2018, the State Administration for Market Regulation (SAMR) was established, patent and trademark management was incorporated into the SIPO, which was renamed the China National Intellectual Property Administration (CNIPA), and CNIPA was incorporated into SAMR. This merger and consolidation could help to improve overall administrative enforcement and coordination across decentralized management.

Decentralized management can result in a lack of coordination among the many central, provincial, and local government bodies governing IP rights, challenging the state's ability to administer IP rights effectively and efficiently. The government has sought to address these challenges. For example, it is strengthening law enforcement cooperation mechanisms in the Beijing-Tianjin-Hebei region, the Yangtze River economic belt, and other regions, to improve the handling of cross-regional cases. However, further reforms are needed. The state could improve the coordination of IP administration and enforcement among relevant state bodies and enhance oversight of subnational IP policy making and strategizing. To handle the large number of patents, the state could expand the size and quality of China's IP administration infrastructure, in terms of staffing and managerial and administrative systems. However, there is an ongoing debate about the extent to which the power of local patent administrative enforcement authorities should be expanded.

Given the significant increase in the number of IP cases, the courts, including specialized IP courts, also need more staff and financial resources. Greater use of technical specialists from outside the court system could address some of the capacity constraints. More resources could be invested in nongovernment arbitration and mediation for IP cases, given that the majority of IP lawsuits in China are being addressed through mediation, if not withdrawn. Procedures could be adopted to encourage greater use of these mechanisms.

Technology start-ups are particularly vulnerable to IP theft, given their lack of capacity to protect their rights and the centrality of IP in their business models. The government could consider targeted measures to improve IP support for technology start-ups. State-backed consulting and financial assistance programs for IP management exist for such firms, but the quality of their consulting services needs to be improved.

Improving the management of innovation policies

Innovation policies would benefit from streamlining and consolidation. Since 2001, China has issued more than 170 innovation support policies at the central level alone, and many more have no doubt been issued at the local level. Policies are formulated and implemented by at least 24 ministries and agencies. The large number of policies and institutions means that innovation policies suffer from institutional fragmentation, duplication, and a lack of focus and prioritization. To streamline and consolidate innovation policies, the government could carry out a public expenditure review of innovation policies and programs. The review would help to identify institutions, policies, and support instruments that could be upgraded, expanded, or—if they are no longer effective—discarded. China also could strengthen its monitoring and evaluation framework to assess systematically the efficiency and effectiveness of innovation policy and adjust policy priorities and public spending accordingly.

Recognizing the need to improve the coordination of innovation policies and programs, in July 2018 the government established the national Science and Technology

Leading Group, led by Premier Li Keqiang. This leading group could consider several possible priorities. It could aim to enhance the administrative efficiency and streamline the funding architecture of innovation support programs to reduce fragmentation and any unnecessary bureaucracy, and to make the programs more user friendly for enterprises to access. It could expand the share

of grant reviews conducted by professionals with the requisite expertise and reduce the share reviewed by government administrators. Finally, it could expand rigorous impact evaluation of innovation support programs to inform public policy and enhance project performance.

Supporting innovation driven by digital diffusion

Global innovation is increasingly driven by digital technology. Digital technology is already an important foundation for China's innovation capabilities and a key driver of China's future growth. The government has prioritized the promotion of digital innovation and aims for the country to become a global leader in key emerging digital technologies, such as artificial intelligence. There are indications that China is well on its way to building the necessary capabilities and environment to promote the digital economy. But much like the overall innovation system, significant potential remains to take advantage of catch-up growth by promoting the diffusion of existing global digital technologies and innovations.

China's digital adoption rate is higher than the average for upper-middle-income countries, but many individual upper-middle-income countries have higher adoption rates, according to the World Bank's digital adoption index[7] (figure 5.6, panels a and b). China's digital adoption rate is also lower than the OECD average, and is, in fact, lower than the rates of all OECD countries estimated. There is a large gap between China and OECD countries in the extent of digital adoption among businesses and individuals, according to indicators such as lower shares of business websites and lower Internet access. By contrast, digital adoption in China's government sector is almost on par with the OECD average and significantly higher than the upper-middle-income-country average. The assessment of the government sector reflects the extent of digital adoption in core government administrative systems and the use of digital identification and online public services.

Among enterprises in China, the use of traditional digital technologies has become

FIGURE 5.6   **Digital adoption index in China and comparator countries, 2017**

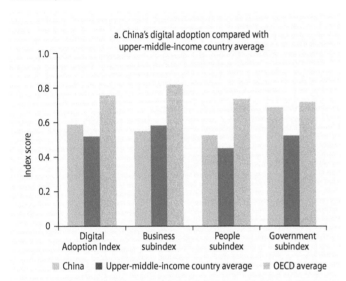

a. China's digital adoption compared with upper-middle-income country average

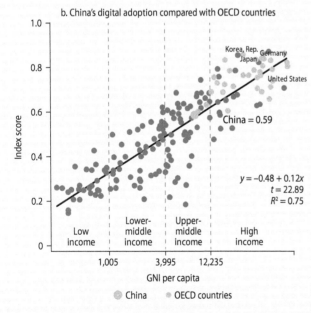

b. China's digital adoption compared with OECD countries

Source: Calculations based on the World Bank digital adoption index.
Note: GNI = gross national income. UMIC = upper-middle-income countries. OECD = Organisation for Economic Co-operation and Development.

nearly universal. In 2016, the latest year for which data are available, 99 percent of enterprises used computers, and 96 percent used the Internet. But more modern digital technologies, such as websites and e-commerce, were still being deployed across the economy. For example, only 45 percent of enterprises used online sales, 46 percent used online procurement, and 39 percent used Internet marketing (CNNIC 2017).

The adoption rate of more modern digital technologies among Chinese enterprises remains significantly lower than that of OECD enterprises. Compared with China, where 49 percent of enterprises have their own website, on average more than three out of four businesses in OECD countries have a website. Even enterprises operating in the most advanced Chinese provinces are still several years behind their global peers, on average, in the use of more modern digital technologies. For example, the percentage of enterprises with a website is highest in Shanghai, at 62 percent, but this is still lower than in 26 of the 33 OECD countries.[8] China's digital adoption rate is closer to that of the poorer OECD countries—such as Latvia, Mexico, Portugal, and Turkey—and far behind OECD leaders, such as Finland and Switzerland.

The diffusion gap in digital technologies between China and OECD countries can be disaggregated into three components: the gap within China, between the lagging and technologically frontier provinces ("x" in figure 5.7); the gap between China's frontier provinces and OECD average countries ("y" in figure 5.7); and the gap between the OECD average countries and the OECD frontier countries, such as Japan, Northern European countries, and the United States ("z" in figure 5.7). The technology diffusion gap exists in all three components. The diffusion gap between China and the OECD countries dominates for the most modern digital technologies. Diffusion within China becomes more important for relatively less modern and more widely available technologies.

Within China, the difference in the rate of adoption between various generations of technologies is considerable. For example, in Heilongjiang Province, 76 percent of enterprises use the Internet for marketing, but only 2.5 percent use it for purchasing goods online. And the diffusion of digital technologies appears to be diverging, with enterprises in poorer provinces adopting technologies at a much slower pace than their counterparts in richer provinces. Regression analysis

FIGURE 5.7   **Disaggregating the digital diffusion lag between China and OECD countries**

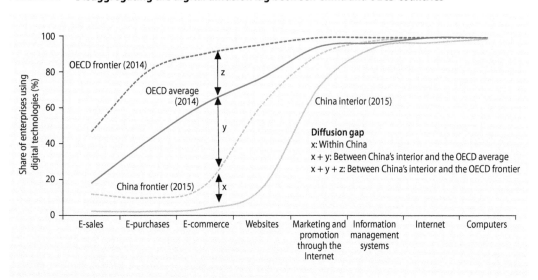

Source: Estimates based on data from the China Statistical Yearbook of Tertiary Industry (various issues).
Note: OECD = Organisation for Economic Co-operation and Development.

indicates that provinces that provide a more supportive business environment—in the form of strong property rights and a more open and diversified local economy—tend to be associated with higher levels of digital technology adoption. By contrast, direct interventions to encourage technology adoption, as measured by R&D spending and patent filings, appear to have much smaller impacts on increasing the adoption of digital technology.[9]

There are also large variations in the degree of digital adoption across industries (McKinsey Global Institute 2017). As in other countries, the most digitized sectors in China are ICT, media, and finance. In ICT, China's Internet companies are rapidly increasing their investments in digital infrastructure. Chinese semiconductor companies have been automating and digitizing facilities to serve global customers. The next set of relatively highly digitized industries includes entertainment and recreation, the retail trade, and government and related sectors, such as health care, education, and utilities. These industries have had to adopt digital technologies in response to consumers' embrace of digitized services, as reflected in the expansion of online sales, smart grids and smart meters for public utilities, digital health (box 5.1), and online education (see chapter 6).

Capital-intensive industries—such as manufacturing, oil and gas, and chemicals and pharmaceuticals—are the next tier of industries to have been digitized. Supply chain and customer management have been largely digitized, but investments in digitization, the stock of digital assets, and the level of automation remain relatively low compared with high-income countries. Similar to other economies, the sectors that lag farthest behind are fragmented and localized industries, such as real estate, agriculture, local services, and construction. But even in lagging sectors, digital solutions are penetrating the industries,

---

BOX 5.1   **Digital health**

Digital technology is transforming the face of health care in China, improving the diagnosis, treatment, and management of patients; the operation of health care providers and insurance agencies; and the supply and use of pharmaceuticals and medical technology devices. Digital health provides health workers and patients with tools to engage more fully with the care process and to improve care management and decision-making, supporting new forms of interactions such as remote physician consultations. These new forms of interactions could help to mitigate the overuse of large hospitals and the underuse of smaller facilities.

The digital health care revolution in China is facilitated by the government's commitment to integrating technology in health sector development. The 13th Five-Year Plan formulated an action plan for a healthy China, identifying smarter health care as a major priority. To promote digital health, China has been making progress in establishing the necessary digital infrastructure, including digital health records and care management systems, and in ensuring the interoperability of digital health tools across facilities and services.

Artificial intelligence (AI) is particularly promising for digital health, and nine priority application areas have been identified: virtual assistants, disease screening, medical imaging, patient record analytics, hospital management, intelligent medical devices, drug development, health management, and genome sequencing analysis. By August 2017, 83 enterprises in China were applying AI in the health care sector, mainly in medical imaging, patient record analytics, and virtual assistants.

China has a comparative advantage in developing AI for the health sector given its vast amount of medical data and generally less restrictive data privacy regulations, compared with Europe and the United States. But most hospital data are unstructured raw data not ready for use in AI systems, and it is unclear whether hospitals would be willing to share their data. The health sector could benefit from more AI talent, since only around 5,000 AI specialists work in the sector. Finally, AI laws and regulations, ethical norms and policy systems, and AI security assessment and control capabilities will eventually be needed to establish policy and ethical norms in the industry.

such as by start-ups offering digital solutions and platforms for restaurants and for residential property sales and rentals.

Promoting data trade and data flow

A fundamental consensus has emerged today that data flows produce significant economic value and can lead to flows of technology, capital, and talent, including across national borders. Therefore, restricting data flows can constrain the benefits for a country's economic development. Digital trade is affected by a wide range of policies, including those on digital services and investments, movement of data, and e-commerce. A digital trade policy framework can be organized into four clusters: fiscal restrictions and market access, establishment restrictions, data restrictions, and trading restrictions (table 5.2) (Ferracana and van der Marel 2017). Each policy can be assessed based on whether it is excessively burdensome (trade distortive) for digital trade and discriminatory against digital, online, and foreign providers. The framework indicates that the overall digital trade policy environment encompasses a wide range of complementary and interrelated factors, including competition policy, intellectual property rights, and fiscal policies.

Data policy is a central component of a country's digital trade policy environment. Data are at the heart of the digital economy and the Fourth Industrial Revolution. They provide the basis for the development of new digital products and services and the refinement of existing ones. Data are often described as infrastructure for the digital economy. There is a growing recognition that data as an infrastructure asset is as important as more traditional infrastructure, such as transport and public utilities. To address data as an infrastructure asset, policies are needed on the management and governance of data, which entail rules, processes, and organizations for the use and maintenance of data.[10]

As nontraditional sources of data become the norm, and data are put to entirely novel uses in the digital economy, questions arise about who owns what data, who can do what with them, and what protections are afforded to whom. Some policies on data flows can be legitimate and necessary to protect the privacy of the individual or to ensure national security. But policies can unnecessarily restrict the free flow of data, and alternative policies may be available that are less restrictive but still allow the government to achieve its policy objectives.

More open data policies tend to be associated with greater data traffic. Restrictions on data can be measured in terms of data policies, intermediary liability, and access to content. Preliminary analysis indicates that China has a relatively restrictive data policy environment and a comparatively low level of data traffic per capita, measured using Cisco's estimates of domestic Internet Protocol traffic per capita. The United States has among the least restrictive data policies and the highest data traffic per capita. Some of the factors that contribute to China's relatively restrictive data policy environment include its policies on data protection and data localization, the lack of a "safe harbor" data transfer regime, and the nationwide "Great Firewall" system.[11] Restrictive data policies can inhibit cross-border innovation and the ability of foreign and domestic Chinese companies to operate global platforms and perform cutting-edge, globally integrated R&D in China. The free flow of data can also support the realization of China's Internet+ and National Big Data strategies.

Data policy is an incompletely developed and still-evolving policy area, both in China

TABLE 5.2 Digital trade policy framework

Fiscal restrictions and market access	Establishment restrictions	Data restrictions	Trading restrictions
• Tariffs and trade defense	• Foreign investment	• Data policies	• Quantitative trade restrictions
• Taxation and subsidies	• Intellectual property rights	• Intermediary liability	• Standards
• Public procurement	• Competition policy	• Content access	• Online sales and transactions
	• Business mobility		

and globally. In a cross-country survey, more than 60 percent of respondents reported having difficulty understanding legal issues related to data protection and privacy. With data policies still being developed across the world, significant opportunities remain to reconsider and adjust the balance between domestic legal and regulatory requirements and the needs of the domestic and international business communities. Major areas of data policy concern personal data protection, data localization requirements, and cybersecurity. There is a need to balance efforts to protect personal data privacy and ensure data security in key sectors, such as banking and health services, with solutions that facilitate and therefore lower the cost of data transfers under all reasonable circumstances. As the volume of cross-border data flows continues to increase, so can the compliance costs associated with data location and data flow restrictions.

Personal data protection

A key element of the data infrastructure is personal data protection. More than 108 countries have data protection laws (UNCTAD 2018). In the nearly 30 percent of countries with no laws in place, personal data receive poor levels of protection, reducing trust and confidence in a wide range of commercial activities. These countries risk being cut off from international trade opportunities, because many trade transactions now involve cross-border data transfers that require adherence to minimum legal requirements for data protection. At least 35 countries are drafting data protection laws to address this gap.

In 2013, the OECD Council adopted revised Recommendations Concerning Guidelines Governing the Protection of Privacy and Trans-Border Flows of Personal Data. This revision updates and modernizes the original 1980 release of the guidelines, in light of changing technologies, markets, and user behavior and the growing importance of digital identities. The new guidelines identify seven governing principles for protecting personal data. They also emphasize the need for greater efforts to address the global dimension of privacy through improved interoperability. Several new concepts were introduced, including national privacy strategies, privacy management programs, and data security breach notification.

In 2016, the EU published the new General Data Protection Regulation to come into force in 2018. It incorporates some of the world's most stringent data regulations.[12] The current EU data regime is based on a 1995 directive. The new regulation exceeds the current provisions in many ways. It greatly enhances individual rights—such as the right to rectify, object to, and erase personal data, and the

---

BOX 5.2   OECD recommendations for protecting data privacy

The OECD, in its Recommendations Concerning Guidelines Governing the Protection of Privacy and Trans-Border Flows of Personal Data (2013), identifies seven governing principles for the protection of personal data:

1. *Notice*. Data subjects should be given notice when their data are being collected.
2. *Purpose*. Data should be used only for the purpose stated and not for any other purposes.
3. *Consent*. Data should not be disclosed without the data subject's consent.

4. *Security*. Collected data should be kept secure from any potential abuses.
5. *Disclosure*. Data subjects should be informed about who is collecting their data.
6. *Access*. Data subjects should be allowed to access their data and make corrections to any inaccurate data.
7. *Accountability*. Data subjects should have a method available for holding data collectors accountable for failing to follow the above principles.

Source: OECD 2013.

rights to data portability and to avoid being subjected to automated profiling. It introduces tougher sanctions for violations, up to 4 percent of the global turnover of violating firms. It expands the definition of personal data to include any data that can identify a person, using "all means reasonably likely to be used." And it widens the territorial scope to apply even to organizations based overseas if their data subjects reside in Europe. It expands investigative powers to include data protection audits and the right to issue public warnings, and it makes it easier for individuals to claim compensation. The new provisions establish higher data processing and management standards and require public organizations and organizations processing large quantities of data to appoint data protection officers. Each EU member state has an independent data protection authority that supervises, through investigative and corrective power, the application of the data protection laws.

In contrast to the harmonization across member states, which is a major goal of the upcoming European legislation, data protection laws in the United States are marked by diversity. The United States does not have a comprehensive national data protection law and instead has more than 20 sector-specific laws, plus hundreds of variations among the 50 states and territories. California alone has 25 state data privacy and protection laws. There is no standard definition of personal data across the states. The definition of sensitive personal data also varies greatly across states, although it typically includes personal health data and financial and creditworthiness data. Unlike the EU, there is no dedicated national data protection authority, although the Federal Trade Commission monitors the data protection policies and related practices of firms. Almost all states require notification of security breaches—a U.S. innovation now being adopted worldwide. Most countries in East Asia have laws protecting personal data and requiring individual consent for data transfers.[13]

Like the United States, China does not have a comprehensive data protection law, but a data protection law is included in the legislative plans of the 13th National People's Congress. The data protection regime is currently managed through the Decision on Strengthening Online Information Protection and the National Standard of Information Security Technology, sometimes collectively referred to as the General Data Protection Law. The new Cybersecurity Law (2017) has significant implications for personal data protection and related cybersecurity practices. It has stronger consumer data protection rights, imposing greater restrictions on the use and trading of personal data and the use of personal information for fraudulent purposes. The law imposes new security and data protection obligations on "network operators." The new cybersecurity measures could improve individual privacy in several ways, by prohibiting firms from collecting information on individuals that is unrelated to business purposes, strengthening data security measures, and requiring encryption tools to protect data. China does not have a separate regulator or commission for data privacy, similar to the United States and many East Asian countries.

High-income countries such as the United States and those in Europe tend to have stronger data privacy concerns, particularly in Europe. China has had a reputation for having a relatively lax data privacy regime and a similarly lax consumer attitude toward data privacy, and these characteristics typically have been considered an advantage in the development of the digital economy. In a 2013 cross-country survey by Boston Consulting Group, three-quarters of respondents outside of China indicated that caution is necessary when sharing personal information online, compared with only half the respondents in China (Boston Consulting Group 2013). But public views may be changing. Concerns about online fraud could be contributing to changing consumer attitudes about data privacy. A 2016 survey by the Internet Society of China found that 71 percent of respondents said that they had suffered some form of online data fraud (China Internet Network Information Center 2017).

Data privacy is not simply a domestic issue for China; it also has implications for China's efforts to globalize its enterprises. The Committee on Foreign Investment in the United States recently rejected China's Ant Financial's proposed acquisition of money transfer provider MoneyGram due to concerns about personal data security. As the exchange of digital data becomes central to the business models of all industries, differences in data privacy and data security regimes can increasingly constrain China's efforts to expand into high-income-country markets.

China's proposed "social credit system" is one example of its unique approach to data privacy and personal data use. The proposed system will rate individual citizens' "trust-worthiness" and adjust access to credit and other public services based on the individual's social credit scores (State Council of China 2014). This approach is a variation of a national digital identification system, widely recognized as being of strategic importance to the future of digital services. Digital identification systems can be developed for specific applications—for example, to manage government health or social programs—or they can be developed as a universal multipurpose system capable of supporting a wide range of needs for legal identity. Among developing countries, only 3 percent have digital identification systems that are universal schemes, as is currently envisioned for China's social credit system. Because digital identifications contain personal data, a critical aspect of any digital identification scheme is the protection of personal privacy and information. Digital identification can raise legal and regulatory concerns about the type, extent, and use of personal information to be collected.

The government is currently experimenting with the social credit system, by providing licenses to private companies to develop the systems and algorithms for social credit scores. Meanwhile, some web operating companies use the data analyses to support their business. One of the best-known examples so far has been Tencent's China Rapid Finance. Another is Ant Financial's Sesame Credit, which determines credit scores based on factors such as the individual's credit history; fulfillment of contractual obligations, such as whether electricity or phone bills are paid on time; personal behavior and preferences, such as shopping habits; and interpersonal relationships.

Data localization and cybersecurity

Data localization laws and regulations refer to requirements that data about a nation's citizens or residents be collected, processed, or stored inside the country, often before being transferred internationally and usually only after meeting local privacy or data protection laws. The goal of such regulations is typically to safeguard the security of citizens' personal information and other important data. In practice, restricting where data are stored and how data are transferred may not be the most effective approach to achieving those goals.

Protecting data requires a strong international consensus on industry standards and access to service providers with proven privacy and security capacity, regardless of whether they have data infrastructure located physically in the local area. Defenders of localization laws cite national security, the local cultural and historical context, and economic nationalism as supportive arguments. Opponents see such laws as a major barrier to trade and competitiveness. There is a fundamental tension between trade liberalization and data localization requirements, as most global businesses depend on the provision of information services across borders.

Countries have increasingly imposed restrictions on the cross-border transfer of data in the form of data localization requirements, storage and processing requirements, and conditional flow regimes in which a firm must fulfill burdensome requirements before it can move data across borders (ECIPE 2017; Stone, Messent, and Flaig 2015). At least 36 jurisdictions have restricted the movement of data across borders, most of them in the last five years, and most commonly through requirements for data localization.

The EU's 1995 Data Protection Directive permits the transfer of personal data only if another jurisdiction provides adequate protection, and the new General Data Protection Regulation permits the transfer of data outside the EU if there are appropriate safeguards, such as binding corporate rules, a valid European Data Protection Seal for both controllers and recipients, standard data protection clauses, or contractual clauses authorized by a state data protection authority. Canadian laws require personal information held by public bodies to be stored and accessed only in Canada, unless certain exceptions apply. In Korea, the Personal Information Protection Act requires information processors to inform and obtain consent from data subjects for transferring personal information to a third party overseas.

China has a variety of national and sector-specific data localization and cybersecurity requirements. The General Principles of Civil Law, promulgated in March 2017, defines the right to personal information as a basic civil right. To obtain personal information, any organization and individual would need to obtain information in accordance with the law and ensure the information's security; should not illegally collect, use, process, or transmit personal information; and should not illegally trade, offer, or disclose personal information.

The new Cybersecurity Law (Network Security Law), which came into effect in June 2017, further changed the landscape for data protection in China. It states core principles on the collection and use of personal information, requires data on consumers in the areas of "key information infrastructure" to be stored within the country, and bans the export of "personal and important data" that could threaten national security or the public interest. This means that multinational corporations operating "key information infrastructure" need to set up data centers physically within China and that the state needs to review and authorize the exporting of any sensitive data "due to business need(s)." Should any violation occur, the government may impose fines on the firm and on individual employees deemed to be responsible for the violation and may revoke or cancel commercial licenses, suspend operations, or shut down a firm's website.

The government believes that data storage and export regulations are necessary to safeguard against threats such as hacking and terrorism. The potential commercial effect of these new requirements—including their impact on innovation, data markets, and cross-border data flows—needs to be monitored carefully. The Cybersecurity Law would also benefit from more detailed regulations to bring greater clarity and transparency to the proposed new requirements and procedures, for example, regarding the proposed review regimes. To the extent possible, requirements for adopting local technology solutions unique to China should ensure compatibility with global standards to facilitate the use of global technology solutions in China.

Improving global cooperation on data policies

With global trade increasingly involving data flows, the wide range of data policies requires a global solution. Government measures that disrupt open exchanges of data can inhibit digital trade. The Internet has become subject to myriad overlapping jurisdictions and conflicting obligations. No single government can tackle the problem on its own. But international Internet governance is complex, and the institutional landscape is crowded and relatively fragmented. There are conflicting priorities among countries and few dedicated spaces in which different stakeholders can interact and devise different solutions.

Achieving policy coherence across countries requires close and sustained international cooperation among all governmental and nongovernmental stakeholders to preserve the cross-border nature of the Internet. A mixture of organizations has emerged to bring together the technical community, businesses, governments, and civil society, such as the Internet Corporation for Assigned Names and Numbers, Internet Engineering Task Force, and World Wide Web Consortium (Bildt 2018). The World Trade Organization and trade agreements have also been identified as ways to deal with fragmentation. For example, the Trans-Pacific Partnership came close to setting new standards for various trade-related aspects of digitalization, including data localization and the accessibility of websites, devices, and apps.

The EU is going in a very different direction from the United States in regulating the transfer and use of data, with more stringent privacy rules and limits on how much data companies can use for AI and in what fashion. Europeans may opt to put data in public "trusts" that private companies could access with public supervision rather than just letting corporations use data for commercial gain. China is emphasizing "cyber sovereignty," the idea that states have the right to manage and control their own Internet without external interference.

ICT telecommunications infrastructure

Telecommunications infrastructure is the physical backbone and key enabler of the digital economy. Affordable, reliable, and widely available high-speed Internet service facilitates the delivery of digital services and transactions across all sectors of the economy. Recognizing the importance of ICT infrastructure, the Chinese government has issued several policy directives to improve access to and the quality and affordability of broadband services. In 2013, the State Council issued the Broadband China Strategy (2013–20) to develop the country's broadband networks, establishing targets for coverage, access, speeds, and subscriptions. Also in 2013, the Ministry of Industry and Information Technology (MIIT) issued the Notice of Implementation of the Broadband China Program. In June 2015, it announced that it would set up a universal service fund to deploy broadband networks

in less profitable rural areas (TeleGeography 2017). And in 2017, it announced that it was working with the Ministry of Finance, local governments, and enterprises on a universal-service pilot to promote broadband in rural and remote areas (MIIT 2017). The 13th Five-Year Plan includes a capital expenditure target of US$290 billion for telecommunications infrastructure investments in 2016–20.

The telecommunications market is dominated by three state-owned enterprises—China Mobile, China Telecom, and China Unicom—which provide the core network infrastructure and fixed, mobile, and Internet services. Other service providers include mobile virtual network operators that offer telecom services over the incumbents' networks and a large number of Internet and social media applications that use the existing telecom infrastructure. Foreign investment in telecommunications is restricted by the share of equity.

China has made significant investments in rolling out mobile broadband for individual users and fixed broadband (optical fiber) with higher data transmission capabilities. As a result, China's access to broadband services is well advanced (table 5.3). There is nearly universal mobile network coverage as well as mobile subscriptions. The percentage of the population with an active mobile broadband subscription, 69.1 percent, is above the Asia-Pacific average but lower than in Brazil, Japan, Korea, and the United States. The percentage of the population with a fixed broadband subscription, 22.9 percent, is also

TABLE 5.3   ICT infrastructure indicators in selected countries

Indicator	China	Brazil	India	Korea, Rep.	Japan	Asia and Pacific	United States
Percentage of population							
Fixed-line subscribers	14.7	20.4	1.9	56.1	50.6	10	37.1
Mobile subscribers	96.9	118.9	87	122.7	131.8	98.9	120.8
Fixed broadband subscribers	22.9	13	1.4	41.1	31.4	11.3	32.4
Active mobile broadband subscribers	69.1	89.5	16.8	111.5	132.3	47.4	124.9
Mobile 3G network coverage	98	96.9	79.7	99	99.9	87.6	99.9
Mobile LTE (4G) network	97	79.6	73.5	99	99	73.6	99.7
Percentage of GNI per capita							
Mobile prices	0.6	1.7	1.8	1.2	1	3.2	0.8
Fixed broadband prices	2.4	2.1	4.8	1.5	0.6	14.5	0.8
Mobile broadband price 1 gigabit	1.1	2.3	3.2	0.4	1.5	5.4	0.3

Source: ITU 2017.
Note: Numbers greater than 100 percent may indicate multiple SIM cards. GNI = gross national income.

above the Asia-Pacific average but lags that in Japan, Korea, and the United States.

China appears to have relatively competitive fixed broadband and mobile prices, compared with other Asia-Pacific countries and higher-income economies.[14] Even though three SOEs dominate both fixed and mobile broadband, economies of scale have enabled lower prices. The government has also played a strong role in lowering prices. For example, in 2015, MIIT issued directives to the telecommunications SOEs to lower prices by at least 30 percent by December 2015. A further price reduction directive was issued in 2016 without specific targets. In March 2017, the government instructed the three major telecom operators to increase speeds, reduce prices, reduce fees for Internet access and leased lines for SMEs and households, phase out domestic long-distance and roaming charges, and reduce prices for international voice calls.

The government plans to make substantial investments in the next generation of networks, known as 5G. MIIT plans to launch 5G commercially by 2020, with large-scale deployments to follow within two to three years. China already claims 97 percent coverage of the population for 4G LTE but plans to leapfrog into 5G to be among the international leaders in the technology. Although 4G standards are supporting current Internet of Things deployment, 5G will become a critical infrastructure to support the hundreds of millions of machine-to-machine and Internet of Things connections.

Remaining challenges and reform options

The main challenge for improving telecommunications access in China is to reduce significant regional disparities in broadband penetration. Consistent with other countries, penetration is highest in larger urban centers and lower in more rural, remote provinces. The mobile broadband penetration rate exceeds 90 percent in the heavily urbanized and prosperous eastern coastal areas of Beijing, Shanghai, and Tianjin, and in the provinces of Guangdong and Zhejiang. Penetration rates are lower in other provinces, particularly in the more rural, remote provinces, but only

in a few provinces, such as Anhui and Jiangxi, does penetration fall below 60 percent.

China could also focus on expanding broadband access for higher bandwidths, allowing faster download and upload speeds. Broadband speed is a proxy for the quality of Internet service and overall network quality and capacity, affecting e-commerce, financial services, and online government services. According to Akamai's *State of the Internet Report 2017*, which provides global benchmarking, Korea has the world's fastest average download speed, at 28.6 megabits per second (Q1 2017; Akamai 2017). China ranks 74 of 100 countries surveyed in average download speeds, at 7.6 megabits per second, but it has among the highest rate of year-over-year increase in average download speed, at 78 percent. China compares reasonably well for broadband adoption rates, at the lower broadband speed of 4 megabits per second (figure 5.8). In particular, China's rate is twice the rate for India, a similarly large country. But both China and India are well behind other countries in the widespread adoption of the higher bandwidths.

China has largely succeeded in expanding access to telecom services, but the massive expansion of Internet use continues alongside slow broadband speed and limited Internet business penetration. The major reform question is whether the current strategies and institutional arrangements are sufficient to address the remaining challenges for China's

FIGURE 5.8 **Broadband adoption in selected countries, by speed, first quarter of 2017**

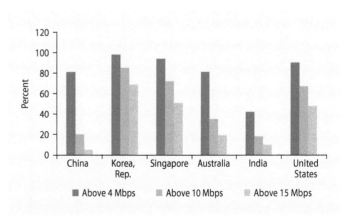

Source: Adapted from Akamai 2017.
Note: Mbps = megabits per second.

telecommunications infrastructure. The policy and regulatory framework is extensive, but can it put sufficient competitive pressure on the incumbent operations? Various policy documents refer to the promotion of private competition. The network infrastructure is essentially regionally distributed among the three telecom operators. There is competition at the services level, by virtual network operators and value-added service providers, such as the Internet service providers. In other countries, greater private sector participation has promoted a more competitive market environment and improved sector performance. Indeed, competition is a critical factor in driving down prices for mobile phone service. Steps toward greater competition could be achieved through gradual market liberalization, combined with procompetitive regulatory reforms.

The government has been experimenting with market liberalization and foreign participation in the telecom sector. In late 2013, it established the China (Shanghai) Pilot Free Trade Zone to promote reforms and experiment with foreign investment in telecommunications, as well as in e-commerce, legal services, logistics, and marine insurance. In 2014, three more pilot free trade zones were established in Fujian, Guangdong, and Tianjin. There are currently 12 pilot free trade zones. A foreign-invested telecommunications enterprise incorporated in the Shanghai free trade zone can have full ownership in an enterprise offering various types of telecommunications-related services, including Internet access and online data and trade processing.

These experiments in market liberalization could be accelerated and replicated in other locations and extended to a range of other Internet services. There could also be an expanded role for the nontraditional service providers—such as Alibaba, Baidu, and Tencent—which already provide extensive "over the top" value added services on existing networks. Their participation could push the sector to improve access, quality, and affordability. Incentive mechanisms may be needed to encourage the new providers to accelerate rollouts in underserved regions.

Greater market competition could be complemented by regulatory reforms. The regulatory framework for telecommunications is quite extensive, top down, and interventionist. Different authorities are responsible for telecom and media, requiring the State Council to coordinate. For example, MIIT is responsible for overall regulation, including licensing. The National Development and Reform Commission is responsible for approvals of investment projects and pricing. While retail prices are market determined, interconnection rates continue to be regulated, and there is frequent conflict over interconnection. The regulatory framework has undergone a series of reforms since China's membership in the World Trade Organization began, and some institutional restructuring has contributed to separating the government's regulatory functions from ownership interests and policy making. The government could consider further steps to separate these functions.

In other countries, major telecom market reforms typically involve de-monopolization and the establishment of an autonomous regulatory authority. The general consensus is that an independent regulator is best positioned to resolve key conflicts, such as interconnections between networks. Moreover, establishing a regulatory authority before de-monopolization increases telecom investments (Wallsten 2002). But regulatory authorities vary in effectiveness. In many countries, the regulator covers both telecom and media, a reflection of the convergence of these technologies; in China, they are separate.

China could consider more incremental reforms to strengthen regulatory oversight of the telecom sector. In addition to taking further action to separate regulatory functions, the regulatory framework could be reoriented toward greater emphasis on the quality of services and public accountability for performance, as in other countries. This reorientation would include reforms to ensure greater public disclosure of data on operational performance. In this regard, in March 2018 MIIT announced that it would establish a public list of "bad" and "untrustworthy" telecom businesses, focusing primarily on the business practices of service providers. However, considerable scope remains for expanding the monitoring and evaluation of the telecommunications sector's performance, including at the subnational level, and for making the relevant data more widely available to increase accountability.

Notes

1. The Patent Cooperation Treaty is an international treaty with more than 145 contracting states. The treaty makes it possible to seek patent protection for an invention simultaneously in many countries by filing a single "international" patent application, instead of filing separate national or regional applications.
2. The Nature Index measures global high-quality research output based on absolute and fractional counts of publication productivity at the institutional and national levels. Weighted fractional count (WFC) accounts for the share of authorship on each article and applies a weighting to adjust for the overrepresentation of papers in astronomy and astrophysics. https://www.nature.com/articles/d41586-018-02904-3.
3. In 2000, 99 percent of Singaporean patents were registered to nonresidents (Dodgson 2000).
4. "China Claims More Patents Than Any Country—Most Are Worthless," *Bloomberg News*, September 27, 2018.
5. Based on the World Management Survey and various industry case studies. See https://worldmanagementsurvey.org/.
6. Statutory damages are damage awards in civil law, in which the amount awarded is stipulated within the statute rather than being calculated based on the degree of harm to the plaintiff.
7. The DAI was developed for the World Bank's *World Development Report 2016: Digital Dividends.* The DAI measures the depth of digital adoption across these three sectors—business, households, and government—for 180 countries around the world. The overall DAI is the average of the subindexes of the three sectors, and each subindex is based on several indicators. Each index is normalized from 0 to 1.
8. More recent data indicate that digital adoption in China may have further increased. A 2017 survey of 500 firms in top five cities in China (Shanghai, Shenzhen, Guiyang, Xi'an, and Shenyang), conducted by the World Bank, indicated that 77 percent of enterprises have their own website, which is comparable to the OECD average.
9. The findings are based on a regression analysis on determinants of provincial DAIs. The quality of the business environment was measured by the proxy variables trademarks issued per capita, to measure strong property rights; trade to GDP ratio, to measure openness; and share of tertiary sector, to measure higher diversified sources of growth.
10. Open Data Institute (https://theodi.org/topic/data-infrastructure/).
11. In a "safe harbor" data transfer regime, a country grants Internet intermediates broad or conditional immunity for third-party content, provided that certain conditions are respected. It is considered critical to the promotion of innovative services, as it provides intermediaries with sufficient legal certainty to provide digital services.
12. See https://www.eugdpr.org/.
13. However, acceptance of contractual obligations typically has been interpreted as consent for transfer of personal data.
14. Making direct comparisons of prices is difficult, especially for mobile services, because the terms, conditions, and quality of services can differ in addition to the prices. As a result, price comparisons can differ across different data sources. For example, International Telecommunications Union data (for 2017) indicate that mobile broadband prices are higher in China than in Korea, but OECD data indicate that they are lower. In addition, the prices should be converted into purchasing power parity to compare the real cost to users.

Bibliography

Akamai. 2017. *State of the Internet Report 2017.* https://www.akamai.com/us/en/multimedia/documents/state-of-the-internet/q1-2017-state-of-the-internet-connectivity-report.pdf.

AMP Steering Committee. 2014. "Accelerating U.S. Advanced Manufacturing." Report to the President. White House: President's Council of Advisors on Science and Technology Policy. https://s3.amazonaws.com/sitesusa/wp-content/uploads/sites/802/2017/06/amp20_report_final.pdf.

Bildt, Carl. 2018. "Securing the Digital Transition." *Project Syndicate,* January 22.

Bloom, Nicholas, Erik Brynjolfsson, Lucia Foster, Ron S. Jarmin, Megha Patnaik, Itay Saporta-Eksten, and John Van Reenen. 2017. "What Drives Differences in Management?" NBER Working Paper No. W23300, National Bureau of Economic Research, Cambridge, MA.

Bloom, Nicholas, Charles I. Jones, John Van Reenen, and Michael Webb. 2019. "Are Ideas

Getting Harder to Find?" Informal. https://web.stanford.edu/~chadj/IdeaPF.pdf.

BMBF (Federal Ministry of Education and Research, Germany). 2017. Please see https://www.bmbf.de/de/zukunftsprojekt-industrie-4-0-848.html.

Boeing, P. 2016. "The Allocation and Effectiveness of China's R&D Subsidies: Evidence from Listed Firms." *Research Policy* 45: 1774–789.

Boeing, P., and E. Mueller. 2019. "Measuring China's Patent Quality: Development and Validation of ISR Indices." *China Economic Review*, 57, 101331.

Boeing, P., E. Mueller, and Sandner. "China's R&D Explosion: Analyzing Productivity Effects Across Ownership Types and Over Time." *Research Policy* 45 (1) 159–76.

Boston Consulting Group. 2013. "Global Consumer Sentiment Survey 2013." https://www.bcg.com/publications/2013/marketing-sales-resilient-consumer-find-growth-amid-gloom.aspx.

Branstetter, Lee, Li Guangwei, and Francisco Veloso. 2014. "The Globalization of R&D: China, India, and the Rise of International Co-invention." Working paper.

Cheng, Hong, Hanbing Fan, Takeo Hoshi, and Dezhuang Hu. 2019. "Do Innovation Subsidies Make Chinese Firms More Innovative? Evidence from the China Employer Employee Survey." NBER Working Paper No. 25432, National Bureau of Economic Research.

China IP Index Report Research Team. 2016a. "Beijing IP Litigation Report 2016" (in Chinese). China IPR Index Report 2016, China Financial and Economic Publishing House.

China IP Index Report. 2016b. "Shanghai IP Litigation Report 2016" (in Chinese). China IPR Index Report 2016, China Financial and Economic Publishing House.

China Internet Network Information Center. 2016.

———. 2017. "Statistical report on internet development in China." http://cnnic.com.cn/IDR/ReportDownloads/201706/P020170608523740585924.pdf.

China Statistical Yearbook of Tertiary Industry. Various issues.

Cicera, Xavier, and William F. Maloney. 2017. *Innovation Paradox: Developing-Country Capabilities and the Unrealized Promise of Technological Catch-Up.* Washington, DC: World Bank Group.

CNNIC (China Internet Network Information Center). 2017. "Statistical Report on Internet Development in China." https://cnnic.com.cn/IDR/ReportDownloads/201706/P020170608523740585924.pdf.

Cornell University, INSEAD, and WIPO. 2016. The Global Innovation Index 2016: *Winning with Global Innovation.* Ithaca, Fontainebleau, and Geneva: Cornell University, INSEAD, and World Intellectual Property Organization. http://www.wipo.int/edocs/pubdocs/en/wipo_pub_gii_2016.pdf.

Dodgson, M. 2000. "Policies for Science, Technology, and Innovation in Asian Newly Industrializing Economies." In *Technology, Learning, and Innovation: Experiences of Newly Industrializing Economies,* edited by L. Kim and R. Nelson. Cambridge: Cambridge University Press.

ECIPE (European Centre for International Political Economy). 2017. "Restrictions on Cross-Border Data Flows: A Taxonomy." By Martina Ferracane. ECIPE Working Paper 1/2017, ECIPE, Brussels.

ElenaNeira.com. 2016. "China Moves a Step Closer to 5G." October 17. http://elenaneira.com/5g/china-moves-a-step-closer-to-5g/#.WKQNMRKGOgy.

Elgar, E., and F. Malerba. 2005. "Sectoral Systems: How and Why Innovation Differs across Sectors." *The Oxford Handbook of Innovation.*

European Commission. 2017. "The 2017 EU Industrial R&D Investment Scoreboard." European Commission, Brussels.

Ezell, S., and R. Atkinson. 2011. *International Benchmarking of Countries' Policies and Programs Supporting SME Manufacturers.* Washington, DC: Information Technology and Innovation Foundation.

Fang, Jing, Hui He, and Nan Li. 2016. "China's Rising IQ (Innovation Quotient) and Growth: Frim-Level Evidence." IMF Working Paper 16/249, International Monetary Fund, Washington, DC.

Fernandes, A., A. Mattoo, H. Nguyen, and M. Schiffbauer. 2017. "The Internet and Chinese Exports in the Pre-Alibaba Era," World Bank Policy Research Working Paper 8262, World Bank, Washington, DC.

Ferracana, M. F., and E. van der Marel. 2017. *Digital Trade Restrictiveness Index.* Brussels: European Centre for International Political Economy.

Foray, Dominique. 2015. *Smart Specialization: Opportunities and Challenges for Regional Innovation Policies.* Routledge Press.

Foray, Dominique, Paul A. David, and Bronwyn Hall. 2009. "Smart Specialisation: The Concept." Knowledge Economists Policy Brief 9.85, 100.

Ghoni, Edwin, and William Maloney. 2017. "Why Don't Poor Countries Do R&D? Varying Rates of Factor Returns across the Development Process." *European Economic Review* 94, issue C, 126–47.

Goh, C, W. Li, and L. Colin. 2015. "R&D Returns, Spillovers, and Firm Incentives: Evidence From China." Policy Research Working Paper, no. WPS 7191, World Bank, Washington, DC.

GTAI (Germany Trade and Invest). 2018. "Incentives in Germany: Supporting Your Investment Project." https://www.gtai.de/GTAI/Content /EN/Invest/SharedDocs/Downloads/GTAI /Brochures/Germany/facts-figures-incentives -in-germany-en.pdf?v=13.

Hu, Albert Guangzhou, and Gary H. Jefferson. 2009. "A Great Wall of Patents: What Is behind China's Recent Patent Explosion?" *Journal of Development Economics* 90 (1): 57–68. http://www.sciencedirect.com/science/ article/pii/S0304387808001120.

ITU (International Telecommunication Union). 2016. "Measuring the Information Society Report." https://www.itu.int/en/ITU-D /Statistics/Documents/publications/misr2016 /MISR2016-w4.pdf.

IP House. 2017a. "ICT Development Index 2017." http://www.itu.int/net4/ITU-D/idi/2017/index .html.

———. 2017b. "Measuring the Information Society Report." https://www.itu.int/en/ITU-D /Statistics/Documents/publications/misr2017 /MISR2017_Volume1.pdf.

Jamrisko, Michelle, and Wei Lu. 2017. "These Are the World's Most Innovative Economies."Bloomberg, January 17. https:// www.bloomberg.com/news/articles /2017 -01-17/sweden-gains-south-korea-reigns -as-world-s-most-innovative-economies.

Judicial Big Data Research Institute. 2017. "Judicial Big Data Report of IP Infringement" (in Chinese). http://www.gdcourts.gov.cn/web /content/37708-?lmdm=2000.

Kelly, Kevin. 2016. *The Inevitable: Understanding the 12 Technological Forces that Will Shape our Future.* New York: Viking.

Kurzweil, Ray. 2015. *The Singularity Is Near.* New York: Penguin Books.

Lam, L, L. Branstetter, and I. Azevedo. 2014. "Too Fast, Too Soon? The Rise of the Chinese Wind Turbine Manufacturing Industry." Informal.

Lee, Keun. 2016. *Economic Catch-Up and Technological Leapfrogging: The Path to Development and Macroeconomic Stability in Korea.* Edward Elgar Publishing.

Liu, Xielin, Sylwia Schwaag Serger, Ulrike Tagscherer, and Amber Chang. 2017. "Beyond Catch-up: Can a New Innovation Policy Help China Overcome the Middle-Income Trap?" *Science and Public Policy*, pp 1-14.

Manyika, James, Jonathan Woetzel, Richard Dobbs, Michael Chui, Peter Bisson, Jacques Bughin, and Dan Aharon. 2015. "The Internet of Things. Mapping the Value Beyond the Hype." McKinsey Global Institute.

McKinsey Global Institute. 2017. "Digital China: Powering the Economy to Global Competitiveness." McKinsey and Company.

MIIT (Ministry of Industry and Information Technology). 2017. http://www.miit.gov.cn /n1278117/n4310819/n4310837/c5452284 /content.html.

Molnar, M. 2017. "Boosting Firm Dynamism and Performance in China." OECD Economics Department Working Paper 1408, OECD Publishing, Paris.

National Science Foundation. 2018. "Science and Engineering Indicators, 2018." Chapter 4 of *Research and Development: U.S. Trends and International Comparisons.* https://www.nsf .gov/statistics/2018/nsb20181/report/sections /research-and-development-u-s-trends-and -international-comparisons/cross-national -comparisons-of-r-d-performance.

Prud'homme, Dan, and Zhang Taolue. 2017. "Evaluation of China's intellectual property regime for innovation." Background paper for this report, World Bank, Washington, DC.

Rong, Z., X. Wu, and P. Boeing. 2017. "The Effect of Institutional Ownership on Firm Innovation: Evidence from Chinese Listed Firms." *Research Policy* 46: 1533–551.

Shanghai Free Trade Zone. 2017. http://en.shftz .gov.cn/.

Shapira, Philip Youtie, and Seokbeom Kwon. 2017. "Tracking the Emergence of Synthetic Biology." *Scientometrics* 112 (3): 1439–69.

State Council of China. 2014. "Planning Outline for the Construction of a Social Credit System," State Council, Beijing, June 14.

Staufen, A. G. 2015. "China—Industrie 4.0 Index 2015." Staufen AG and Weg zür Spitzenleistung, Köngen. https://www.staufen.ag/file admin/HQ/02-Company/05-Media/2-Studies /STAUFEN.-studie-china-industrie-4.0-index -2015-de_DE.pdf.

Stone, S., J. Messent, and D. Flaig. 2015. "Emerging Policy Issues: Localization Barriers to Trade." OECD Trade Policy Paper 180, OECD Publishing, Paris.

TeleGeography (database). 2017. Globalcomms Database, China https://www.telegeography.

com/products/globalcomms/data/country
-profiles/ap/china/china.pdf.

UNCTAD (United Nations Conference on Trade
and Development). 2018.

Wallsten, Scott. 2002. "Does Sequencing Matter?
Regulation and Privatization in Telecommunications Reforms." World Bank. http://info
.worldbank.org/etools/docs/voddocs/152/334
/sequencing.pdf.

Wei, Shang-Jin, Zhuan Xie, and Xiaobo Zhang.
2017. "From 'Made in China' to 'Innovated in
China': Necessity, Prospect, and Challenges."
Journal of Economic Perspectives 31(1) 49–70.

White House. 2011. "Report to the President on
Ensuring American Leadership in Advanced
Manufacturing." https://obamawhitehouse

.archives.gov/sites/default/files/microsites/ostp
/pcast-advanced-manufacturing-june2011.pdf.

WIPO (World International Patent Office).
2018. "Statistical Country Profiles: China."
December.

World Bank. 2012. "China 2030: Building a
Modern, Harmonious, and Creative Society."
February 27. https://www.worldbank.org
/en/news/feature/2012/02/27/china-2030
-executive-summary.

———. 2016. "Toward an Innovative Poland:
Entrepreneurial Discovery Process and Business Needs Analysis." World Bank, Washington, DC.

World Management Survey. 2012. Various industry case studies.

6

Building Human Capital

Human capital investment is essential for promoting the second and third of the three D's. It facilitates the diffusion of innovation and technology (the second D) by enhancing the capability of the workforce to use, adopt, and disseminate technologies. A more capable workforce would help to foster new discoveries and innovations (the third D) and strengthen the research capabilities of China's universities, research institutes, and enterprises. Prioritizing human capital investments and strengthening China's education and training system will be essential for transitioning to innovation- and productivity-led growth. Investing in each worker is particularly urgent for China, given its shrinking and aging workforce. China needs to focus on ensuring that no child is left behind and that each child has education opportunities at all stages of schooling, starting from early childhood education. China also needs to think ahead and consider the expected impact of rapid technological changes on the future economy and how best its education and training system could prepare workers for the future workplace. Reforms of the education and training system will need to be considered together with complementary active labor market and social protection policies

that help workers adjust to a more dynamic modern workplace.

China has made considerable progress in strengthening its education system and expanding education opportunities. Over the past three decades, China has made primary education universal and expanded access to education at all levels. China runs one of the world's largest education systems, with more than 270 million students enrolled at various levels. Yet much remains to be done. Gross enrollment rates across all levels are now comparable to those in upper-middle-income countries, but enrollments in upper-secondary (88.8 percent) and tertiary education (48.1 percent) still lag enrollments in high-income countries in 2018. Overall, the educational attainment of China's labor force lags well behind that of comparator countries (figure 6.1).

A record 7 million students will graduate from Chinese universities in 2017, nearly 10 times the figure in 1997 and more than twice the number in the United States in 2017. When the Republic of Korea reached China's current gross domestic product (GDP) per capita in 1992, its gross tertiary enrollment was 40 percent, similar to that of China today. Korea's subsequent transition

FIGURE 6.1   **Educational attainment of the labor force in China and comparator countries, 2015**

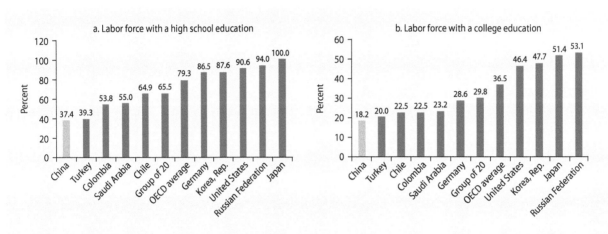

Source: Li et al. 2017.
Note: OECD = Organisation for Economic Co-operation and Development.

to high income was supported by a growing supply of university graduates. By 2004, two decades later, Korea's gross enrollment rate had reached 90 percent. This was accomplished with the underpinning of universal access to quality basic education.

Although the number of university graduates has increased rapidly in China, enterprises still identify skill shortages as a major constraint. In a survey of entrepreneurs conducted for this report, up to three-fourths of respondents indicated that finding workers with technical and managerial skills was difficult. So China needs to close the investment gaps in basic education and learning, especially in rural areas and among disadvantaged populations, and to ensure the quality of postsecondary education.

Different types of skills will be emphasized in the future workplace, shaped by technology. China's education and training system will need to prepare its workers for the future workplace by equipping them with nonroutine, cognitive, and interactive social skills. Technical education and short-term training need to be geared more toward jobs in the services sector, and lifetime learning will be increasingly critical for workers to keep up with changing technology. The whole postsecondary system needs to mainstream more work-based learning and focus on the full

range of skills needed to adapt to new job requirements, not just on a narrow range of vocational or occupational skills.

Technology's impact on China's labor market

Technological advances are expected to change the world's labor markets, including China's, by automating a large share of tasks performed by labor. Electronic and information technologies have already automated many routines and noncognitive tasks. Advances in big data analytics and machine learning could automate more cognitive tasks—such as driving, analyzing texts, and recognizing faces. In the United States, over 2005–14, traditional occupations declined to about half of total employment in manufacturing, while more highly skilled occupations grew the fastest, such as architecture, engineering, business, finance, management, sales, and computer and mathematical occupations (Oldenski 2015).

Robot density is expected to increase rapidly in China. Industrial robots can displace local jobs much faster than the local economy can create other jobs. In the United States, they have reduced local employment and lowered wages in local labor markets, indicating insufficient offsetting gains in local employment (Acemoglu and Restrepo 2017). It is estimated that adopting one new industrial robot would displace six to seven workers in the United States, but the impact in China may differ, given the vast differences in country context.

Technology can displace workers by automating their tasks, but it also can increase demand for labor by improving productivity and creating new jobs and tasks. The net effect of technology on jobs will depend on both factors. Studies of the displacement effect vary widely in their estimates. Some estimates suggest that up to half (47 percent) of U.S. jobs can eventually be displaced by automation (Frey and Osborne 2017). *World Development Report 2016: Digital Dividends* estimates that up to two-thirds of the jobs in developing countries (and possibly a somewhat higher proportion in China) can be automated, and potentially 57 percent of jobs in the Organisation for Economic Co-operation and Development (OECD) countries (World Bank 2016).

However, the rate of technology adoption depends on many factors and does not necessarily translate into actual automation. As automation increases, labor becomes cheaper, lowering the incentives for firms to automate. In response, labor also can adjust and specialize in complementary tasks that are difficult to automate. Studies that account for delays in technology adoption, offsetting employment gains, wage adjustments, and the heterogeneity of tasks within an occupation find a much smaller net impact of technology on jobs, often several times smaller. Offsetting employment gains in other parts of the economy—and the creation of new jobs and industries enabled by technology—can absorb the displaced labor and significantly reduce the net impact on employment. Accounting for such factors, the estimate of jobs at risk of full automation in OECD countries falls to only 9 percent (Arntz, Gregory, and Zierahn 2016). In general, the difficulty of predicting future jobs and industries makes estimating the impact of technology on jobs extremely challenging.

Instead, it may be more helpful to consider how technological advances and automation will change the types of skills demanded and the nature of tasks that humans perform. A number of studies indicate that modern work will increasingly deemphasize the skills needed for routine tasks, which are easier to automate, and instead require cognitive and socioemotional skills required for nonroutine tasks. In high-income countries and in most low- and middle-income countries with data, the share of middle-skill jobs, intensive in routine tasks, has been declining, and the share of high- and low-skill jobs has been growing—described as "job polarization" (Autor, Levy, and Murnane 2003).

In Western European countries, much of job polarization has been attributed to technological change, to the impact of outsourcing, or to other competing factors (Goos, Manning, and Salomons 2014). Several studies confirm that polarization is due largely to technologies that displace routine tasks and increase labor productivity in high-skill, abstract tasks—and less to technological disruptions in low-skill occupations' intensive in nonroutine manual tasks. Industries and countries that have seen faster growth of information and communication technology (ICT) have increased the demand for college-educated workers and lowered the demand for workers with middle-level skills, without necessarily displacing the low-skill and least-educated workers (Michaels, Natraj, and Van Reenen 2014). In many countries, the polarization has also translated into wage polarization, with less-educated employees experiencing smaller increases in earnings and more-educated employees experiencing larger gains. This suggests that middle-skill workers have difficulty acquiring the more complex skills required in nonroutine tasks and thus take on jobs in occupations below their education level, driving down wages.

Until recently, China was an exception to the global trend of job polarization. Unlike many other countries in the 2000s, China's share of middle-skill occupations (World Bank 2016), such as clerks, craft and related trade workers, and plant and machine operators and assemblers, increased. Also in the 2000s, the employment share of workers in the middle ranges of wage distribution and

FIGURE 6.2 **Employment shares in China, by wage and skill distribution, 2000–15**

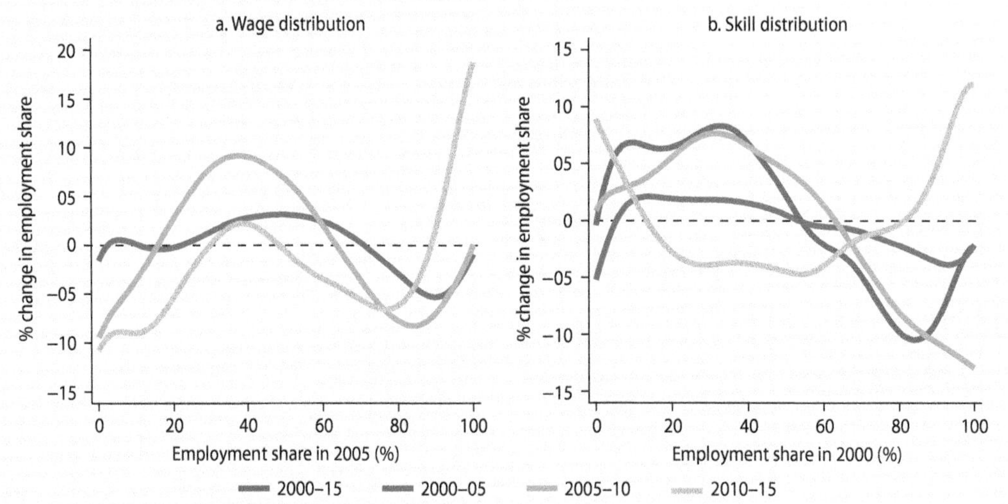

a. Wage distribution

b. Skill distribution

2000–15   2000–05   2005–10   2010–15

Sources: National Bureau of Statistics census and intercensal survey data, from Du and Park 2017.

education experienced the largest increase, providing further evidence that the share of middle-skill jobs had increased (figure 6.2; Du and Park 2017). This most likely reflects the expansion of China's manufacturing sector and the associated expansion of middle-skill jobs in the 2000s, as China benefited from the outsourcing of manufacturing production from high-income economies.

In more recent years, China has started to show signs of labor market polarization. Since 2010, the share of higher-wage employees has increased significantly, much more than that of lower-wage employees and in previous years (figure 6.2, panel a). Also, after 2010, the employment share of workers with the highest and lowest education levels increased the most (figure 6.2, panel b). Such indications of labor market polarization are also evident in the changing demand for skills in the labor market. Since 2010, as in most high-income and middle-income economies, in China work has become less manual and more intensive in cognitive and interpersonal skills (figure 6.3). The share of workers with manual skills increased in 2010, but then declined in 2015, the largest decline among workers of all skill levels. Nonroutine manual interpersonal skills increased the most in 2015, followed by routine cognitive

FIGURE 6.3 **Evolution of the skill content of Chinese jobs, 2000–15**

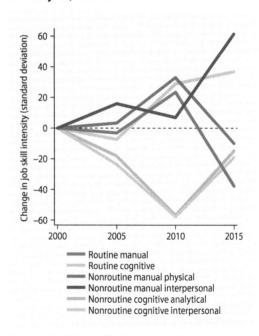

Routine manual
Routine cognitive
Nonroutine manual physical
Nonroutine manual interpersonal
Nonroutine cognitive analytical
Nonroutine cognitive interpersonal

Sources: National Bureau of Statistics census and intercensal survey data, from Du and Park 2017.

skills. This change may reflect the growth of jobs in services.

Labor market polarization is likely to deepen in China with the advance and adoption of technology. In particular, China's rapid adoption of industrial robots and its large number of manufacturing jobs could make displacement much more severe than in many other countries. In China, more than 40 percent of the country's manufacturing workers are employed in firms with automation equipment, and some 10 percent are employed in firms with robots. By 2015, China had become the world's largest user of robots. Industrial robots, which accounted for 27 percent of new robots globally, are projected to constitute 40 percent of global sales by 2019. But robot density—the number of industrial robots per 10,000 workers in manufacturing jobs—is still low in China (49) compared with Korea (531), Singapore (389), Japan (305), Germany (301), the United States (176), and the United Kingdom (71).

Technological upgrading also can change the demand for manufacturing jobs and skills by changing how manufacturing production is organized. It can lead to a global redistribution of manufacturing jobs, potentially affecting China. Over the past decades, firms in high-income countries have been offshoring their manufacturing capacity to lower-income countries to take advantage of lower labor costs and to gain efficiency through expanding global value chains. China has been one of the prime beneficiaries of this process, allowing it to become a global manufacturing base and contributing to the increasing share of middle-skill jobs. But these favorable trends could start to reverse for China. Advances in technology could enable the reshoring of jobs to local and regional hubs closer to final-consumer markets. China could be hit hard given the large share of its manufacturing exports attributed to foreign-invested firms and its rising labor costs.

But further work is needed to assess global reshoring. Anecdotal evidence based on firm surveys is fragmented and incomplete, and the results vary widely (De Backer et al. 2016). Aggregate data on the activities of U.S. multinational enterprises show no signs that the home share of employment is increasing, but they do provide some evidence that capital investment is increasingly concentrated in the United States. Home employment shares of European multinationals[1] have been stable in recent years, suggesting that any reshoring is being canceled out by offshoring. In general, offshoring continues and appears to remain more important than reshoring. Despite rising labor costs, offshoring to China could continue, as companies seek access to China's large and emerging domestic market.

Building universal foundational skills

Reforms to prepare students for the future workplace will be necessary across the entire education system. China needs to build the universal foundational skills of all students by addressing the remaining disparities in educational attainment. And it needs to support the most vulnerable individuals who drop out and fail to acquire critical foundational skills throughout basic education.

For the early years and compulsory primary education, China needs to close the investment gaps in education and learning, especially in rural areas and among disadvantaged populations. In 2016, the gross enrollment rate for preschool education was around 77.4 percent,[1] but rural and migrant children have been starting their education significantly later than their urban peers, contributing to large differences in length of attendance. This is critical because cognitive and interpersonal skills as well as creative thinking begin to take root early in life. The 2015 Program for International Student Assessment (PISA) science results indicate that Chinese students with early child development (ECD) perform 2.5 years ahead of those with no ECD.

OECD countries already spend, on average, 2.3 percent of GDP on services for families and for children ages 0 to 6 years, which allows many of them to provide ECD services for free. China's investment in ECD has increased over the years, and it reached 0.4 percent of overall GDP in 2016. Seventy-seven percent of children attended preprimary school, but only 60 percent in rural areas attended, compared with nearly 100 percent in urban areas (2015).[2] Large differences in educational inputs, such as the pupil-to-teacher ratio, indicate that children in rural areas are likely to receive a lower-quality preprimary education.

For compulsory basic education, poor nutrition and health among disadvantaged children, including left-behind children and migrant children in elementary school, have been linked to poor cognitive performance and lower well-being. These learning deficits linger from earlier stages of education, and a significant number of students, particularly from rural and migrant families, do not complete a full cycle of high school education. Rural children also exhibit lower progression to the academic stream of senior-secondary schools and therefore are less likely to apply to tertiary institutions. In 2015, 78 percent of junior-secondary school graduates in urban areas entered the academic stream of senior-secondary school, compared with only 45 percent in rural areas.[3]

Whether China can significantly increase the average level of educational attainment will depend critically on younger cohorts staying in school longer. As the education of the first nine years is compulsory and nearly universal, raising the level of educational attainment requires moving students on to upper-secondary school. Over the years, the transition rate from lower-secondary education to higher-secondary education has increased significantly, driven mostly by improved access for rural students. However, the transition rate has been declining somewhat since 2014. Despite the overall increase in access to upper-secondary school, the central and western rural areas continue to experience significant student dropouts, highlighting retention and equity challenges.

The costs (tuition and fees) of an upper-secondary education and the opportunity costs of work are important barriers to attaining upper-secondary schooling, particularly for the poor and the underserved. Furthermore, there is a significant urban-rural divide, with only 47 percent of rural youth having completed upper-secondary school at the age of 20 (2015).[4] These are major challenges for the government's goal of universalizing secondary education. Different provinces and regions also demonstrate large variations in the average years of schooling of their labor force, highlighting regional gaps in access to upper-secondary schooling.

Creating a world-class higher education system

A world-class higher education system will help China join the ranks of global innovation and technology leaders. China's higher education system has undergone major expansion and transformation over the past two decades. In 1999, the government decided to expand university admissions, and since then the number of new college students has risen rapidly—from 1.6 million in that year to 7.5 million in 2016 (figure 6.4). In the same period, the number of tertiary institutions (universities offering four-year bachelor's degrees and two- and three-year colleges offering certificates) also increased rapidly—from 1,071 in 1999 to 2,596 in 2016. Hence, the number of tertiary institutions more than doubled, and the enrollment of college students almost quintupled.

China now has one of the world's largest tertiary education systems, with 27 million students in its universities and colleges (including 16.1 million in technical or specialized short-cycle programs), 2 million in graduate schools and research institutes, and 5.8 million in 284 tertiary institutions for adult education. Public higher educational institutions, where 86.5 percent of students are enrolled, are overseen by either the central ministries or the provincial ministries. All of the institutions under the central ministries are full universities; the majority of the most prestigious universities are overseen by the Ministry of Education.[5]

As university enrollments in China continue to increase, the number of young (ages 25 to 34) college graduates with tertiary degrees in China is projected to rise a further 300 percent by 2030, compared with an increase of about 30 percent in Europe and the United States (OECD 2015). In 2013, China already accounted for 17 percent of all young college graduates across OECD and Group of 20 countries, the largest share among all countries, and this share is expected to reach 27 percent by 2030. China's contribution to the pool of scientists and skilled technicians will be even greater; its share is projected to reach 37 percent by

2030, due to the greater share of Chinese students graduating in STEM subjects (science, technology, engineering, and mathematics). In 2013, 40 percent of Chinese university graduates completed their studies in STEM subjects, compared with less than a third in countries such as France, Germany, the United Kingdom, and the United States.

Government spending on tertiary education, at 0.87 percent of GDP, is comparable to spending in Japan and Korea, but lower than spending in other high-enrollment countries such as Brazil, India, the United Kingdom, and the United States (figure 6.5). Maintaining adequate resources across the tertiary system has been a struggle in the face of the rapid growth in the number of institutions. For example, while enrollment has quadrupled, the full-time faculty has increased only 1.7 times. As in most countries, the traditional model of state-supported higher education in China has long since given way to a model of cost sharing by students, raising concerns about affordability, access, and equity. Despite extensive efforts to improve tertiary education opportunities worldwide, access to and success at this level of education tends to be highly inequitable.

China's top universities have moved up in the global rankings. In the QS World University Rankings (2018), which is used by the global innovation index, China has six universities among the top 100 in the world and seven among the top 200. In the Times Higher Education World University Rankings (2018), China has two universities among the top 100 (Peking University and Tsinghua University) and seven among the top 200. The seven among the top 200 in both rankings are the same.[6] Both rankings are dominated by U.K. and U.S. universities. According to the Academic Ranking of World Universities, originally produced by Shanghai Jiao Tong University, the number of Chinese universities in the top 300 increased from 0 in 2000 to 6 in 2008 and to 18 in 2017.[7]

Creating world-class universities has been a long-standing priority for China, which has been upgrading its top universities through targeted programs. The "211" and "985" projects were launched in the 1990s

FIGURE 6.4 **Number of postsecondary students and tertiary institutions in China, 1985–2017**

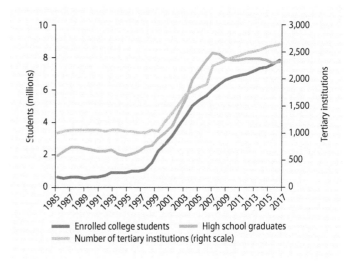

Source: National Bureau of Statistics.

FIGURE 6.5 **Government spending on tertiary education in selected countries**

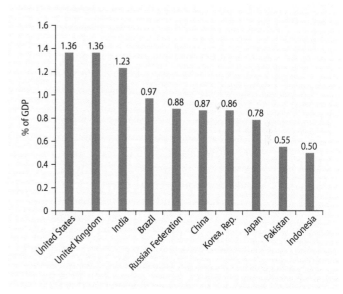

Sources: For China, calculations based on 2016 government data; for other countries, calculations based on World Bank Edstats data (most recent year, 2013–16).

to strengthen the country's top 100 higher education institutions, particularly their research capacity. In 2015, China announced the Double World Class Project, to succeed the earlier programs tasked with promoting the best universities to world class. A total of 42 universities and 95 subjects were selected to receive funding from central and local governments to improve facilities and infrastructure, conduct research and development, and attract high-level academics.

Creating world-class research universities is an expensive endeavor. The key is to ensure the balanced development of the entire higher education system. China has experienced significant regional disparities in resources and enrollment within the higher education system: many universities supported by the Double World Class Project are in the eastern region, while universities in poorer areas struggle to mobilize adequate resources and quality faculty. The disparity is reflected in the significant variation in spending per student, from RMB 64,850 in Beijing to RMB 21,678 in Guizhou province in 2016.[8]

Disparities in the tertiary education institutions have obvious implications for overall quality. Across countries, the rapid expansion of tertiary education systems has posed significant challenges to ensuring quality across the system. In China, the massive college expansion has induced many to attend college, but the returns to a college education have been more moderate and flattening since the mid-2000s, consistent with the deteriorating quality of colleges. And returns are much lower in rural areas (8 percent annual returns) than in urban areas (21 percent).[9] A sizable portion of college graduates in China are getting very low returns to college education, and those returns are not necessarily justified by the cost of a college education. Accounting for private expenditures on college education, about 10 percent of college graduates earn a negative net return on their investments in college education. If public expenditures are added, this share would be higher.

Governance reforms to modernize China's higher education system

Good governance has been identified as an important determinant of high-quality universities. University autonomy is considered a key aspect of good governance, and its importance increases as the tertiary education system expands and becomes more complex (Altbach and Salmi 2011; Salmi 2009).

Over the past decades, China has carried out higher education governance reforms that granted more autonomy to higher education institutions. Other East Asian countries have also carried out reforms to grant greater autonomy to higher education institutions, starting with reforms in the 1990s by Indonesia, Korea, Malaysia, and Thailand, followed by a second wave of reforms in the 2000s in Japan and Singapore. However, some of the reforms to grant greater institutional autonomy have been partial and incomplete (World Bank 2012).

In China, the governance reforms are also considered an unfinished agenda. The Higher Education Law (1998) established the legal status of higher education institutions and provided regulations regarding institutional autonomy for admission, programs, majors, and course instructions. The National Outline for Medium- and Long-Term Educational Reform and Development (2010–20) attempted to clarify the relationship between the government and higher education institutions and advocated building a "modern school system" based on "self-governance" for the education institutions. Direct management of higher education institutions has declined except for certain national universities. But regulations remain extensive, and government approval is still required for many managerial decisions. In a 2010 expert survey of East Asian countries by the World Bank, higher education institutions in China were assessed as having no autonomy or only partial autonomy on various indicators of higher education autonomy: setting academic and course structure and content; determining salaries and hiring and dismissing faculty; owning buildings and equipment; and determining the size and composition of student enrollment (World Bank 2012).

Chinese universities essentially have a dual governance structure. The university president, although formally the leader and legal representative of the institution, shares the authority to appoint members of the senior academic and administrative team with a Communist Party of China (CPC) secretary, who in many cases is the chair of the university board. CPC secretaries also are often directly involved in daily management and administration, in some cases acting like a co-president. The president is selected and appointed by the government, and members of the board are either selected or approved by the government. To provide the faculty with a greater role in university management, universities in other countries have established academic councils or faculty senates that decide on academic matters. The university president, who is also the council president, coordinates administrative and academic decisions and implements the council's decisions. As part of its strategy to become a world-class university, Shanghai Jiao Tong University established an academic council in 2008.

China could consider developing a strategic plan for higher education to establish a modern tertiary education governance framework with governance reforms to support greater autonomy of tertiary education (box 6.1). Tertiary education institutions could be provided greater organizational, financial, human resource, and academic autonomy. Reforms could be piloted first in universities with adequate institutional capacity and

leadership. Updating the Higher Education Law would provide the legal basis for modernizing higher education governance. Such laws should be updated at least every 10 years (the law in China dates to 1998). One model to consider for the higher education strategic plan is the California Master Plan for Higher Education (Altbach and Salmi 2011), which is considered a pioneer in systemwide governance frameworks for higher education. The plan emphasizes the balanced growth of California's three-tier public higher education system, while also committing to the excellence of its top-tier research universities. Academic freedom is at the core of the plan, and all appointments and promotions of faculty are rigorously meritocratic. Internal governance of the university is mainly in the hands of professors, and key administrative decisions on academic policies receive input from academics.

Granting greater autonomy and decision-making authority to higher education institutions requires increasing their institutional capacity and leadership to handle their increased responsibilities. Across countries, granting this authority typically involves

---

BOX 6.1   **A modern tertiary education governance framework**

A modern tertiary education governance framework supports the autonomy of tertiary education institutions through four main dimensions: organizational, financial, human resource, and academic. These four dimensions were first introduced by the European University Association in its Lisbon Declaration in 2007 and are supported by various research programs on the importance of autonomy for successful universities in Europe and the United States. They are also core elements of an assessment (benchmarking) framework of tertiary education systems developed by the World Bank:

- *Organizational autonomy* refers to the roles, functions, and authority of the governing board of the university. It is characterized by an independent university board with external representation and

the authority to approve strategic plans and annual budgets and to recruit the university president (chief administrator). The university leader and the leadership team (deans and so on) are selected competitively according to professional criteria, using an external search committee.

- *Financial autonomy* is the freedom to mobilize, manage, and use financial resources, including the freedom to determine tuition and fees and to own and manage properties.
- *Human resources autonomy* is the freedom to recruit and dismiss faculty and set salaries unencumbered by civil service requirements. Human resource policy is based on meritocratic and competitive recruitment and retention of staff.
- *Academic autonomy* is the freedom to define academic structure, programs, and course content.

Source: Altbach and Salmi 2011.

establishing and empowering the governing boards. Modern governing boards are responsible for providing strategic vision, selecting the university president (chief executive), approving strategic plans and annual budgets, and establishing a system of risk management and the parameters of financial autonomy. In East Asia, the trend has been to establish modern governing boards or university councils and to strengthen their authority. China has not moved in this direction, as its institutional arrangements reflect the country's unique governance and institutions.

On their own, autonomy and a stronger governing board are unlikely to achieve higher education's potential without a well-functioning accountability and quality assurance mechanism. Strengthening an accountability and quality assurance mechanism would also allow the government to reduce direct control over how universities should be run. With greater autonomy, universities would have to be accountable for their use of public resources, the alignment of their operations with public policy goals, and their overall performance in educating students. China recognizes the importance of ensuring the performance and quality of tertiary education institutions. China's National Outline for Medium- and Long-Term Educational Reform and Development (2010–20) stated, "Raising quality is at the heart of higher education development, and it is a basic requirement of building a strong nation of higher education."

Establishing an independent quality assurance agency would help to ensure the quality standards of higher education institutions. Compliance with such standards would play a significant role in determining the accreditation status of an institution. Accreditation also could be a prerequisite to qualify for public and private funds, maintain legal institutional status, attract students, and recruit a qualified faculty. In most countries in East Asia, including high-income countries such as Japan and Korea, the quality assurance agencies are independent. In China, this agency is a semiautonomous agency under the Ministry of Education. In addition, fewer than a quarter of tertiary institutions are evaluated or accredited, compared with three-quarters and above for countries such as Japan and Korea, and very few institutions publish their evaluation or accreditation results.

Publishing evaluation results and collecting and disseminating performance data are key aspects of a higher education quality assurance system. Making such institutional performance and outcome data available to the public enhances the transparency and accountability of tertiary systems and helps students and parents make informed choices. Systematically gathering information about indicators of educational quality can help policy makers and universities evaluate progress and develop strategic plans. The systematic monitoring of graduates' transition into the workforce is essential to evaluate the relevance of tertiary education offerings to labor market needs. Such information would help tertiary institutions assess their own performance accurately and respond to the changing demand for skills. Finally, annual publication of university rankings is common in many OECD countries and is becoming increasingly common in Eastern and Central Europe and Latin America.

New issues are emerging in China's higher education system. China plans to turn about 600 general universities into "universities of applied learning," more commonly called polytechnic universities or institutes of technology in other countries. Such institutions typically specialize in engineering, technology, and applied sciences and emphasize teaching rather than research. Also, with a new Private Education Law (2017), China will formally introduce for-profit universities, recognizing the expanding and thriving private education sector that caters to millions of Chinese youth from lower- and middle-income families. Both applied and for-profit universities will require clear and comprehensive regulatory frameworks and quality assurance mechanisms. Such frameworks are particularly critical for for-profit universities, which, in other countries, have at times performed poorly in an inadequately regulated environment.[10] In this regard, ensuring public access to information on school performance, and linking performance standards and finance mechanisms to job market performance, could be helpful.

Teaching creative thinking and problem solving

The future workplace will have greater demand for cognitive and interpersonal skills, and pedagogy and curricula will need to be reoriented to provide those skills. Recognizing the need for reforms, countries such as Finland, Korea, and Singapore are moving to more balanced curricula, with greater attention to developing socioemotional and other higher-order skills. Singapore is shifting from an education model emphasizing academic performance to a "positive education" approach downplaying academic grades and focusing on specific skills that assist students in strengthening their relationships, build positive emotions, enhance personal resilience, promote mindfulness, and encourage a healthy lifestyle. Korea's revised national curriculum aims to nurture "creative and integrative" learners by promoting socioemotional competencies, knowledge-information processing skills, creative thinking skills, communication skills, and civic competency—for example, by integrating liberal arts and natural science tracks in high schools. Finland's new national core curriculum introduced collaborative classroom practices that are multidisciplinary and problem and project based, with students expected to participate in the planning of schoolwork. Students are expected to take a more active role in Finland's core curriculum, devising their own individual learning goals, while teachers provide an enabling learning environment and support them in their individual study plans.

In China, the higher education system emphasizes professional and specialized skills that are more directly applicable to the job market, and this emphasis may be hindering the development of a broader perspective that can be helpful for creative and cognitive thinking. Universities focus on specialized skills directly relevant to the job market in response to demands by students and their families. China's tertiary education system also requires students to specialize very early. Unlike in systems in many Western countries, students already select a major when they apply to college, and almost from the moment they step onto campus,

higher education tends to be very narrow and focused. Reforming this approach, by allowing students greater freedom to select or alter their educational path, could expose students to a broader education and provide them with the foundational knowledge and skills to think creatively and enter any profession.

Universities are taking a more pragmatic approach to striking a balance between narrow professional skills and broader foundational skills. Universities in Australia, Europe, and the United States are increasingly promoting more multidisciplinary courses and majors. Such multidisciplinary courses have become increasingly popular in universities in high-income countries for equipping graduates to learn and think across a broad range of fields while also developing in-depth academic skills. Multidisciplinary courses often follow a problem-centered approach and use case studies to solve complex problems. Many emerging research fields tend to be multidisciplinary.

In China, education incentives are driven strongly by university entrance exams, which can impact incentives for creative and broader learning.[11] Such exams are common in East Asian countries, including Japan and Korea, where students have historically scored high on international assessments, such as the OECD's PISA test. The school exam system has been criticized for creating strong incentives for students and teachers to focus on testing skills, rather than on problem solving, curiosity, or creativity. A common view is that, compared with other leading systems, East Asian education systems often inhibit creativity and emphasize rote memorization. However, the OECD's assessment of the creative problem-solving component of the 2012 PISA test found that East Asian students, including students from China, outperformed students from other countries. In addition, there is evidence that exam-driven systems develop persistence ("grit"), goal orientation, self-control, and willpower that can help students in their careers and lives (Baumeister, Vohs, and Tice 2007; Choi 2014; Duckworth et al. 2007). The success of East Asian emigrants in Silicon Valley, where China and Japan are among the top five source countries for immigrant entrepreneurs, also suggests that growing up in an exam-driven system may not inhibit creativity.

However, exam-driven systems also can inhibit intrinsic motivation, stifle creativity, and have significant psychological and social costs. For example, the stress levels of Korean students are quite high by international standards and are linked to high adolescent suicide rates. In Korea, the system also has led to high financial costs for families in the form of private tutoring expenditures; such costs risk exacerbating social inequality. Exam-driven systems also can engender a relatively narrow, homogeneous set of aspirations and metrics.

Using technology to teach creativity and problem solving

China's burgeoning educational technology industry and the associated new digital technologies can potentially be harnessed to reorient teaching and learning. In China, the rate of adopting new digital technologies in education is accelerating. The number of monthly users of online education platforms is now 170 million for children's education, 95 million for foreign language learning, and 45 million for professional education (China Internet Watch 2017). Technology-aided instruction has the potential to improve learning when it aids teachers and gives students an individual learning experience. The following six are among the most promising technologies:

1. Artificial intelligence (AI) in education aims to improve teaching and learning by enhancing students' metacognition, fostering collaborative learning, spreading effective pedagogies, and relieving teachers of tedious tasks. By augmenting personalized learning, it could provide students with insights that promote self-directed learning and allow teachers to identify patterns to improve their pedagogies. AI also can help to broaden learning assessment systems by including socioemotional skills through game-based learning assessments. In China, AI systems are being developed that can engage in conversations and

provide emphatic responses—and even take the national college entrance exam (*Gaokao*). Such systems can then be used to provide support for individualized learning and for teaching children with autism-spectrum disorders.

2. Educational applications of Internet- and sensor-enabled technologies help track learner information and student achievement. Besides tracking attendance, smart identification cards could determine how learners move through the school during the day and with whom they interact—and how these actions affect student learning and achievement. For instance, facial recognition software may be used to generate feedback on student engagement, which could help teachers to improve their pedagogic strategies and understand areas where students are struggling or could benefit from more challenges.

3. Adaptive learning software, based on advances in data analytics, can personalize instruction and measure student learning through interactive and real-time metrics that adjust to students' level of subject mastery. It allows teachers to gain insight into the trajectory of individual learners. Myriad adaptive learning platforms exist, including Yuanfudao (offering a test data pool uniquely adapted to China's testing system and online courses inspired by the Khan Academy), TutorGroup (connecting anytime from anywhere to synchronous tutoring with a live tutor), and Kidaptive (cloud-based adaptive learning that creates learner profiles and actionable feedback for parents and teachers).

4. Maker Education, or learning through making, is a workshop environment, similar to Makerspaces, using technologies to promote hands-on learning and creation. Typical activities include painting, cooking, three-dimensional printing, and robotics. Teachers are expected to facilitate students' self-directed hands-on learning. These environments are said to foster socioemotional skills like persistence, resilience, and collaboration as well as higher-order skills like problem solving and creativity. China is investing heavily

in Maker Education spaces, and, since their first appearance in 2010, they have spread throughout China. The China-U.S. Youth Maker Competition has been sponsored over the last few years by the Ministry of Education, in partnership with Intel and Tsinghua University.

5. Start-ups like DFRobot and Senfu are developing applications of robotics education for young and adolescent children. The applications include kits for students to assemble a simple robot as well as more open-ended interactive hardware and a multidisciplinary curriculum and associated teacher training in robotics. The hands-on contact with modern technology encourages critical and computational skills early on. Robotics competitions, which are increasingly common, offer children opportunities to apply their skills in solution-oriented projects.

6. Virtual reality, enabling firsthand simulated experiences for learning, is used in schools to teach abstract concepts in science (such as observing blood circulation), geography, and history in more engaging ways, transporting students to classrooms in other places or simulating a visit to distant, unreachable locations. It also nurtures socioemotional skills like empathy through immersive experiences that reward greater collaboration. New start-ups in China are developing ways to combine virtual reality with adaptive learning to customize instruction for each student and increase student engagement.

Despite the hype, the potential of new educational technologies has yet to materialize fully. Many big investments have failed to deliver clear learning gains. The new technologies work best when they complement teachers rather than seek to replace them. Technology-enabled instruction to improve pedagogy and allow students to learn at their own pace have so far achieved better results. Using technology to give students a dynamic learning experience seems to improve learning. Hardware-focused interventions that provide computers at home or at school have not necessarily had a significant impact on learning outcomes. China would benefit from embracing the promise of new technologies in education, using a gradual approach of testing and experimentation that determines the most effective approaches. This effort could be complemented by regulations to safeguard the privacy and security issues arising from the use of these technologies in education.

Strengthening technical and vocational education and training

Technical and vocational education and training (TVET) is an important source of skilled labor for the economy. Secondary and tertiary vocational-track students account for about 40 percent of all students.[12] The government has a policy goal of reaching an enrollment ratio for vocational to academic programs of 50:50. China's target ratio is similar to that of Europe. The share of students on the vocational track is determined by many factors and is not necessarily proportional to a country's income status. But, on average, only 29 percent of upper-secondary students in OECD countries are enrolled in the vocational track. For upper-middle-income countries and middle-income countries, the ratios are 34 percent and 21 percent, respectively.[13] So, China's 40 percent share of students in vocational programs is comparatively high.

China's high share of students in vocational programs reflects lower costs. Since 2011, the central government has prioritized investments in vocational education, and mobilized additional subnational investments. Vocational education has thus become more affordable for students from rural or disadvantaged backgrounds. More than 90 percent of vocational school students enrolled at the secondary level receive tuition waivers in addition to other financial assistance. At the tertiary level, scholarships are provided to 30 percent of all students and financial assistance to 25 percent. At the secondary level, the financial resources for vocational programs are on par with those for academic programs, but vocational programs only receive 18 percent of all tertiary funding—far below the share of vocational students.

The State Council issued an action plan in 2014 to create a modern, demand-driven TVET system. To provide more market-oriented vocational training, it targets 80 percent of large and medium enterprises to enter official cooperation agreements with vocational schools and colleges. Provincial and local governments have more freedom to adjust the training course offered by vocational colleges to meet the requirements of local companies. To complement government vocational colleges, the government promotes expanding private vocational colleges. It also calls for treating higher vocational training the same as university studies, allowing for easier transfers between the two streams.[14]

Many challenges remain in building a modern TVET system in China. The government has rolled out initiatives to enhance school-industry collaboration, the market relevancy of TVET curricula, and improved pedagogy. As a result, there are certainly examples of successful vocational schools, in some cases schools that have benefited from cooperation with international companies and international organizations (box 6.2). But the practical relevance of vocational training still needs to be improved. TVET needs to acquire greater market relevance through closer private sector involvement. Public-private partnerships to foster enterprise participation in curricular design, delivery, and practical training opportunities have been used in other countries, such as the Meister schools in Korea and the apprentice system in Germany. There are also significant disparities in the quality of facilities and staff across schools, with only 35 percent of teachers having industry experience.[15] TVET governance and management are fragmented across public agencies; quality is uneven across schools; courses need to adapt to a more service-oriented economy; and TVET funding needs to be driven more by outputs than by inputs.

A key policy priority is to integrate technical and academic streams more fully. Vocational programs with an excessive technical focus do not provide an ideal learning environment for young learners to acquire core competencies for long-term career development. Global evidence indicates that youth

---

BOX 6.2   Lessons from recent World Bank TVET projects in China

In the past decade, the World Bank has implemented several provincial TVET projects and accumulated experience in the reforms of TVET. Since 2007, the Bank's key investments in the education sector have been skill development projects in targeted provinces, ranging from the more developed Guangdong Province to the less developed western provinces such as Gansu, Xinjiang, and Yunnan. The projects showcased these good practices on building modern TVET schools and improving systems through piloting and institutionalizing reforms:

- *Strengthen school-industry links.* Training success is tied to how closely the programs are linked to the real demands of the labor market, which requires employers to be involved in teaching and learning at the school level. Industry-led skill councils can guide curriculum development based on specific skills demanded, and school-led "school-industry committees" can steer broad-based school reforms of curricula, pedagogy, and assessment.

- *Ensure government buy-in.* Systematic provincial reforms help to achieve objectives and to sustain results in the long run. School reforms need to be accompanied by structural and institutional reforms to avoid setbacks in reform.

- *Customize a teacher training plan.* To enhance the effectiveness of instructor training, schools should develop a customized training plan, based on the instructor's professional development, and that accurately reflects needs, skill demands, and good training practices.

- *Promote modular, competency-based training for lifelong learning.* Modular courses promote flexible entry to and exit from training over a worker's career and are inherently demand driven. They promote student-centered pedagogy and competency-based evaluation instruments to assess students' learning outcomes and teachers' effectiveness.

- *Build pathways for further study.* Opening pathways to tertiary studies can increase the demand for secondary technical and vocational education.

employment rates are higher for individuals with TVET education than for those with academic education at the initial point of transition from education to work. That advantage decreases with age, however, as the narrow technical skills that initially helped in obtaining work become outdated and the absence of more general competencies for adapting and lifelong learning becomes a constraint (Hanushek, Woessmann, and Zhang 2011). Therefore, the technical and academic streams should be viewed not as separate programs but as part of an integrated system, to allow students in the technical stream greater access to a broader education. Students should be allowed to shift more easily between streams and should receive credit for skills acquired in either stream.

Pathways for skills acquisition need to be diversified. While options for post-TVET education have increased in recent years, some programs lack opportunities for graduates to continue to study in higher education. It is possible for qualified graduates of secondary vocational schools to be admitted to tertiary vocational programs, but such programs are generally considered less prestigious than regular universities. Considering that a large majority of TVET students are from rural, migrant, and blue-collar families, having more post-TVET options would provide more opportunities for social mobility. As more universities are turned into universities of applied learning, pathways can be explored for vocational students to enter them.

The government can coordinate managing the TVET sector. Currently, both the Ministry of Education and the Ministry of Human Resources and Social Security and their local departments are involved in overseeing TVET. Reforms will require improving coordination between the two ministries. Other line ministries are also involved in delivering sector-specific training. The government could pursue greater coordination among agencies for TVET—perhaps by establishing a new skills development authority—to tighten the links between schools and enterprises, to facilitate the provision of work-based training, especially by small and medium enterprises, and to update the qualifications framework for technical and vocational schools, with standards and

competencies that reflect changing labor market demand. Examples of countries with national training authorities include Australia, Brazil, New Zealand, the Philippines, South Africa, and the United Kingdom.

A national qualifications framework for technical and vocational schools could also be considered. China has a quality assurance and accreditation system, but it needs to be updated to ensure relevant and reliable standards for quality improvement. Occupations and the associated competencies have been changing rapidly, and curriculum and standards require inputs from industry to stay relevant. In addition to outdated standards, the following impediments make it difficult for training to stay relevant: teachers typically lack industry connection and therefore are not equipped with the most up-to-date technical knowledge; pedagogy tends to be teacher-oriented rather than student-centered, making students less likely to engage actively during training; and facilities tend to be outdated, constraining student acquisition of hands-on experience.

TVET needs to move toward preparing workers increasingly for employment outside the manufacturing sector, such as in the services sector and self-employment. This process begins with reforms of course offerings, which only recently started incorporating the entrepreneurship and core business skills training that is directly relevant for self-employment, the management of small enterprises, and services. The required skills encompass costing, pricing, preparing financial statements, keeping business records, project management, marketing, sales, and preparing business plans, among others. Promising programs in Korea and other countries are introducing entrepreneurship, work readiness skills, and experiential applied teaching methodologies in secondary schools and are developing new TVET curricula with a focus on skills for self-employment.

Promoting lifelong learning

With rapid technological development, job transitions throughout working lives will become the norm. The labor market is expected to become more dynamic, with more frequent job transitions, requiring workers to learn new skills throughout their lifetimes. A system of lifelong learning can prepare workers—notably adult workers—for the expected impact of changes in technology in the labor market. Adult workers need to learn job-related skills quickly, which means higher demand for modular competencies-based training. These training providers will need to be more responsive to the diverse age and experience profiles of workers experiencing job transitions.

Building a demand-driven system for lifelong adult learning will require establishing the institutional conditions for a well-regulated market of private and public providers that deliver training services with the close involvement of employers. Successful systems require a high degree of coordination and partnership between government agencies and the private sector, as well as provide businesses a strong voice in determining training policy. The government provides oversight by monitoring data on program quality, encouraging autonomy and accountability, and ensuring efficiency and results-orientation in government financing. Building demand-side buy-in from employers is a key challenge. The United Kingdom and some other European countries provide useful insights for setting up sector employer councils (box 6.3), while East Asian countries have established

independent apex training authorities, such as Singapore's Institute for Technical Education, that have strong partnerships with employers and other stakeholders.

China has been increasing its investments in adult and labor force training programs, with an emphasis on clear links to employer demands. The higher education system has institutions for adult education, including universities offering education via radio and television; schools of higher education for professional staff, workers, and agricultural workers; colleges for management cadres; pedagogical colleges; independent correspondence colleges; and evening schools or correspondence courses provided by institutions of higher education. Similar to formal higher education, adult continuing education also expanded after 1999, but the expansion was mainly in evening schools and correspondence courses of higher education institutions.

Workplace learning and on-the-job training are important sources of skills formation, and an integral part of lifelong learning. Work-based training, while a government-mandated requirement, is uneven across enterprises, and small and medium enterprises, in particular, face disincentives and capacity constraints in training their employees. If labor turnover is high, employers have less incentive to train their workers. To

---

BOX 6.3   **Adult learning in the United Kingdom**

The United Kingdom has a Skills Strategy, overseen by the Skills Alliance, a ministerial-led group made up of stakeholders in the sector, including representatives of employers, the Skills for Business Network, and the National Employment Panel. Training is organized and funded by learning skills councils at the national, regional, and local levels, in partnership with regional skills partnerships and colleges, training providers, and other key stakeholders. Providers include publicly funded bodies, nonprofit agencies, and private providers.

The planning involves taking stock of the existing learning environment, drawing on different sources of labor market intelligence, and consulting with key partners, including employers and training providers. Implementation involves regional learning skills councils that secure training by open bidding. Audits

of the adult learning system assess the performance of the system and make necessary adjustments.

Semiautonomous, nongovernmental bodies often provide information and career advice to workers—in particular, the unemployed and low skilled. Jobcentre Plus identifies the skill needs of job seekers who have been unemployed and inactive for six months (its functions have since been absorbed into the government). Learndirect offers personalized advice, information, and guidance tailored to the needs of adult clients with lower-level skills. Learning ambassadors are local volunteers who, having themselves undergone training, identify and work with people in similar situations. A new government website, Universal Jobmatch, allows job seekers to search for employment and employers to upload and manage their own vacancies and search for prospective employees.

counter such perceptions, the government could provide incentives for workplace learning and on-the-job training. One option is to promote "training contracts" by establishing a legal framework to incentivize firms and workers to invest in training. Worker-retention rules could be embedded in such training contracts, depending on the nature of the investment; the worker either has to pay back the cost of training or has to stay in the job for a certain period in return for benefiting from employer training.

China's new education sector strategy

China would benefit from having a new education sector strategy to develop the workforce for an innovative China. To implement Made in China 2025, China will need a new Education 2035 Strategy to meet the labor market's changing demands. By 2035, China will be the leading contributor to the world's talent pool. But the quality of China's human capital, not the quantity, will need to be the cornerstone of the knowledge economy. How might Education 2035 differ from China's current education sector strategy, the National Outline for Medium- and Long-Term Educational Reform and Development (2010–20)?

One, the new strategy would provide an in-depth road map for modernizing tertiary education. The strategy would provide a comprehensive and coherent plan and policy framework for the balanced and sustainable development of a multitiered tertiary education system that would aim for quality, equity, and efficiency. World-class universities would continue to be promoted, but their development would be integrated with the rest of the higher education system to ensure the balanced development of all tiers of the system. Key measures could include amendment of the Higher Education Law (1998) to bring it in line with a modern tertiary education system; reforms to strengthen the autonomy, accountability, and quality assurance of universities; new regulations to promote the expansion and healthy development of private higher education providers and the new applied universities; and curricular and pedagogical reforms to promote higher-order skills, such as critical thinking and creativity,

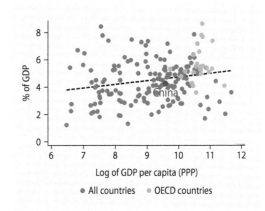

FIGURE 6.6 **Cross-country public spending in education, 2015**

Sources: Calculations based on World Development Indicators for the most recent year available; China's education expenditure data are from the Ministry of Finance.
Note: PPP = purchasing power parity. OECD = Organisation for Economic Co-operation and Development.

and socioemotional skills, such as empathy and teamwork.

Two, the new strategy would outline a plan to increase public investments in education and address spending and quality disparities across the education system. Countries generally increase their education expenditures as they develop, and China has more than doubled its public education spending over the last 15 years. However, its current public spending on education, at 4.1 percent of GDP (2018), is lower than predicted by its GDP per capita and lower than most OECD countries (figure 6.6).

Increased education spending will be needed to finance the following major reforms: closing the gaps in quality ECD, undertaking curricula and pedagogical reforms in basic education, universalizing upper-secondary education, strengthening TVET and establishing a comprehensive lifelong adult training system, and addressing socioeconomic disparities across the education system. Universalizing upper-secondary education could be achieved by reducing or eliminating tuition fees for both the vocational and academic streams in a fiscally sustainable manner. This effort would extend compulsory education to the upper-secondary level and help China to catch up with the secondary school enrollment rates of high-income countries. Increasing investments provides an opportunity to address the significant disparities across regions and tiers of the education system. All of these reforms will require more spending on education.

Three, the new education strategy could outline a strategy and a new policy and regulatory framework for a more market-driven TVET and lifelong learning. This approach could build on ongoing initiatives to strengthen school-industry collaboration, the market relevance of postsecondary vocational education and training, and pedagogical improvements to make training more modular and better geared to a service-oriented economy. The governance and management of TVET and higher education could be more integrated across public agencies, enabling a smoother transition by students between tertiary TVET tracks and university careers. In addition, public funding could be made output rather than input driven.

Four, increased education spending would need to be complemented by a more transparent monitoring system to ensure the efficiency and impact of the spending, with greater public access to information on the education sector and school performance data. China could address the gaps in internationally comparable data on learning outcomes and key input information at the provincial level. In recent years, the government has developed its own national assessment to monitor learning results at the national and subnational levels. Making this information publicly available would help to ensure more accountability at the local level and could serve as a medium-term solution before all provinces join international learning assessments, such as PISA.

Notes

1. See http://www.moe.edu.cn/srcsite/A03/s180 /moe_633/201607/t20160706_270976.html.
2. See http://theory.people.com.cn/n1/2017 /0323/c40531-29162998.html.
3. Calculation based on Ministry of Education data. The database is accessible at http://www.moe.gov.cn/s78/A03/moe_560 /jytjsj_2015/. The ratio is calculated using the number of junior secondary school graduates divided by the number of entrants in regular senior secondary schools in urban and rural areas, respectively.

4. UNICEF report based on the 2015 1% National Population Sample Survey conducted by the National Bureau of Statistics (https://www.unicef.cn/en/reports/population -status-children-china-2015).
5. *China Statistical Yearbook* various years and Ministry of Education website (http://www .moe.gov.cn/jyb_zzjg/moe_347/201508 /t20150824_202647.html).
6. Fudan University, Nanjing University, Peking University, Shanghai Jiao Tong University, Tsinghua University, University of Science and Technology of China, and Zhejiang University.
7. These rankings have been criticized for simplifying the measurement of the complex and multifaceted qualities of these institutions, putting too much focus on research and not enough on student learning outcomes, teaching, the relevance of education, and other aspects of universities.
8. China Education Finance Statistical Yearbook, 2017.
9. Analysis of the returns to college education was carried out by World Bank staff, based on Chinese Household Income Project survey data.
10. For-profit schools and universities have had challenges even in high-income economies, including the poor quality of instruction and the labor market performance of graduates, high accumulation of student debt, and various forms of consumer abuse. The failures of large for-profit institutions, such as Corinthian Colleges in the United States and Universidad del Mar in Chile, illustrate the potential for predatory practices among for-profit providers in an insufficiently or inadequately regulated environment.
11. Discussion of college entrance examination systems is drawn from King and Rogers (2014).
12. At the upper-secondary-school stage, where students are selected into academic and TVET tracks of study, 16.0 million students are on the vocational track, accounting for 40 percent of students at the upper-secondary level. At the tertiary level, the number students enrolled in short-cycle courses, most of which are vocational programs, reached 10.8 million in 2016, accounting for 40 percent of all undergraduate students as well.
13. World Bank Edstats data. The data points quoted are from 2014, which are the latest available information.
14. Off target: China's vocational education and training system threatens the country's rise

to industrial superpower status. Mercator Institute for China Studies (MERICS), *China Monitor* 24, October 2, 2015.

15. Mercator Institute for China Studies (MERICS), *China Monitor*.

Bibliography

Acemoglu, D., and P. Restrepo. 2017. "Robots and Jobs: Evidence from U.S. Labor Markets." NBER Working Paper 23285, National Bureau of Economic Research, Cambridge, MA. https://www.nber.org/papers/w23285.pdf.

———. 2018. "The Race between Machine and Man: Implications of Technology for Growth, Factor Shares and Employment." *American Economic Review.* 108 (6): 1488–542.

Altbach, Philip G., and Jamil Salmi. 2011. *The Road to Academic Excellence: The Making of World-Class Research Universities.* Washington, DC: World Bank. http://documents.world bank.org/curated/en/688061468337210820 /pdf/The-road-to-academic-excellence-the -making-of-world-class-research-universities .pdf.

Arntz, M., T. Gregory, and U. Zierahn. 2016. "The Risk of Automation for Jobs in OECD Countries: A Comparative Analysis." OECD Social, Employment, and Migration Working Paper 189, OECD, Paris. https://www.oecd -ilibrary.org/docserver/5jlz9h56dvq7-en.pdf?ex pires=1565980074&id=id&accname=guest& checksum=B51050A3BDBFF284EEE29C34B 3A9DF65.

Autor, D. H., and M. J. Handel. 2013. "Putting Tasks to the Test: Human Capital, Job Tasks, and Wages." *Journal of Labor Economics* 31(S1): S59–S96.

Autor, D. H., F. Levy, and R. J. Murnane. 2003. "The Skill Content of Recent Technological Change: An Empirical Exploration." *Quarterly Journal of Economics* 118 (4): 1279–1333.

Baumeister, R. F., K. D. Vohs, and D. M. Tice. 2007. "The Strength Model of Self-Control." *Current Directions in Psychological Science* 16 (6): 351–55.

Bodewig, C., and S. Hirshleifer. 2011. "Advancing Adult Learning in Eastern Europe and Central Asia." Social Protection and Labor Discussion Paper no. 1108, World Bank, Washington, DC.

British Council and World Bank. 2015. "Managing Large Systems: A Comparative Analysis— Challenges and Opportunities for Large Higher Education Systems." http://documents.world bank.org/curated/en/504751496328578948 /pdf/115401-WP-PUBLIC-PUB-DATE-JUNE -2015-SABER-TED-Managing-Large-Systems .pdf.

Brynjolfsson, E., and A. McAfee. 2014. *The Second Machine Age: Work, Progress, and Prosperity in a Time of Brilliant Technologies.* WW Norton & Company.

China Internet Watch. https://www.chinainternet watch.com/.

Choi, A. 2014. "What the Best Education Systems Are Doing Right." Ideas. TED.com (September 4).

David, H. 2015. "Why Are There Still So Many Jobs? The History and Future of Workplace Automation." *Journal of Economic Perspectives* 29 (3): 3–30.

De Backer, K., C. Menon, I. Desnoyers-James, and L. Moussiegt. 2016. "Reshoring: Myth or Reality?" OECD Science, Technology, and Industry Policy Paper 27, OECD Publishing, Paris.

Du, Y., and A. Park. 2017. "Changing Demand for Tasks and Skills in China." Background paper for this report, World Bank, Washington, DC.

Duckworth, A. L., C. Peterson, M. D. Matthews, and D. R. Kelly. 2007. "Grit: Perseverance and Passion for Long-Term Goals." *Journal of Personality and Social Psychology* 92 (6): 1087–1101.

Frey, C. B., and M. A. Osborne. 2017. "The Future of Employment: How Susceptible Are Jobs to Computerisation?" *Technological Forecasting and Social Change* 114: 254–280.

Gao, Q., H. Yi, H. Wang, Y. Shi, C. Abbey, and S. Rozzelle. 2017. "Student Confidence in Reading in Rural China." Rural Education Action Program Working Paper.

Goos, M., A. Manning, and A. Salomons. 2014. "Explaining Job Polarization: Routine-Biased Technological Change and Offshoring." *American Economic Review,* 104(8): 2509–526.

Graetz, G., and G. Michaels. 2015. Robots at Work. *CEP Discussion Paper No. 1335.*

Hanushek, A. Eric, Ludger Woessmann , and Lei Zhang. 2011. "General Education, Vocational Education, and Labor-Market Outcomes over the Life-Cycle." NBER Working Paper 17504, National Bureau of Economic Research, Cambridge, MA.

Khor, N., L. Pang, C. Liu, F. Chang, D. Mo, P. Loyalka, and S. Rozelle. 2016. "China's Looming Human Capital Crisis: Upper Secondary Educational Attainment Rates and the Middle-income Trap." *China Quarterly* (228): 905–26.

King, Elizabeth, and Halsey Rogers. 2014. "Intelligence, Personality, and Creativity: Unleashing the Power of Intelligence and Personality

Traits to Build a Creative and Innovative Economy." World Bank background paper for the November 2014 Seoul Education Symposium.

Klorer, Elena, and Matthias Stepan. 2015. "Off-Target: China's Vocational Education and Training System Threatens the Country's Rise to Industrial Superpower Status." *Mercator Institute for China Studies* 24 (2 October). https://www.merics.org/sites/default/files/2019-08/China_Monitor_24_Vocational_Education_EN.pdf.

Lee, S., and B. A. Malin. 2013. "Education's Role in China's Structural Transformation." *Journal of Development Economics* (101): 148–66.

Li, H., P. Loyalka, S. Rozelle, and B. Wu. 2017. "Human Capital and China's Future Growth." *Journal of Economic Perspectives* 31 (1): 25–47.

Li, S., and C. Xing. 2016. "China's Key Labor Market Trends, Challenges, and Policy Implications: Employment, Wage Structure, and Labor Productivity." Background paper for this report, World Bank, Washington, DC.

Maloney, W. F., and C. Molina. 2016. "Are Automation and Trade Polarizing Developing Country Labor Markets, Too? Policy Research Working Paper Series, no. 7922, World Bank, Washington, DC.

Meng, Xin. 2014. "China's Labour Market Tensions and Future Urbanisation Challenges" In L. Song, R. Garnaut, and C. Fang (eds), *Deepening Reform for China's Long-Term Growth and Development* (pp. 379–406). Australian National University Press.

Mercator Institute for China Studies (MERICS). 2015. *China Monitor* 24, October 2.

Michaels, G., A. Natraj, and J. Van Reenen. 2014. "Has ICT Polarized Skill Demand? Evidence from Eleven Countries over Twenty-Five Years." *Review of Economics and Statistics* 96 (1): 60–77.

National Bureau of Statistics. Various years. *China Statistical Yearbook of the Tertiary Industry.* Beijing: China Statistics Press.

OECD (Organisation of Economic Co-operation and Development). 2015. "How Is the Global Talent Pool Changing (2013, 2030)?" *Education Indicators in Focus,* No. 31, OECD Publishing, Paris, https://doi.org/10.1787/5js33lf9jk41-en.

Oldenski, Lindsay. 2015. "Reshoring by US Firms: What Do the Data Say?" Peterson Institute for International Economics, Number PB15-14, September. https://www.piie.com/publications/pb/pb15-14.pdf.

Salmi, Jamil. 2009. *The Challenge of Establishing World-Class Universities.* Washington, DC: World Bank. https://openknowledge.worldbank.org/handle/10986/2600.

Shi, Yaojiang, Linxiu Zhang, Yue Ma, Hongmei Yi, Chengfang Liu, Natalie Johnson, James Chu, Prashant Loyalka, and Scott Rozelle. 2015. "Dropout in Rural China's Secondary Schools: A Mixed-Methods Study." *China Quarterly* 224: 1048–69.

Schweinhart, L. J., J. Montie, Z. Xiang, W. S. Barnett, C. R. Belfield, and M. Nores. 2005. "Lifetime Effects: The High/Scope Perry Preschool Study through Age 40." High/Scope Educational Research Foundation.

Wang, X., B. M. Fleisher, H. Li, and S. Li. 2014. Access to College and Heterogeneous Returns to Education in China. *Economics of Education Review* 42: 78–92.

World Bank. 2012. *Putting Higher Education to Work: Skills and Research for Growth in East Asia.* Washington, DC: World Bank.

———. 2016. *World Development Report 2016: Digital Dividends.* Washington, DC: World Bank.

———. 2017. *Growing Smarter: Education Quality and Economic Growth in East Asia and the Pacific.* Washington, DC: The World Bank.

Yi, H. M., G. R. Li, L. Y. Li, L. X. Zhang, J. J. Xu, E. Kardanova, H. Shi, J. Chu, and P. Loyalka. 2018. "Assessing the Quality of Upper-Secondary Vocational Education and Training: Evidence from China." *Comparative Education Review,* vol. 62, no. 2.

Zhou, Chengchao, Sean Sylvia, Linxiu Zhang, Renfu Luo, Hongmei Yi, Chengfang Liu, Yaojiang Shi, Prashant Loyalka, James Chu, Alexis Medina, and Scott Rozelle. 2015. "China's Left-Behind Children: Impact of Parental Migration on Health, Nutrition, and Educational Outcomes." *Health Affairs* 34(11): 1964–971.

7

Allocating Resources Efficiently

China's financial sector developments

China's financial system has mobilized significant resources to support investment-led growth. Its financial sector has expanded rapidly, giving the country some of the world's largest banks and stock and bond markets. As a result of this rapid increase, some in China have questioned whether the financial sector has gotten "too big," resulting in an imbalance between the financial and real sectors. China's financial sector has indeed grown quite large, particularly when considering the country's level of development (figure 7.1). This has also raised concerns about whether the financial sector is adequately serving the real sector. However, the critical issue is to ensure that the financial sector efficiently allocates financial resources for the most productive uses in the economy.

China's financial system remains dominated largely by the banking industry. The five largest commercial banks in China accounted for the majority of assets before the global financial crisis, but their share of total bank assets had declined to only 36.8 percent at the end of 2017. The development and policy banks and the Postal Saving Bank of China account for another 13.7 percent of banking assets; and other banks, including regional banks, now hold nearly half of banking assets. During 2010–16, the rate of asset growth of smaller banks was twice that of the five big banks, with substantial off-balance-sheet exposure and shadow credit.

The rapid expansion of China's financial system has taken place alongside significant accumulation of debt in the economy, raising financial vulnerabilities. China's authorities recognize the need to address the total stock of debt—state-owned enterprise (SOE), private, general government, and household—which increased to 251.3 percent of gross domestic product (GDP) at the end of 2018. The rapid growth and risk exposure of many smaller regional banks may make them especially vulnerable to tightened financial conditions and hardened budget constraints. Local governments can influence the credit allocation of regional banks, which can hinder market-driven financial intermediation. Reforms to reduce the financial vulnerabilities of regional banks and improve their credit allocation would need to minimize disruptions to financial markets.

The expansion of innovative financial products has increased the complexity of

FIGURE 7.1 **Financial sector share of GDP in selected countries**

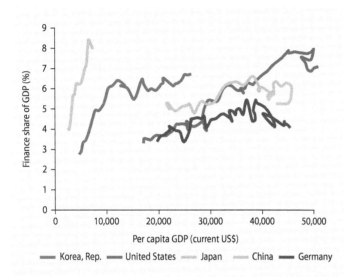

Sources: Calculations based on KLEMS, World Development Indicators, and Bank of Korea data.

the financial sector and made bank balance sheets less transparent. Nonbank financial intermediaries—including trusts, security companies, subsidiaries of fund companies, and asset management companies—are channeling resources from depositors and investors looking for higher yields to borrowers having difficulty accessing formal credit. The government recently emphasized the need to address accumulated financial risks by deleveraging the economy, including measures to tighten shadow credit and the creation of the Financial Stability and Development Committee of the State Council to enhance policy coordination and harmonization.

Since the global financial crisis, financial allocative efficiency may have deteriorated. A rising share of new commercial credit has gone to infrastructure and real estate, including mortgage loans and construction. These sectors now account for roughly half of China's outstanding debt, and their returns on capital have been declining (see discussions in chapter 2). The increase in credit-financed investment in infrastructure has been matched by a sharp increase in the share of commercial credit to state-owned enterprises and a sharp decline in the share of credit to the private sector (figure 7.2). SOEs

have accounted for a large share of increased leverage in recent years, as their debt climbed from 73 percent of GDP in 2012 to 103 percent in 2016. Public-benefit SOEs (local government financing vehicles) accounted for the majority of the increase in debt (and bonds) as a share of GDP.[1] Since 2016, authorities have worked to contain leverage in the SOE sector and to channel more credit to the private sector.

Because China's financial system remains dominated largely by the banking industry, it is important to promote greater competition in the banking sector and to diversify the financial system by expanding nonbank financial institutions. To promote greater competition, the government has announced its intention to open up the financial sector further to foreign investments. Complementary reforms could include strengthening the corporate governance of commercial banks, the management of state-owned capital in banks, and the overall supervision and regulation of the banking sector.

China's capital markets have grown rapidly in recent decades, indicating a significant expansion in the nonfinancial sector's use of equity and corporate bond markets since the early 2000s. The combined market capitalization of these two markets increased

FIGURE 7.2 **Share of the net credit growth of SOEs and non-SOEs, 2011–16**

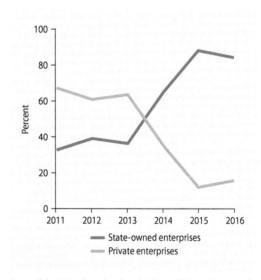

Source: Calculations based on People's Bank of China's Almanac of China's Finance and Banking data.

to 158.1 percent of GDP at the end of 2017, surpassing India and Mexico and comparable to Germany, although still significantly smaller than Japan, the United Kingdom, and the United States. The amount raised in equity markets (16.9 percent of GDP) was the highest among a sample of both high-income and low- and middle-income nations during 2010–16, and the amount raised in bond markets (6.2 percent of GDP) was the third highest after the United States and the United Kingdom.[2] Foreign investors have a limited presence in China's financial markets, and Chinese firms raise most of their capital domestically.

Capital market development in China was accompanied by an increasing number of issuing firms in the equity and bond markets. The average number of firms issuing equity each year in China increased more than three times, from 161 in 2000–07 to 659 in 2010–16. The number of issuers in Chinese bond markets increased 24-fold, from 45 to 1,100. Very large corporations and SOEs account for the bulk of transactions in capital markets. SOEs accounted for 22 percent and 51 percent of the firms active in the equity and bond markets, respectively, and 61 percent and 78 percent of the amounts raised in each market, respectively. The major capital markets are also dominated by a select number of industries, including manufacturing, finance, transport, and energy.

Listings in China's capital markets are limited by relatively high standards for initial public offerings (IPOs). Most developed capital markets have a registration-based system, in which the market decides the scale, valuation, and timing of IPOs. Instead, in order to protect the interests of small and medium investors and ensure the quality of IPO companies, China uses an approval-based system, in which the China Securities Regulatory Commission (CSRC) thoroughly evaluates firms before granting approval to go public. This system is used to control the level of IPOs and stabilize prices in capital markets, by tightening IPO approvals during periods of declining prices and relaxing them during market booms. At certain times, these interventions lead to long delays in IPO approvals, limiting the access of new firms to

capital markets. For example, at the start of 2017, more than 600 firms were queuing for approval, with wait times longer than two years (Reuters 2017). However, the average wait time had declined sharply, to less than 10 months as of May 2018.

Financing small and medium enterprises and entrepreneurs

Small and medium enterprises (SMEs) in China account for more than 90 percent of firms, employ more than 80 percent of total urban workers, and contribute more than 60 percent of GDP—but fewer than 30 percent of them have access to credit.[3] Large corporations have relatively easier access to financing through both banks and capital markets. Low access to and high costs of financing for SMEs are a major bottleneck. According to World Bank Enterprise Surveys, more than one in five firms in China rate access to finance as their most significant business constraint (2012). Fewer than a quarter of small firms that need a loan actually have access to bank credit, compared with approximately half of medium firms and two-thirds of large firms (figure 7.3). Lending to SOEs, given their implicit guarantees and lower information asymmetries, is considered less risky. By contrast, private firms have less access to credit due to information asymmetries, modest collateral, shorter credit histories, and perceived higher risk exposure. As a result, private firms are almost twice as likely as SOEs to have been turned down for a loan.

In recent years, regulatory authorities have encouraged commercial banks and other financial service providers to expand lending to SMEs. They have implemented differentiated monetary and credit policies, risk compensation funds, and government guarantee funds and tax incentives. For example, commercial banks are allowed to issue financial bonds specifically for SME loans, increasing banks' available funding for SME lending. When calculating loan-to-deposit ratios for SME business lines, the SME loans that correspond to such bonds can be deducted from the numerator. At the end of 2015, 66 commercial banks nationwide had issued RMB 549 billion (US$83 billion) in financial bonds

FIGURE 7.3   Access to credit in China and comparator regions, by size of firm, 2012

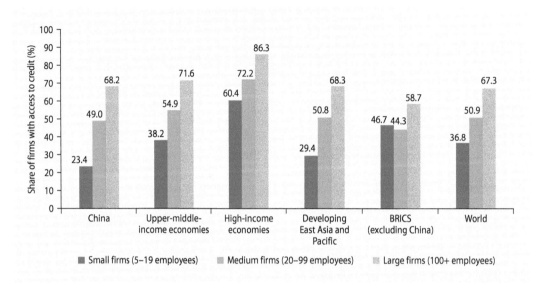

Source: World Bank Enterprise Surveys.
Note: BRICS = Brazil, Russia, India, China, and South Africa.

specifically for SME lending. The China Banking and Insurance Regulatory Commission (CBIRC) allows nonperforming loan ratios for SME loans up to 2 percent higher than industrywide targets.[4] CBIRC issued Guidelines on Financial Services for Micro and Small Enterprises in 2015, which specifies that the growth of SME loans should be no less than the average growth of all loans, the number of SMEs receiving loans should be no less than the previous year, and the approval rate of SME loan applications should be no less than the previous year.

Instead of such top-down quantitative targets for lending to SMEs, a more sustainable and effective approach requires market-oriented reforms to alter banks' risk-return profile for lending to SMEs. Supported by a stronger financial infrastructure, banks need to develop the culture and skills to price risk accurately among SMEs. The government could strengthen the financial infrastructure in several ways. It could upgrade credit registries. It could strengthen credit information systems, including expanding the use of information from nonfinancial sources for credit scores. It could establish a national electronic registry for movable collateral. It could establish platforms for accounts receivables and strengthen out-of-court enforcement

mechanisms. It also could consider expanding dedicated SME lines of credit and partial credit guarantees, securitizing loans, and pooling SME risks.

In recent years, the People's Bank of China (PBOC) has been developing a credit-reporting system to reduce information asymmetries between lenders and borrowers, mainly through the Credit Reference Center of PBOC (CCRC), a public credit registry established in 2006. The CCRC collects data from more than 3,000 financial service providers, including banks, rural credit cooperatives, microcredit companies, insurance companies, and other nonbank financial service providers. The CCRC distributes information to these institutions in response to inquiries. At the end of June 2017, the CCRC covered 930 million individuals, including 450 million persons with a borrowing history, and 24 million legal entities, including 6.6 million entities with a borrowing history.

PBOC recognizes that the private sector, including new fintech companies, could improve China's credit information infrastructure, but there had been concerns about corporate governance, independence, and conflicts of interest. The first credit bureau license to a private firm was issued by PBOC in 2018 to Baihang, located in Shenzhen.

More work is needed to clarify the licensing requirements for credit bureaus and to distinguish more clearly between credit bureaus and credit scoring and data analytics companies, since each type of company provides supplemental data that help overcome information asymmetries. In addition, greater access to public information could benefit financial inclusion. Government agencies—such as tax, commerce, and judicial authorities—hold vast amounts of valuable data on both individuals and SMEs, but such information is difficult to access. A comprehensive legal framework on data protection and privacy for the financial sector is needed in China to address data issues, including public access to information and the use of big data and alternative data.

In the past 15 years, CBIRC and PBOC have encouraged commercial banks and other financial service providers to use movable assets—including receivables, inventory, equipment, and title documents—as the basis for lending or issuing debt instruments. A basic legal framework and a registry system for secured transactions were established in the mid-2000s, spurring the development of a movable asset finance market and a collateral management industry. PBOC established a modern collateral registry, the Integrated Movables Financing Registration System, under the CCRC in 2013. The system began as an Internet-based filing system for security interests on accounts receivables and has now expanded to cover most movable assets.

In recent years, with the support of the International Finance Corporation, CCRC has continued to improve its registry services and to promote movable asset finance more generally through complementary initiatives, including extensive training of financial sector authorities and lenders, the development of a collateral management industry, and the creation of a digital supply chain finance platform under CCRC. This has stimulated the market and increased lender confidence, especially to SMEs, which are 70 percent of the borrowers and lessees in the system. At the end of 2016, loans involving movable assets represented about 40 percent of outstanding commercial loans in China, up from 12 percent in 2004. The second-generation information technology (IT) registry system is expected to launch soon. The next challenge for the CCRC will be to achieve a truly integrated registration system.

Around the world, credit guarantee schemes have become an increasingly popular way to promote financing to SMEs. China has a decentralized system, with a large number of provincial and municipal guarantee funds, many of them dedicated to attaining specific social goals. There were 7,340 credit guarantee companies in China at the end of 2015, serving 2.74 trillion guaranteed loans (almost 3 percent of all bank loans). Guarantees are established and operated by both the public sector (provincial and municipal governments) and the private sector. In 2015, loans to SMEs were 84 percent of all guaranteed loans, but it would be useful to assess whether more established and mature SMEs benefited disproportionately from loan guarantees.

Historically, China's public sector guarantees were the prevailing form in the industry, but the percentage of guarantee funds that received government financing had fallen to about 19 percent in 2011 before rebounding to 30 percent at the end of 2015. In many countries, credit guarantees for small and medium enterprises tend to be a policy-supported business, with private guarantee companies playing more of an auxiliary role. Since 2015, China has expanded efforts to build a government-supported guarantee system. Many private guarantee companies are still in the process of finding a sustainable business model. Consolidating and scaling up the industry may help to improve profitability and coverage. The regulatory and supervisory framework may also benefit from consolidation and streamlining.

State participation in the guarantee industry is typically justified as a means to pursue policy objectives, such as creating employment or preventing the failure of unprofitable businesses, but it has undermined incentives to allocate guarantees efficiently. Local governments often set a cap on fees that funds can charge for their services, which limits the growth of funds that do not have government support. And despite agreements on paper to share risks, in practice guarantee funds often assume a disproportionate share of losses—in some instances, full coverage of the credit risks—creating moral hazard and undermining bank incentives to assess credit quality and monitor borrowing firms.

Promoting capital market financing to SMEs has been a recurrent topic on the government's agenda since the early 2000s. Given that the main capital markets are not adequately serving smaller firms, China developed secondary exchanges to support direct financing of SMEs. The goal of these markets is to offer listing and regulatory requirements that are less stringent than those in the main exchanges. Currently, there are three main SME capital markets in China, the Shenzhen Stock Exchange: ChiNext, the SME Board, and the National Equities Exchange and Quotations (NEEQ).

The SME Board is aimed at SMEs at a relatively mature stage of development and with stable profitability, giving priority to high-technology companies. By contrast, ChiNext targets innovative and high-growth start-ups and offers less strict listing requirements. The third main SME capital market is the National Equities Exchange and Quotations (NEEQ), an over-the-counter market that provides financing options for SMEs. It targets innovative start-ups with high growth prospects, particularly in information technology. It encourages the listing of small firms by offering less stringent listing requirements, such as no profitability requirement; a rapid application process; and the possibility to list without issuing securities.

SME capital markets in China have expanded significantly over the years, reaching a combined total market capitalization of US$1,280 billion (about 12 percent of GDP) at the end of 2016, higher as a ratio of GDP than in most other economies, including mature SME capital markets in both low- and middle-income as well as high-income economies (figure 7.4). However, the number of firms listed in these markets represents less

FIGURE 7.4   **SME capital markets in selected countries**

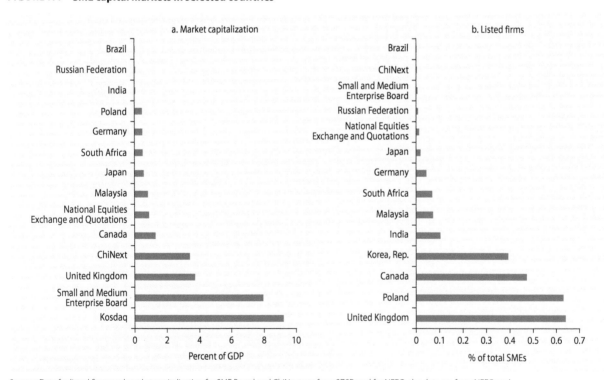

Sources: Data for listed firms and market capitalization for SME Board and ChiNext are from SZSE; and for NEEQ, the data are from NEEQ and China Money Network (2016). For the rest of the SME capital markets, data are from WFE (2015). Data on total SMEs are from the World Bank MSME Country Indicators. Data on total GDP are from the World Bank.
Note: NEEQ = National Equities Exchange and Quotations. SME = small and medium enterprises.

than 0.1 percent of all SMEs in China, which is relatively low.[5] Hence, SME capital markets are larger in China than in other countries but focus on a smaller group of SMEs, despite the fact that the three SME markets combined have 11,555 listed firms, compared with 1,660 in the main markets (as of the end of 2016).

SME markets are oriented more to private enterprises than the main markets, with a smaller share of SOEs. Manufacturing accounts for the largest share of firms in both SME capital markets and the main markets. SME markets also appeal to different industries than the main markets, giving greater emphasis to IT enterprises. So SME capital markets are better suited than the main markets to providing alternative financing to new, growing, and smaller private firms in alternative industries. In addition, SMEs listed on ChiNext and the SME Board tend to be larger, and firms listed on ChiNext are large enough to list on the main markets. The exception seems to be NEEQ, where smaller firms are listed.

Fintech

China is at the global forefront of financial technology (fintech) and the digital finance revolution.[6] It has the world's largest fintech credit market, and its fintech has expanded rapidly to provide an alternative source of financing for SMEs and entrepreneurs that have been relatively neglected by traditional financial institutions. About US$9 billion was invested in China's fintech industry between June 2015 and 2016 alone, and China is home to some of the world's largest fintech lending companies. In 2016, 8 of 27 fintech firms worldwide, valued at more than US$1 billion, were in China (World Bank 2018).

China is now the world's biggest market for digital payments and home to diverse and innovative enterprises in Internet lending, Internet insurance, and Internet fund management. These enterprises are leveraging network effects, economies of scale, and advanced technology, such as big data analytics, to provide diversified and customized financial services. The entrance of new fintech providers has encouraged traditional providers to innovate and reconsider underserved segments of the market previously considered commercially nonviable. Fintech companies are also working with traditional financial service providers. For example, new fintech companies are providing credit-scoring services and improving creditworthiness assessments and risk management systems of traditional financial service providers.

Chinese regulatory authorities have sought to maintain a balanced policy approach to the entrance and scaling up of fintech companies. The objective of this approach has been to encourage innovation while introducing moderate and proportionate levels of supervision. This balanced approach is referenced in the 2015 Guidelines on Promoting Sound Development of Internet Finance, which note the need to "give ample room for innovations in Internet finance," while also highlighting the need for "ensuring the healthy development of Internet finance so that Internet finance can better serve the real economy." How much authorities have adhered to these principles has varied by provider and product.

Digital payment, or third-party payment, has emerged in China with the explosive growth of online e-commerce and social network platforms. Third-party payment refers to payments that a payer makes through a nonbank payment platform. For industry leaders Alipay (Alibaba) and Tenpay (Tencent), the rapid growth of payments in China was made possible by integrating payment functionality into existing e-commerce (Alibaba's Taobao and Tmall) and social media (Tencent's QQ and WeChat) platforms with their large user networks. Following the introduction of Alipay in 2004 and Tenpay in 2005 and their mobile platforms in 2009, the volume of nonbank digital payment transactions increased rapidly to RMB 208.07 trillion (US$29.5 trillion) in 2018, through 254 e-payment providers (PBOC 2018).

Despite the rapid growth, Chinese regulatory authorities initially took a "wait and see" approach to the regulation of fintech. Regulations were first issued six years after the launch of Alipay. Fuller regulations were only issued in 2015—covering minimum capital requirements, investor requirements, caps on monthly payment activities, and customer identification and data privacy requirements. Although this wait-and-see approach allowed the emerging industry to innovate and grow with relatively few restrictions, it also entailed risks, such as inadequate regulation, monitoring, and oversight of some of the potential risks of digital payments, including fraud and money laundering.

Online peer-to-peer (P2P) lending also has increased rapidly in China—these are direct person-to-person loans transacted on an Internet platform by matching borrowers with potential lenders (investors). P2P lending takes advantage of information technology to reduce information asymmetry between debtors and creditors, thereby lowering the costs of matching. At the end of 2016, the total outstanding loan balance of P2P lending reached RMB 816.2 billion (US$122.4 billion), equivalent to 4.3 percent of the balance of household loans issued by deposit-taking financial service providers, and the total volume of transactions reached RMB 2.1 trillion (US$309.6 billion).

Similar to digital payments, the authorities initially took a relatively light wait-and-see regulatory approach toward P2P lending. But contrary to existing regulations, many P2P platforms started providing credit guarantees and setting up pools of funds, while other platforms engaged in outright fraud.[7] Many investors have lost money through fraudulent P2P service providers in China. In response, the authorities issued new regulations ("interim rules") in 2016 to clarify that P2Ps are information intermediaries; established business rules, risk management requirements, and procedures to protect consumers, such as information disclosure requirements; introduced joint and coordinated supervisory arrangements; and specified prohibited activities, including accepting savings (deposits), managing pools of funds, and providing guarantees.

Internet-based microlending and Internet banks have the potential to significantly expand access to financing for SMEs, entrepreneurs, and individuals, but so far their operations have been fairly limited. Internet-based microlending refers to small loans provided by Internet companies to their customers. An example is MYbank, a subsidiary of Ant Financial, which claims to have provided unsecured lending to 12.3 million small businesses and RMB 47.7 billion in new loans in 2018 (MYbank 2018). Internet banks have banking licenses but have no physical outlets or counter services. There are now three Internet banks in China,[8] which have been established by e-commerce and digital payment enterprises that leverage their technology, large customer base, and data to target individuals and SMEs.

Internet bank operations have so far been constrained by regulations that restrict the functionality of bank accounts opened remotely, which are the type of accounts offered by these banks. Remotely opened accounts could eventually become fully functional if the necessary remote identification technology becomes available. As the technology develops, the authorities can address any undue regulatory restrictions on the use of remote identification to access fully functional accounts.

The outcome of the initial wait-and-see approach to regulating the fintech industry has been a large, dynamic, and competitive industry. With a larger and more mature industry, policy makers in China have increasingly recognized the need to manage the risks of fintech and establish a more comprehensive regulatory framework. The 2015 Guidelines on Promoting Sound Development of Internet Finance represent a significant step in the development of a comprehensive regulatory framework for fintech. They specifically encourage the development of existing and new types of digital financial services, but emphasize that these services should be limited to small-value transactions. They clarify the regulatory mandates of different financial sector authorities and note several areas where additional regulation is required, including areas related to reserve fund management, information security, anti–money laundering, and disclosure and transparency.

Financial sector authorities could consider a "regulatory sandbox," which provides more structure than the wait-and-see approach, while still providing the flexibility for innovation. The regulatory sandbox is a piloting approach for introducing and testing new technologies in a market under waived or modified regulations but with clear restrictions, such as number of customers, type or value of products and services, and specialized monitoring and reporting requirements. The testing may continue for a certain period (such as 6 to 12 months), after which the financial sector authorities may develop rules based on the experience and risks assessed.[9]

Various laws and regulations have been issued in recent years to protect financial consumers.[10] The legal and regulatory framework now requires further adaptation to ensure that consumer protection risks in fintech and digital finance are covered comprehensively. Fintech provides many benefits to the underserved, but consumers also face a variety of risks, including lack of transparency about product terms and conditions, violations of data privacy, and false, misleading promotions.

A comprehensive legal framework for data protection and privacy is needed. Rules regarding disclosure and transparency, sales and marketing, the safety of funds, and dispute resolution should be expanded to include new fintech companies and adapted as necessary to digital finance business models. Supervision efforts require further strengthening—as does coordination across PBOC, CBIRC, and CSRC—because many financial consumer protection issues for fintech cut across markets and products. Enforcement of violations is still relatively weak.

Effective financial education is also needed to raise the financial capabilities of the consumers of financial services. According to PBOC's 2017 Financial Consumers' Capability Survey, consumers' overall financial knowledge is relatively low, and a significant imbalance in financial knowledge exists between rural and urban areas and among different regions. Consumers also have limited understanding of contracts and statements of financial products and services. Digital technologies could be leveraged further to deliver financial education efficiently and effectively.

Venture capital

Venture capital funding has surged in recent years, and China is now the second-largest global market after the United States, with a quarter of all global venture capital investments. In 2016, almost 40 percent of venture capital by value was focused on early-stage deals (classified as products developed but not yet commercialized), up from 8 percent in 2010. Venture capital investments are most prevalent in higher-income areas; Beijing, Guangdong, Jiangsu, Shanghai, and Zhejiang accounted for almost 70 percent of invested venture capital from 2006 to 2016. But venture capital investors are increasingly directing capital to earlier-stage companies and to less-developed regions. Government guidance funds have the potential to be an important source of venture financing. There are more than 1,000 government guidance funds—yuan-denominated government-led funds that include venture capital and private equity funds. But less than 10 percent of the target capital of government guidance funds is in venture capital funds, with the rest in industry funds and infrastructure funds.

The rapid growth of venture capital financing and government guidance funds may present challenges for the quality of fund management. The increasing supply of capital and the ensuing competition for deals have pushed up valuations. Management of equity financing—early-stage equity financing, particularly—requires appropriate managerial expertise. Given the rapid growth in the number of funds and the volume of financing available, the government would want to ensure that the quality of fund management keeps pace.

The focus of government guidance funds for innovation should be sharpened to address key market failures in an environment with a strong supply of venture capital. These funds need to maintain market-oriented principles to avoid crowding out private financing. There is a well-established international model of government intervention in early-stage financing, based most commonly on Israel's experience. It appears that many of China's government guidance funds do not necessarily adhere to this model. The international model considered best practice features funds that are at least 10+2 years in duration (allowing sufficiently long investment cycles), are not required to make a positive return to government, and provide at least 50 percent of funding to anchor co-investment funds. They have incentive structures to crowd in private investors (who receive preference on returns). They are outsourced to independent management teams and investment committees in which government plays no role. They have remuneration and incentives aligned with the private sector. And they are generally not sector or region specific by design, although funds themselves often have a specific business model that specializes in regions or sectors.

For their part, venture capital funds need to have enough high-quality deals, particularly those with relatively short investment cycles. Therefore, before establishing early-stage risk-focused government guidance funds, it is important to assess the flow of local deals and the maturity of the ecosystem to develop this flow. Government guidance funds are subject to a complex authorizing environment, as well as regulation and supervision by multiple agencies, which can subject these funds to conflicting messages that can blur their strategic objectives. Therefore, streamlining the governance structure and policy environment is critical. Finally, venture capital–backed companies in China tend to seek their exit in public markets rather than in private sales, whereas the latter are more frequent in high-income countries. Therefore, ensuring that IPOs are not delayed unnecessarily would support the growth of venture firms. In addition, there may be a need to explore reforms that aim to ensure that private sales are a viable alternative for venture capital exits.

Facilitating free flows of labor

With the working population expected to decline, China will need to access the underutilized labor in agriculture, increase female labor force participation, and fully use labor throughout adult working lives. A key aspect will be to promote labor mobility, allowing labor to flow to places and uses where it can

be most productive. Improving the spatial allocative efficiency of labor can ensure that businesses get the workers they need. Assisting people to relocate to jobs will be more effective than moving jobs to people, such as through government "industrial relocation" programs. Major opportunities remain for a more efficient movement of labor in the economy.

Hukou, China's household registration system, is a major determinant of labor mobility and has important implications for the country's socioeconomic development and modernization. The implication of the *hukou* system is that a proportion of the urban population—those without urban *hukou*—may not have full access to public services in cities. This leads to two definitions of urbanization in China—one for urban residents, the other for the urban *hukou* population.

The flagship report *Urban China* (World Bank and Development Research Center of the State Council 2014) recommended comprehensive *hukou* reforms centered on transforming the household registration system from an origin-based to a residence-based system. Since then, a series of policy changes have been made to deepen *hukou* reform, including the issuance of a national framework and guidelines for the transition to a residence-based system and a program to integrate 100 million migrants into cities.[11]

In particular, the 2014 State Council policy initiative—Opinions on Further Promoting *Hukou* Reform—marked a new era for reforming the *hukou* and managing internal labor mobility and migration in China. This policy initiative has five key aspects: (1) adjusting *hukou* conversion policy; (2) unifying the urban and rural *hukou* registration system; (3) introducing a residence permit system; (4) establishing a national basic population database; and (5) increasing the coverage of basic public services to the residential population in cities. The 2014 *hukou* policy explicitly sets different limits for *hukou* conversion by city size—the larger the size of a city, the higher the threshold of *hukou* conversion. As a result, the *hukou* has essentially been liberalized in medium and small cities, but the threshold for large cities and megacities remains very high, which discourages migration and constrains labor

FIGURE 7.5   Resident and *hukou* population as a share of total population in China, 2011–20

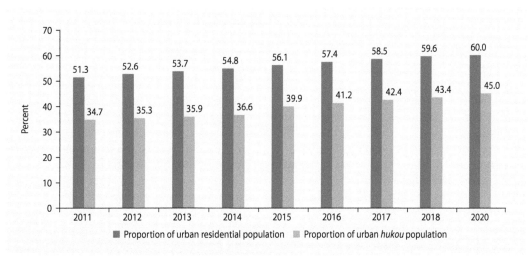

Sources: Based on National Statistical Bureau and Ministry of Public Security data.
Note: The numbers for 2018 are estimates, and those for 2020 are policy targets.

mobility. In 2016, the State Council issued the Provisional Regulation on the Residence Permit System, detailing guidelines for implementing the transition to a residence-based system.

By the end of 2016, 25 provinces had introduced detailed plans to implement the residence permit system. Government administrative data show that 28.9 million residence permits were issued by the end of 2016, and the proportion of urban residents with a local *hukou* rose to 42 percent. A key next step would be to decouple basic public services from the urban *hukou*, especially in large cities, to open access to all residents regardless of their *hukou* status. *Hukou* reform would likely require reforms of the intergovernmental fiscal transfer arrangements between central and local governments to share the cost of providing public services to migrants and to promote equality of public services across regions and between rural and urban areas. In the medium term, reforms in social services and public finance could allow a nationwide common service standard, irrespective of location. The portability and sustainability of pension benefits are particularly important and eventually would require central administration.

In line with the progress made by the *hukou* reforms, urbanization has been rising, and the urbanization gap, measured by the difference between the urban resident population and urban *hukou* population, has been narrowing, although it has stabilized somewhat since 2015 (figure 7.5). In 2018, the proportion of resident population and *hukou* population was 59.6 percent and 43.4 percent of the total urban population, respectively.[12] The government proposed to increase the proportion of urban *hukou* population by 1 percentage point in 2018.

While important strides are being made on *hukou* reforms, more actions are needed to meet the government's ambitious plan to settle 100 million people in cities. Local governments have been piloting various "quasi-*hukou*" status categories as a transitional solution that provides partial access to urban public services and welfare. The goal is to establish a residence-based *hukou* system, which would not need a separate residence permit system. But *hukou* restrictions in large cities and megacities remain high. Conversion rules in large cities and megacities depend on several specific requirements, which in many cases only allow highly qualified migrants to move in.

Pension and social security reforms

A nationwide pension and social security system would enhance labor mobility. China's broad social security system covers social insurance, social assistance, and social welfare. The social insurance programs include pension, medical, unemployment, work-injury, and maternity insurance. Among the five insurance programs, only pension insurance has achieved a provincial pooling of pension funds through either a partial pooling approach in most cases or a full pooling approach in a few provinces; for the other social insurance programs, the social insurance funds are pooled at the prefecture or county level.

A very low level of pooling of social insurance funds and a fragmented social insurance information system have constrained the portability of social insurance entitlements and benefits when workers move across cities or provinces (box 7.1). Recognizing this challenge, the 2011 Social Insurance Law called for pooling pension funds at the national level and other social insurance funds at the provincial level. In 2018, the Chinese authorities established a central fund adjustment system by following a partial pooling

approach—that is, collecting social contributions from individual localities and reallocating them at the national level. This is encouraging, and similar reforms should be considered for the other social insurance programs.

A more sustainable pension system with an automatic balancing mechanism and adequate pension levels could reduce precautionary savings, boost domestic consumption, remove fiscal pressure, and promote macroeconomic stability. In 2014, the total social insurance contribution rate was over 40 percent in China, among the highest in the world.[13] Lowering that rate would increase disposable income, which in turn would promote higher household consumption. This will become increasingly important since China is rebalancing toward greater reliance on consumption. The contribution rates have been reduced 4 percent since 2015 as a temporary measure in response to the economic

---

BOX 7.1   An integrated system delivers better social insurance services

A pioneer in China's reform, Guangdong Province has the country's largest economy and the largest number of both residential population and migrants. Guangdong is now shifting from traditional low-cost manufacturing to more knowledge-intensive goods and services, resulting in a growing demand for skilled workers. However, movement across cities and between rural and urban areas within the province and beyond incurred significant welfare costs, as pension portability could not be assured, the mechanism for reimbursement of insured health services was inefficient, and access to employment services was limited because of the fragmented social security system both across individual social insurance programs and spatially across and within provinces.

Since 2013, the World Bank has been supporting Guangdong to establish a centralized and integrated management information system (MIS) for social insurance and labor programs. This project has helped Guangdong develop an overall architecture design for the integrated provincial MIS, which

would integrate data management across its major business lines—including social insurance, employment services, and human resources management—and across the 21 prefectures in Guangdong Province. This will allow rural and urban residents in Guangdong to have access to social security and employment services anywhere from local one-stop service stations in the province and independent of the person's household registration.

In 2017, the provincial MIS was successfully piloted at the largest prefecture municipality—Qingyuan. With this success, Guangdong plans to scale up the integrated provincial MIS to the entire province by 2020, benefiting all of the urban and rural residents enrolled in social insurance programs. With its centralized data support, Guangdong has already initiated reforms to pool pension and other social insurance funds fully at the provincial level. Guangdong provides an interesting model as China works to develop a national integrated social security information system.

Source: "In Guangdong, China, an Integrated System Delivers Better Social Insurance Services," *World Bank News,* February 14, 2018, http://www.worldbank.org/en/news/feature/2018/02/14/in-guangdong-china-an-integrated-system-delivers-better-social-insurance-services.

slowdown. If the legacy costs of the earlier, more generous pension liabilities are financed separately, pension contribution rates could drop from the current 28 percent to 15–16 percent, according to a World Bank study.

Wider reforms should be undertaken to help achieve full coverage by 2020, to promote portability and equity, and to strengthen the long-term sustainability of the pension system. The Chinese government has developed an overall design for pension system reform, although the design has not been released to the public. Indications are that the authorities would consider introducing both parametric and structural reforms. For the former, possible reform measures could include gradually raising retirement ages and unifying them for men and women; establishing pension indexation adjustment mechanisms; and lengthening the reference period of wages used in determining basic monthly benefits.

Several reform measures have already been undertaken. In 2017, a notional interest[14] for individual accounts was introduced for the urban worker pension scheme and the public sector pension scheme, suggesting that a notional defined-contribution approach could eventually be adopted to the urban worker pension scheme. Also in 2017, the State Council announced plans to transfer 10 percent of SOE equity into the social security funds to help address the shortfall of pension funds and thereby strengthen the fiscal sustainability of the funds. Transferring SOE shares and dividends into the social security funds could help to lower social insurance contributions.

These announcements indicate that reforms are generally on the right track. What is needed now is an overall strategy and reform agenda to show how all of the various reforms fit within a comprehensively designed reform program. Considering the country's rapid urbanization and population aging, China's pension reform needs to follow an integrated framework and introduce a built-in actuarial balancing mechanism to establish a "clean" system,[15] which would respond automatically to future demographic, social, and economic as well as technological changes. Moving toward a clean system also requires a

road map for transitioning from the existing system. During the transition, a strategy for fully pooling pension funds at the national level is crucial. Also, it is vital to develop a financing strategy for the legacy costs that could make the contributions sufficiently affordable to ensure broad worker coverage and financial sustainability.

Encouraging and supporting labor force participation

Firms have expressed concerns about high labor turnover. However, analysis for this flagship report concluded that the average job tenure in China is comparable to Organisation of Economic Co-operation and Development (OECD) countries, indicating relatively low turnover (figure 7.6). In the SOE sector, job tenures are longer and increase with education, reflecting the high job security offered by the public sector. In non-SOE (private) sectors in urban areas, job tenure is shorter but very similar to that in Europe and North America. Shorter job tenure is to be expected among employees with more highly demanded skills and is not seen as a problem in the United States. Silicon Valley, for example, is noted for its high rates of employee turnover and its dynamic labor market.[16] A reasonable turnover rate is a symptom of a healthy economy, as it provides an avenue for improving the match between employers and employees. Also, the option to leave provides firms with appropriate incentives to compensate their workers for their contributions, thereby making worker pay competitive. A key issue is whether firms, perceiving high rates of labor turnover, hold back on investing in employee training.

Despite concerns about skill shortages, college graduates in China cannot always find jobs commensurate with their education and training, and many end up in part-time, low-paid jobs, at least initially. Analysis for this report indicates that college graduates are increasingly ending up in jobs in middle-skill occupations with lower earnings potential. Given enterprises' views of a skills shortage, this finding may indicate low allocative efficiency in the labor market. It

FIGURE 7.6 **Average job tenure in selected countries and within China**

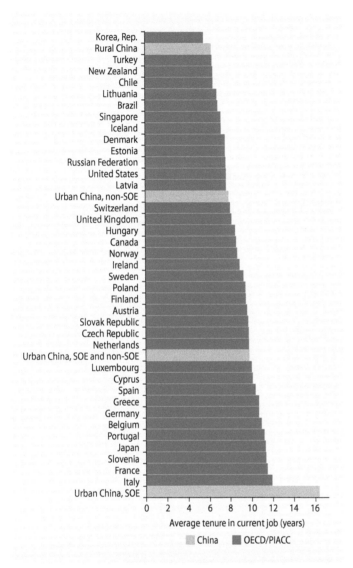

Average tenure in current job (years)

China OECD/PIACC

Sources: Calculations based on China Household Income Project 2013 data, Organisation for Economic Co-operation and Development (OECD) reports; and Program for the International Assessment of Adult Competencies (PIACC) survey data. For countries where both the OECD and PIACC estimates are available, the OECD reported measure is used.

institutions and the broader social insurance system to fit new forms of employment and to prepare for the impacts of technology and population aging. Many recent labor law reforms in OECD countries—including Germany, Italy, and Spain—have moved toward more unified labor contracts and simplified regulations that, while maintaining fundamental worker protections, enhance firms' flexibility in managing their human resources and reduce regulatory ambiguities and thus labor disputes.

Longer life expectancy means that individuals can productively engage in the labor market at older ages. But urban Chinese workers, both men and women, withdraw much earlier from the labor market than workers in other countries. Due to early retirement policies, women withdraw even sooner than men. The participation rate of urban women over age 45 is much lower in China than in high-income economies, even though the participation rate of younger women is comparable. Although an increasing body of work has shown that participation of the elderly does not crowd out employment of the younger cohort, a large degree of unsubstantiated skepticism remains about policies that allow workers to phase or defer retirement.

China could address the shrinking labor force by tapping the underused labor of adult women and the elderly. Policies that promote longer and more flexible working lives, as well as complementary policies in areas of pensions and elder care, would encourage older workers to contribute more productively to the economy. In addition, policies that allow a more gradual transition from work into retirement could reduce the burden on the workforce that currently supports them. Changes in regulations surrounding retirement could be complemented by policies that incentivize firms to employ elderly workers either fully or partially. Many believe that this policy could also delay the retirement of their spouses since retirement decisions are often made jointly. Developing the child and elderly care market could free up time for labor market participation by family members, especially adult women, who spend a considerable amount of time caring for the children and elderly in their families.

also could reflect inadequate quality in some tertiary institutions, following a period of rapid expansion.

Labor laws could be reformed to enhance flexibility in human resource management while ensuring fundamental worker protection, including for informal employment. China's labor contract law is considered less restrictive than the OECD average with regard to hiring and firing. The government could consider changes to labor market

Active labor market policies could be used more extensively and systematically in China to assist displaced workers, for example, those in overcapacity heavy industries and industries affected by labor-saving technologies. The policy instruments could be selected and designed according to local conditions. These policies can encourage the movement of labor from sunset to sunrise industries and increase reemployment and earnings prospects for workers affected by technological changes.

International experience offers some clues for active labor market practices. Job search assistance and counseling—delivered by public or commercial agencies—can be cost-effective but of little use where labor demand is weak. Training programs with strong employer involvement have proven the most effective. Wage subsidies can help to offset the short-term impacts of temporary negative shocks but are less good at increasing employment over the longer term—and accurate targeting and design are important to avoid simply displacing existing workers. With large-scale displacement and few wage opportunities in the locality, support for self-employment, such as credit and technical assistance, and incentives for mobility can be more effective interventions.

Whichever instruments are chosen, competition in program delivery generally improves efficiency and effectiveness. Options include performance-based contracts with service providers and vouchers that can be redeemed at different training providers. Suitable targeting, through statistical and case profiling of laid-off workers, is essential for identifying what would help each worker find new employment.

Notes

1. Estimates of government debt, household debt, and nonfinancial corporate debt are based on data from the Bank for International Settlements (BIS). The estimates of the composition of corporate debt by private firms, local government financing vehicles(LGFVs), and non-LGFV SOEs were based on the following: (a) PBOC's Almanac of China's Finance and Banking, to estimate loans outstanding for private firms and SOEs; (b) Wind database, to estimate bonds outstanding by private firms, LGFVs, and non-LGFV SOEs; and (c) national audit results for bank loans outstanding issued to LGFVs for 2012, and then bank loans outstanding issued to LGFVs in subsequent years estimated by applying the growth rate of bank loans outstanding of the WIND sample of LGFVs, and bank loans outstanding to LGFVs.

2. China was compared to Brazil, Germany, India, Japan, Mexico, the Russian Federation, the United Kingdom, and the United States.

3. These estimates are from the 2018 meeting on SMEs, chaired by Liu He: http://www.gov.cn /guowuyuan/2018-08/20/content_5315204 .htm.

4. The CBIRC was established in April 2018 by the merger of the China Banking Regulatory Commission (CBRC) and the China Insurance Regulatory Commission (CIRC).

5. In China, SMEs are defined as firms with fewer than 1,000 employees, which is larger than in most countries. Using an alternative definition of SME might produce an even lower ratio. See the World Bank micro, small, and medium enterprise indicators for a definitions of SMEs in different countries.

6. Partly drawn from the World Bank and PBOC, *Toward Universal Financial Inclusion in China: Models, Challenges, and Global Lessons*, 2018.

7. One high-profile case was Ezubao, which the authorities shut down in 2015 after it was discovered to have operated a Ponzi scheme, selling fraudulent investment products to nearly 1 million investors and defrauding them of more than US$7.6 billion.

8. WeBank (Tencent), MYbank (Alibaba/Ant Financial), and XW Bank.

9. Such an approach has been used in Malaysia, Singapore, and the United Kingdom, among others.

10. In 2014, China's National People's Congress revised the Law of the PRC [People's Republic of China] on the Protection of Consumer Rights and Interests. In 2015, the General Office of China's State Council of China issued the Guidelines on Strengthening the Protection of Rights and Interests of Financial Consumers. In 2016, PBOC issued the Implementation Rules on the Protection of Rights and Interests of Financial Consumers.

11. Provisional Regulation on the Residence Permit System by the State Council in 2016; Opinions on Promoting the Development of a New-Type Urbanization; and the Program to Promote the Settlement of 100 Million

Migrants into Cities announced by the State Council.

12. Data are from National Bureau of Statistics (2019).

13. State Council Office, 2019. "A Notice on the Comprehensive Proposal of Reducing Social Insurance Contribution Rates," no. 13, April 1, 2019.

14. In 2017, a joint regulation of the Ministry of Finance and the Ministry of Human Resources and Social Security established an administratively determined annual rate of return on individual accounts, indicating that the authorities are considering financing the individual accounts on a pay-as-you-go basis.

15. See more discussions in World Bank (2013) and World Bank and Development Research Center of the State Council (2014).

16. Also, certain segments in China, such as unregistered migrant workers, may exhibit a high turnover.

Bibliography

Beck, Thorsten, Asli Demirgüç-Kunt, and María Soledad Martínez Peria. 2011. "Bank Financing for SMEs: Evidence Across Countries and Bank Ownership Types." *Journal of Financial Services Research* 39 (1): 35-54.

Berger, Allen, and Gregory Udell. 2006. "A More Complete Conceptual Framework for SME Finance." *Journal of Banking and Finance* 30 (11): 2945-66.

Bu, Di, and Yin Liao. 2016. "The Small and Medium Enterprises and the Credit Reporting System in China." *Global Credit Review* 6: 41-8.

Calice, Pietro. 2016. "Assessing Implementation of the Principles for Public Credit Guarantees for SMEs: A Global Survey." Policy Research Working Paper No. 7753, World Bank, Washington, DC.

CFPB (Consumer Financial Protection Bureau). 2017. "CFPB Explores Impact of Alternative Data on Credit Access for Consumers Who Are Credit Invisible."

CGFS (Committee on the Global Financial System) and FSB (Financial Stability Board). 2017. "FinTech Credit: Market Structure, Business Models and Financial Stability Implications." Bank for International Settlements, Financial Stability Board, Basel.

Cowan, Kevin, Alejandro Drexler, and Álvaro Yañez. 2015. "The Effect of Credit Guarantees on Credit Availability and Delinquency Rates." *Journal of Banking and Finance* 59 (C): 98-110.

DRC (Development Research Center of the State Council). 2019. "Policy Options on Promoting the Reform of China's Movable-Assets-Based Financing Market." No. 59 (in Chinese). http://en.drc.gov.cn/2019-06/04/content_37477078.htm.

The Economist. 2017. "In Fintech, China Shows the Way." February 25.

Fleisig, Heywood, Mehnaz Safavian, and Nuria de la Peña. 2006. *Reforming Collateral Laws to Expand Access to Finance.* Washington, DC: World Bank.

Gozzi, J. C., and S. L. Schmukler. 2015. "Public Credit Guarantees and Access to Finance." *European Economy: Banks, Regulation, and the Real Sector* 2: 101-17.

Harwood, Alison, and Tanya Konidaris. 2015. "SME Exchanges in Emerging Market Economies: A Stocktaking of Development Practices." Policy Research Working Paper No. 7160, World Bank, Washington, DC.

Huang, F. 2017. "The Future of Chinese Capital Markets." Unpublished Manuscript.

IFC (International Finance Corporation). 2012. *IFC Secured Transactions Advisory Project in China.* Washington, DC: IFC.

Kuntchev, Veselin, Rita Ramalho, Jorge Rodríguez-Meza, and Judy Yang. 2014. "What Have We Learned from the Enterprise Surveys Regarding Access to Finance by SMEs?" Policy Research Working Paper No. 6670, World Bank, Washington, DC.

Love, Inessa, María Soledad Martinez Peria, and Sandeep Singh. 2016. "Collateral Registries for Movable Assets: Does Their Introduction Spur Firms' Access to Bank Finance?" *Journal of Financial Services Research* 49 (1): 1-37.

MYBank. 2018. Annual Report. (in Chinese). https://render.mybank.cn/p/f/mybank/info.htm.

OECD (Organisation for Economic Co-operation and Development). 2015. *New Approaches to SME and Entrepreneurship Financing: Broadening the Range of Instruments.* Paris: OECD.

PBOC (People's Bank of China). 2017. "Financial Consumers' Capability Survey." http://www.yd96688.com/HdAtt/att/2018/08/20180807171840851.pdf.

———. 2018. Overall "Operation of the Payment System in 2018." http://www.pbc.gov.cn/zhifujiesuansi/128525/128545/128643/3787878/index.html.

PBOC and nine other ministries and commissions. 2015. "Guiding Opinions on Promoting the Healthy Development of Internet Finance." http://www.cbrc.gov.cn/chinese/home/doc DOC_ReadView/DD36A6654C7E4D0D9D6 58E712BFB46C5.html.

Reuters. 2017. "Chinese IPOs Surge After Regulator Eases Flow." February 1.

Stein, Peer, Oya Pinar Ardic, and Martin Hommes. 2013. *Closing the Credit Gap for Formal and Informal Micro, Small, and Medium Enterprises.* Washington, DC: IFC.

Wehinger, Gert. 2014. "SMEs and the Credit Crunch: Current Financing Difficulties, Policy Measures and a Review of Literature." OECD Journal: Financial Market Trends Volume 2013/2, OECD, Paris.

WFE (World Federation of Exchanges). 2015. *WFE Report on SME Exchanges.* Paris: WFE.

World Bank. 2013a. *Global Financial Development Report 2013: Rethinking the Role of the State in Finance.* Washington, DC: World Bank.

———. 2013b. *World Bank Doing Business 2013.* Washington, DC: World Bank.

———. 2014. *Global Financial Development Report 2014: Financial Inclusion.* Washington, DC: World Bank.

———. 2015. "Small and Medium Enterprises (SMEs) Finance," World Bank Brief, September 1.

———. 2018a. *Global Economic Prospects: Broad-Based Upturn, but for How Long?* Washington, DC: World Bank.

———. 2018b. *Global Financial Development Report 2017/2018: Bankers without Borders.* Washington, DC: World Bank.

World Bank, and Development Research Center of the State Council. 2014. *Urban China.* Flagship report. Washington, DC: World Bank.

World Bank, and People's Bank of China. 2018. *Toward Universal Financial Inclusion in China: Models, Challenges, and Global Lessons.* Washington and Beijing: World Bank and People's Bank of China.

8

Leveraging Regional Development and Integration

Regional planning and development have been a key national strategy since China's reform and opening up. Four regional strategies—Western Region Development, Northeast Region Revitalization, Rise of the Central Region, and Leading Development in the Coastal Region—were deployed as national strategies to optimize spatial development, cultivate new growth poles, and foster territorial cooperation. Since China's 18th Plenum in 2012, three major regional strategies have been proposed to complement the original four: Belt and Road Initiative (BRI), Jing-Jin-Ji Coordinated Development, and Yangtze River Economic Belt. These "place-based" strategies (initiatives) have focused on developing new growth poles, increasing efficiency in the spatial allocation of production factors, and enhancing regional specialization. Considering the large population in the central and western regions, alongside natural resource abundance, the development of growth poles in these regions is seen as an opportunity to unlock untapped potential and support new drivers of growth.

These initiatives build on fundamental principles of spatial development where density and proximity are key ingredients, as seen in the tendency of economic activities to cluster and grow unevenly across space (Duranton and Venables 2018; World Bank 2008). The benefits of proximity arise from the direct savings in transport and communication costs from being close together, and economies of scale that arise as firms and infrastructure operate at scale. Furthermore, the provision of networked infrastructure (such as transport and energy) is much cheaper, per person, in dense urban areas than in dispersed rural ones. The other driver is the agglomeration economies that are generated by close and intense economic interaction. These economies arise through several different mechanisms. Thick labor markets enable better matching of workers to firms' skill requirements. Better communication between firms and their customers and suppliers enables knowledge spillovers, better product design, and timely production. A larger local market enables the development of a larger network or more specialized suppliers. Fundamentally, larger and denser markets allow for both scale and specialization.

Institutional and regulatory constraints can create spatial inefficiencies. In principle, the constraints could be removed economywide, but in practice this is difficult because of the fiscal cost (for example, costs of investments in infrastructure) and the politi-cally challenging nature of the reforms (for example, reforms to redevelop land from industrial to commercial use and relax con-straints on labor mobility across regions). Place-based strategies and associated invest-ments in growth poles, transport corridors, and infrastructure also run the risk of creat-ing stranded assets with little economic value unless they are based on a careful assessment of demand and address underlying market and coordination failures.

China has been highly successful in lever-aging spatial transformation for economic development over the past 40 years. Rapid urbanization has supported density and proximity, with rising concentrations of people in cities and metropolitan areas. Cit-ies with more than 1 million urban residents accounted for 260 million people in 2010 (20 percent of China's population) based on the latest available population census, up from 183 million in 2000 (14 percent). The urban populations of Beijing and Shanghai grew almost 50 percent during this period, as did those of Chongqing and Shenzhen (47 per-cent), while the 10 cities with 5 million to 10 million urban residents grew 41 percent. In terms of regions, the largest gains in popula-tion shares from 2000 to 2010 were in the Yangtze River Delta, the Pearl River Delta, and the Beijing-Tianjin region. Together, these three regions absorbed 45 percent of China's additional 91.5 million people. The spatial concentration of people has also been accompanied by rising prosperity; the com-bined economies of Beijing, Guangzhou, Shanghai, Shenzhen, and Tianjin amounted to US$1 trillion in 2010, twice the size of the economies of Norway and Sweden and close to that of the Republic of Korea in 2010.

As China looks toward spatial develop-ment to support future drivers of growth, three sets of policy and investment choices need to be considered carefully. The first is the pace and magnitude of urbanization. There is still room to quicken the pace and improve the efficiency of urbanization, with China being about 8 percentage points less urbanized than other countries for its level of income.[1] Reducing spatial frictions in factor markets will be central to enhancing the pace and efficiency of urbanization.

The second set of choices pertains to the development of economic clusters, which include reforms to enhance linkages within dynamic regions, such as the Yangtze River Economic Belt, and redeveloping regions that have fallen behind. China's investments as part of the BRI could potentially provide new development opportunities for towns and cities in the western region, but there is a need to ensure that economies of scale and specialization are reaped and that a package of complementary investments and policies is implemented in a coordinated manner.

The third set of choices includes the man-agement and strategic redevelopment of existing cities and metropolitan areas such that the urban fabric is dense and connected. Improving urban and metropolitan manage-ment will support density; reduce congestion in transport, housing, and services; and allow cities to take on new economic vocations.

In summary, greater scale and special-ization will be critical for China to leverage regional development to support new drivers of growth. These goals will require reducing spatial frictions in factor markets, developing and expanding economic clusters, improving urban management, and redeveloping cities in a strategic manner.

Reducing spatial frictions in factor markets

Inefficiencies in how labor, land, and capital are being distributed across China's terri-tory are holding down China's urbanization and spatial development. Policy reforms in each factor market would not only enhance returns to that factor but also, given comple-mentarities across factors, enhance the per-formance of other factor markets. Research done for this report shows that simultane-ously reducing the costs of interprovincial labor migration and freeing up the spatial allocation of capital can result in welfare gains of more than 27 percent. Chapter 7 dis-cusses inefficiencies in the flow of labor. The following paragraphs discuss the allocation of capital and land.

Capital should be allocated where it is expected to maximize returns and contribute to growth. Research done for this report indicates a mismatch between the regional supply of capital and local economic activities, in the form of the rising price of capital in eastern urban areas where economic expansion has been taking place. By contrast, the price of capital in the western and central regions relative to the eastern region fell between 2007 and 2014. Econometric analysis done for this report shows that increasing the supply of and access to capital for cities in the eastern region, where greater economic activities are taking place, can improve efficiency in the use of capital as well as contribute to greater output. An important driver of the spatial misallocation of capital and the development of regional clusters are the barriers that small and medium enterprises (SMEs) face in accessing credit from state-owned commercial banks. Even though SMEs generate more employment than large businesses and contribute meaningfully to gross domestic product (GDP), commercial banks nonetheless can favor large borrowers. In 2018, only about 18 percent of bank loans were extended to small and micro enterprises, according to World Bank estimates using People's Bank of China (PBOC) statistics.[2]

Food security concerns have led to national policies inhibiting the conversion of farmland to urban land. The national allocation process places constraints on total new urban and rural land for construction. As China's largest cities try to reorient their economic landscape to support high-end services and innovation, they will need to change their land use policies to allow firms to benefit from economies of density and proximity (agglomeration economies). At the same time, secondary cities in their vicinity will need to make land available for standardized manufacturing to relocate.

There are significant spatial mismatches between urban growth (population and economy) and urban land. Despite little growth in the urban population (0.3 percent), the northeast region witnessed sizable expansion of urban land between 2013 and 2016 (13.1 percent). In the eastern region, urban land areas also grew rapidly (8.3 percent), but at a slower

pace than the urban population (10.5 percent). Henderson, Lall, and Venables (2017) show that inland cities are being allocated more land for urban construction than they can convert, while cities in the eastern region are converting more land for urban construction than originally planned. Empirical research shows that reallocating 30 percent of the land supply from low-productivity cities to high-productivity cities would add between 0.5 and 2.6 percent to China's total GDP.

Policy reforms that constitute a national trading market can enable high-growth cities to trade urban land development rights with jurisdictions with abundant farmland and agriculture-based economic activities. In fact, land quota exchanges between jurisdictions have been piloted in Chengdu and Chongqing and have delivered positive outcomes. This mechanism would allow for a market-based determination of the location and intensity of new development and lead to a more effective allocation of land resources toward the highest and best uses. Scaling up this practice can potentially unlock huge efficiency gains and contribute to economic growth.

Nurturing and connecting economic clusters

China's leaders are putting in place strategies and investments to enhance the development of growth poles and development corridors in different parts of the country. In particular, there is a considerable push for the development of the western region, revitalization of the northeast region, and rise of the central region, adding to regional development plans for the Pearl River Delta, the Yangtze River Delta, and the Beijing-Tianjin-Hebei (Jing-Jin-Ji) region. China's leaders could consider three key principles as they roll out place-based policies to develop clusters to accelerate growth in specific regions.

Reinforce agglomeration economies

Firms in most sectors strongly value agglomeration, which facilitates co-location with other firms and promotes the supply of relevant inputs and knowledge spillovers. Firms are unlikely to move by themselves to "green-field" locations, even if they are offered multiple advantages such as quality infrastructure and institutions. More important to a firm's decision to move is the expectation that complementary firms and inputs, such as skilled labor, will move with it. This complementarity would support scale and specialization.

In fact, China's economic geography has undergone dramatic changes over the past 40 years to reinforce agglomeration economies, with rising clustering and concentration of people and economic activity. Market forces have pushed China toward concentrating industry in its large metropolitan areas, with the Yangtze River Delta and Pearl River Delta emerging as dominant industrial hubs. The clustering of economic activity has accelerated the pace of economic growth and helped to reduce rural-urban inequalities by increasing the incomes of rural residents (Guo et al. 2017). Moreover, according to research carried out for this report, the locations of economic activity have been changing over the past decade. Data at the enterprise level show a decline of manufacturing employment growth in the eastern region (particularly provincial capitals) and an increase in such employment in prefecture-level cities in the central region. The geographic center of manufacturing firms has been moving from the east toward the center of the country since around 2008.

China's investments through the BRI can potentially have profound spatial impacts within China, in addition to the other BRI-connected countries. BRI investments that reduce transport costs between western China and cross-border markets in Central Asia are likely to encourage population and economic growth around border regions such as Urumqi (El-Hifnawy, Lall, and Lebrand 2018). This pattern is consistent with previous episodes of external integration where trade openness can induce concentrations of economic activity near border areas, such as occurred along the border between Mexico and the United States as a result of the North American Free Trade Agreement (Hanson 1998).

Given the changing nature of industrial geography, policies and multisectoral investments will be needed to support scale and spatially clustered development so that benefits from agglomeration can be reaped. Then firms can choose their location based on commercial factors. This would be a bottom-up approach, as opposed to a more top-down, centrally planned approach.

As the growth of manufacturing has slowed in large cities and metropolitan areas in the east, innovative activities have begun to concentrate in these cities. International experience suggests that agglomeration in innovative core areas leads to greater concentration of innovation (McCann and Ortega-Argilés 2011). Regions with large cities—dense with skilled people, well-endowed infrastructure, and burgeoning economic activity—are more innovative. The agglomeration benefits of knowledge and research and development (R&D) spillovers decline rapidly with distance, and dense and well-connected urban areas are the most conducive for nurturing innovation. China's innovative activity is highly concentrated in the coastal region's largest metropolitan areas. For instance, Guangdong contributed 19.3 percent of the total patents granted in 2017, the largest among provinces, followed by Jiangsu and Zhejiang. Provinces in the central and western regions tend to be among the least innovative.

Shenzhen's successful economic transformation from a provincial region of small towns and fishing villages in the 1980s to a manufacturing center, and now a technology and innovation hub, offers valuable lessons for other regions considering spatial and economic transformation. After years of being a manufacturing center for iPhones and other electronics, Shenzhen has established a comprehensive, high-technology, industrial value chain, including key parts such as chips, memory, gyroscopes, Bluetooth, displays, and touch modules. As a result, Shenzhen has a strong basis for hardware innovations that can take advantage of future technology trends in artificial intelligence, virtual reality, drones, and the Internet of Things. Of the various lessons offered by Shenzhen, two key insights for promoting local economies are the focus on establishing a business climate that encourages entrepreneurship and the promotion of inward migration. First, innovation has been led by private companies' investment in R&D. Most enterprises in Shenzhen have a private ownership structure, represented by some of the most dynamic and innovative private enterprises in China, such as BYD, DJI, Huawei, Tencent, and the gene-mapping company BGI. In Shenzhen, more than 90 percent of the R&D institutions are located within private enterprises; more than 90 percent of researchers are concentrated in private enterprises; more than 90 percent of R&D funding comes from private enterprises; and more than 90 percent of patents originate from private enterprises. Shenzhen has also established an R&D culture, reportedly spending US$10 billion, or 4 percent of GDP, on R&D, more than Singapore and Hong Kong SAR, China, combined.

Second, Shenzhen has actively welcomed migrants. Ninety-five percent of its population are migrants who have forged the region's entrepreneurial spirit. Other cities, such as Beijing and Shanghai, have certain areas with high proportions of migrants, but none has the level of migrant concentration of Shenzhen. This level of concentration has enabled Shenzhen to develop a local culture that encourages risk taking, tolerates failure, and rewards talented people regardless of their background.

Coordinate investment and policies across several sectors

Locations that lag in development often face multiple deprivations of relevance to prospective investors, including with regard to human capital, institutional quality, infrastructure, distance to ports, and presence of agglomerations. These deprivations make it particularly difficult to counteract existing spatial concentration, and resolving just one deprivation is rarely enough to make the location attractive to productive firms. For example, firms cannot take advantage of transport investments if logistics are not efficient, and the power supply is lacking. Strong information and communication technology infrastructure will fail to attract a high-technology sector without a local pool of skilled labor and complementary business services. Overcoming these barriers to investment would require coordinated policy responses, strong skills in planning and execution across a broad range of local

government functions, and active collaboration among subnational governments (provincial and local) as well as with national line ministries.

The northeast region highlights the need for a package of coordinated actions. The three northeastern provinces—Heilongjiang, Jilin, and Liaoning—were once the center of heavy industry in China. However, the region has been a relative laggard in economic performance in recent decades, despite several rounds of regional revival efforts. A coordinated and integrated approach, focused on market-oriented reforms, is needed to help the region get out of stagnation. The economy clearly needs to diversify by promoting new sectors. The northeast provinces could streamline their administrative procedures as part of an overall effort to improve the local business climate and promote market-oriented reforms. The region could consider a more market-oriented approach to promoting the local economy, by benchmarking other regions where the market economy thrives. For example, the government of Shenzhen is highly efficient and service oriented, focused on supporting local markets. Its policies, such as online registration of firms, are designed to encourage market competition, innovation, and entrepreneurship. Revitalizing the local economy will also require promoting and retaining local talent, attracting new talent, and promoting entrepreneurship.

Infrastructure investment has been a big part of regional development initiatives so far in China, and there are plans for additional public investment to support regional development. In 1990, almost all goods were transported either by rail or by river. The road system was underdeveloped and had limited access to many places. By 2010, China had constructed an extensive highway system serving the entire country. As transport costs fell, and access to markets improved, regions could specialize and gain from trade. In the longer term, transport infrastructure can help firms relocate, supporting spatial development. However, going forward, given the large infrastructure investments so far and the resulting significant improvements in the country's infrastructure, infrastructure may no longer be as significant of a bottleneck as in the past. This would also mean that investments in infrastructure may not need to be as high as in the past.

What China needs now is not simply more investments in infrastructure but also smart ways to plan, utilize, and manage its infrastructure investments. For example, the priority for the energy sector should not be simply more infrastructure investments but also sectoral reforms to ensure that the investments in power generation—in particular, renewable energy—can be efficiently used and transmitted. In the transport sector, for example, expansion of the network needs to be complemented by enhanced logistics operations, which are currently highly fragmented and unorganized. There are 78,000 road logistics companies in China that are unable to optimize routes, avoid unloaded trips, employ well-trained staff, or share information with infrastructure operators, logistics service providers, and logistics customers. The cost of logistics was RMB 11.1 trillion, or 15 percent of GDP, in 2016, which is high compared with the cost in other countries (NDRC and CFLP 2017). There are also untapped opportunities to use inland water transport and railways in the system. Only 1.3 percent of container traffic through China's ports involves trains, with

85 percent of all containers entering or leaving the ports on trucks. The lack of logistics hubs for multimodal transportation is one of the main reasons for the low use of rail transportation.

In addition to investment and policy coordination, there is room to enhance the extent to which existing economic clusters are connected so that individual towns and cities can specialize, trade goods and services within the cluster, and develop scale economies. Such localization and intracluster linkages can enhance overall efficiency and productivity. In the case of the Yangtze River Economic Belt, empirical analysis conducted for this report indicates a low degree of economic integration between cities in the upper, middle, and lower reaches of the region. Much of the trade in the region takes place within each province as opposed to between provinces, thus missing opportunities to leverage the regional market and interprovincial trade (figure 8.1). To benefit from spatial development, there is a need to enhance trade and linkages across the Yangtze River Economic Belt.

The policy simulations carried out for this report indicate that a combination of infrastructure investments and spatially targeted

FIGURE 8.1   **Trade within and between provinces in the Yangtze River Economic Belt of China**

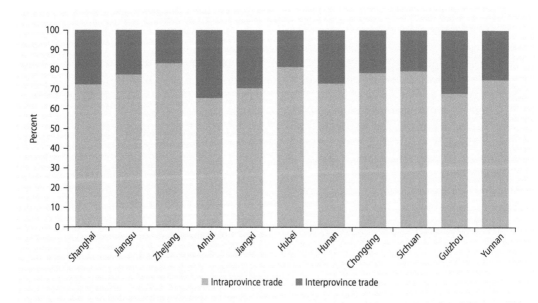

Source: Calculations based on World Bank data.

fiscal policies can support market integration and industrial upgrading of the Yangtze River Economic Belt. There is significant opportunity for economic integration and transformation along the Yangtze River Economic Belt to support the upgrading of industries and services within the belt, anchored by the Yangtze River Delta and Shanghai, and the development of innovation hubs.

Regional cooperation is also constrained by intergovernmental fiscal arrangements and performance assessment systems of local government officials, which tend to encourage local protectionism and market segmentation. Under the existing "tax assignment system" that regulates the financial and taxation relationship between the central and local governments, most local government revenues are generated locally. The supply of public services and the salaries of civil servants are closely related to local fiscal revenues. As a result, local governments are strongly incentivized to focus on developing their local economies, including by taking protectionist measures to promote local enterprises that provide tax revenues. In addition, the government's performance assessment system has tied the promotion of officials closely to local economic performance, and competition between local officials has become, to a considerable extent, a contest of local economic growth. In such an institutional arrangement, regions may focus on competition instead of cooperation and often tend to take a "beggar-thy-neighbor" approach.

Therefore, the government could aim to reform its performance appraisal mechanism and the intergovernmental fiscal and taxation relationship to provide more incentives for local governments to cooperate and collaborate on matters such as the integration of traffic facilities, environmental protection, public service provision, reduction of trade barriers, and the opening of local markets to support regionally coordinated development.

Engage in strategic urban management

In China, limits on urban density are keeping agglomeration economies down and pushing housing prices up. Density-restricting floor area ratio (FAR) regulation is one of the most important land use regulations in urban China. FAR regulation takes the form of an upper-bound constraint on the ratio of a building's total floor area to the lot size of the building. By law, any land parcel to be auctioned off must have a designated regulatory FAR level. The FAR regulation is constraining the efficient development of Chinese cities, as the cities with rapid population growth have lower FARs imposed on newly developed residential land than other cities. This regulation adds to the challenges posed by low land conversion quotas in cities with high population growth, as discussed earlier. In addition to raising the cost of housing and encouraging urban sprawl (as land cannot be developed at scale due to conversion quotas), such regulations are exacerbating congestion and environmental degradation.

The FAR issue is one of many challenges that need to be addressed to improve urban management. A critical issue in the development of high-density and high-quality urban environments is the reform of urban planning and significant improvement of urban design. Cities will need to update their planning regulations to build urban amenities and public services that meet the spatial needs of the new drivers of growth. Flexible manufacturing and customized production often require small spaces at convenient, easily accessible locations. Most services favor a certain population density and quality of life. The expansion of massive public transit networks in Chinese cities, combined with visionary land use plans, presents unprecedented opportunities to get the urban form right.

To address the challenges and ensure an inclusive and efficient urban future, the government could consider the following priorities:

• Reform the process and procedures for how cities determine the type of land uses allowed and the related detailed development restrictions, such as the regulatory FAR limit, building height, and green area rate. Such reforms would aim to improve land use intensity and density in cities. In particular, local governments could reform the decision-making process that limits the FAR for new residential areas in growing cities, and introduce efficiencies and transparency in the process for applying for changes in the FAR and in the land compensation fee to adjust the FAR.

- Introduce zoning regulations that encourage compact and mixed-use urban development connected by high-quality public transport, where residents have easy access to jobs, shops, schools, and other public facilities in a walkable environment. Cities need to invest in advanced urban planning, progressive architecture, urban regeneration, and people-oriented design.
- Develop new planning and design principles and techniques, applied at multiple levels from region and city to subdistrict and local community, that can create livable high-quality urban space for the modern services economy.
- Prepare the type of strategic planning of physical infrastructure and public services that can foster new types of business opportunities, such as shared mobility (including cars and bikes), shared office spaces, and renewable energy vehicles (for example, planning for charging stations for electric cars).
- Improve real estate transparency and urban architectural design to enhance the business operating environment, raise new capital, and contribute to the quality of urban life, making cities more globally competitive.
- Introduce new policies and regulations to improve land use efficiencies by encouraging the use of underutilized land in urban centers and discouraging the oversupply of industrial land on the city's periphery.

Notes

1. Based on a comparison of incomes and urbanization with all countries globally, using World Development Indicators data for 2016.
2. The estimate is based on micro enterprises, as opposed to medium enterprises, because PBOC defines the size (number of employees) of micro enterprises similar to what other countries designate as medium enterprises.

Bibliography

Baum-Snow, Henderson, Brandt, et al. 2017. "Highways, Market Access, and Urban Growth in China." Processed. https://economics .smu.edu.sg/sites/economics.smu.edu.sg/files /economics/pdf/Seminar/2017/20170313.pdf.

Carlino, G., and W. Kerr. 2014. "Agglomeration and Innovation." NBER working paper 20367, National Bureau of Economic Research.

Duranton, Gilles, and Anthony J. Venables. 2018. "Place-Based Policies for Development." Policy Research Working Paper WPS8410, World Bank, Washington, DC.

Fu, Shihe, Xiaocong Xu, and Junfu Zhang. 2018. "Land Conversion and Misallocation across Cities in China." Background paper for this report, World Bank, Washington, DC.

Guo, D., U. Deichmann, and S. V. Lall. 2017. "The Geography of Industrial Development in China." Background paper for this report, World Bank, Washington, DC.

Guo, Di, Kun Jiang, Cheng-Gang Xu, and Xiyi Yang. 2017. "Clustering, Growth, and Inequality in China." CEPR Discussion Paper no. DP12543, Center for Economic and Policy Research. https://ssrn.com/abstract=3095593.

Hanson, Gordon. 1998. "North American Economic Integration and Industry Location." *Oxford Review of Economic Policy* 14 (2): 30–44.

Henderson, J. Vernon, Somik Lall, and Anthony Venables. 2017. *Africa's Cities: Opening Doors to the World.* Washington, DC. World Bank.

Henderson, J. D. Su, Q. Zhang, and S. Zheng. 2017. "A Note on Migration Costs in China." Background paper for this report, World Bank, Washington, DC.

Kochendorfer-Lucius, Gudrun, and Boris Pleskovic. 2009. "Spatial Disparities and Development Policy." Berlin Workshop Series 2009, World Bank, Washington, DC.

Lall, Somik V., and Mathilde Sylvie Maria Lebrand. 2019. "Who Wins, Who Loses ? Understanding the Spatially Differentiated Effects of the Belt and Road Initiative." Policy Research working paper no. WPS 8806, World Bank, Washington, DC. http://documents.worldbank .org/curated/en/292161554727963020/Who -Wins-Who-Loses-Understanding-the-Spatially -Differentiated-Effects-of-the-Belt-and-Road -Initiative.

Lau, Alan, and Min Su. 2017. "China's E-Commerce Soft Spot: Logistics." Retrieved from https://www.mckinsey.com/industries /high-tech/our-insights/chinas-e-commerce -soft.

Liu, Bing-lian, Jian-hua Xiao, Zhi-lun Jiao, Shao-ju Lee, and Ling Wang (eds). 2013. "Contemporary Logistics in China: Transformation and Revitalization." Current Chinese Economic Report Series, Springer-Verlag, Heidelberg.

McCann, Philip, and Raquel Ortega-Argilés. 2011. "Smart Specialisation, Regional Growth and Applications to EU Cohesion Policy." *Regional Studies* 49 (8) January.

MEP (Ministry of Environmental Protection). 2017. "China Vehicle Environmental Management Annual Report." http://dqhj.mep.gov.cn/jdchjgl/zhgldt/201706/P020170605550637870889.pdf.

NDRC (National Development and Reform Commission) and CFLP (China Federation of Logistics and Purchasing). 2017. "Briefing on National Logistics Operation in 2016" (in Chinese).

World Bank. 2008. *World Development Report 2009: Reshaping Economic Geography.* Washington, DC: World Bank.

Yanlin, Li. 2017. "The Study on Logistics Performance Evaluation in China" (in Chinese). Retrieved from http://www.transformcn.com/Topics/img/site22/20170925/c81f661ac8d91b32af6522.pdf.

9

Promoting International Competitiveness and Economic Globalization

Integration into the global economy has been a major driver of China's economic growth and development. China achieved economic globalization through reforms to open up its economy to global trade and investments, becoming the world's largest trader of manufactured goods and a major destination for foreign investments. China is now an essential part of the global economic landscape, and its production, trade, and investments are deeply integrated in global value chains (GVCs). Foreign-invested enterprises helped China to expand its exports rapidly through the processing and assembly of manufactured goods. China now seeks to promote globally competitive indigenous enterprises and move to higher-value-added parts of GVCs.

Continued reforms to open its economy further will be critical for China to achieve its aspirations to become a more innovative and productive economy. The 3rd Plenary Session of the 18th Communist Party of China (CPC) Central Committee proposed to reform and open the economy further, outlining a series of policy measures to support China's industrial upgrading and economic transformation under the "new normal." Being outwardly oriented with innovative domestic firms engaged in global trade and investments will help to improve China's long-term competitiveness and prosperity. China's deep integration in GVCs helps domestic enterprises access the global supply of advanced components, technologies, and services. As China approaches the global technology frontier, it will increasingly need to access frontier technologies. Foreign direct investment (FDI) and outward direct investment (ODI) in advanced manufacturing and high-end services can drive technological innovation and industrial upgrading in China.

Given China's importance to the global economy, it will be increasingly looked upon to support an open global economy, promote shared global prosperity, and collaborate on global public goods. International cooperation and coordination are becoming more critical as rapid technological advancement is creating closer links among nations. China's growth was a significant contributor to global growth following the global financial crisis, and it remains an important source of global economic growth. China also believes that the Belt and Road Initiative (BRI), an ambitious effort to improve cross-country economic integration and connectivity on a transcontinental scale, will make a major contribution to the global economy. To achieve "win-win cooperation that promotes shared development and prosperity," BRI will require a multilateral approach based on transparency, accountability, and investments that are financially, environmentally, and socially sustainable.

China faces three major global dynamics that present both challenges and opportunities. First, rising global trade tensions and the challenges of sustaining global growth have created a more uncertain and challenging external environment for China's open development. Second, China's traditional areas of labor-intensive comparative advantage may be weakening, while its new areas of comparative advantage are still evolving. Third, the influence of emerging economies, including China, on the global economy is rising, and therefore international coordination will require a wider consensus. China's policy choices will have a considerable impact on global economic developments and international economic and trade relations. Therefore, China and the rest of the world will need to work together to address emerging challenges and ensure shared global prosperity.

China's integration into the global economy and rising competitiveness

China's unprecedented economic growth and rapid development have been driven by 40 years of reforms since 1978 and the opening up of its economy. China has benefited greatly by integrating into the global economy and leveraging its comparative advantages in global trade and investments. China has become the world's largest international trader of manufacturing goods and the second-largest trader in services. China's exports have soared in dollar terms—17 percent annually in the past two decades—and its export market shares for both gross trade and added value have risen significantly (figure 9.1). The contribution of China's exports to its growth has been falling with the slowdown in global trade since the global financial crisis of 2008, but its share of global trade has been rising. China's share of global exports of goods increased from only 3.9 percent in 2000 to 14.6 percent in 2017.

China has evolved from being a peripheral actor to being one of the three major global manufacturing hubs for GVCs, along with Germany and the United States (figure 9.2). China is a prime example of using GVCs to improve supply-side productivity and competitiveness. To facilitate its integration into GVCs, China has invested heavily in transportation, the Internet, and information and communication technology (ICT)–related infrastructure and carried out reforms to promote foreign investment, improve trade and investment facilitation, and strengthen the business environment.

Foreign investments have been critical for China's export growth and international competitiveness. Foreign-invested enterprises contributed to nearly half of China's imports and exports, one-fourth of industrial output, and one-fifth of tax revenue in 2017. China was the second-largest destination for FDI in the world, after the United States, in 2018. According to the *World Investment Report 2017* (UNCTAD 2017), multinational firms consider China the second-most-preferred destination for cross-border investment in the world.

China has evolved from being a net importer of FDI to a net exporter in 2016 (figure 9.3). Despite experiencing a sharp decline in 2017, China's outbound investments were the third-largest in the world. Regional connectivity programs, such as the BRI, have

FIGURE 9.1   **China's share of global exports of goods, 1993–2017**

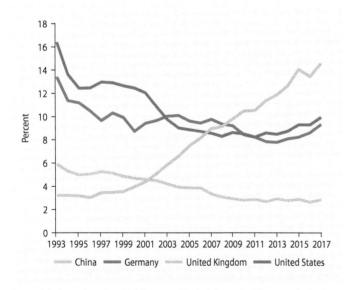

Sources: Calculations based on World Integrated Trade Solutions (WITS)–Comtrade database for 1992–2016 and International Monetary Fund Direction of Trade Statistics (DOTS) for 2017.

FIGURE 9.2   **Global network of intermediate trade (minimum-spanning-tree method), 1995 and 2016**

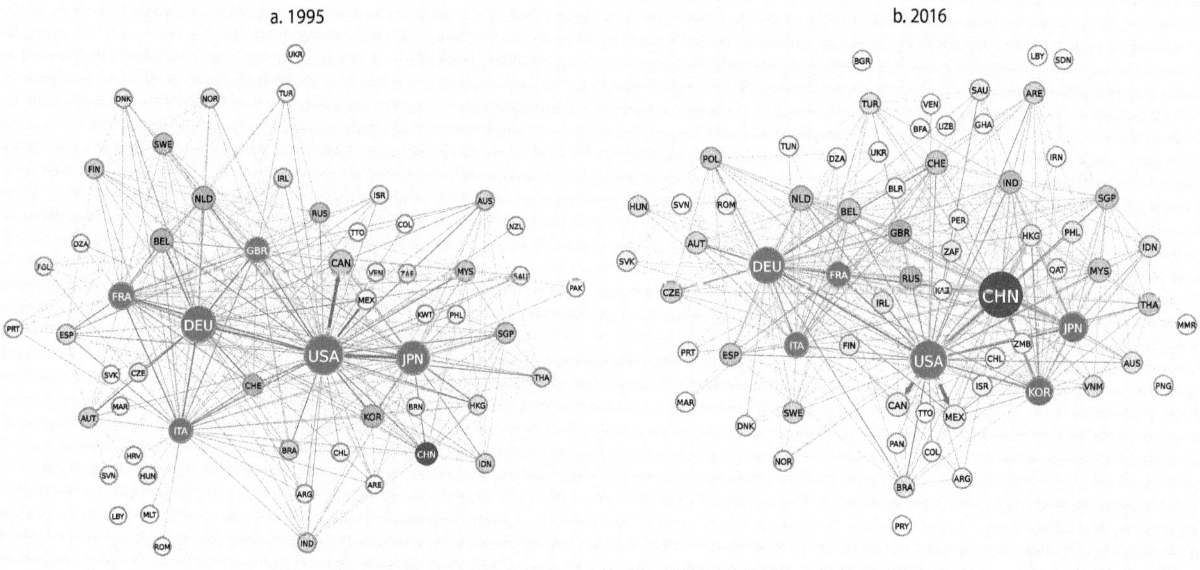

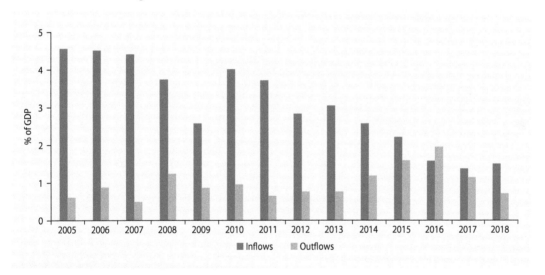

a. 1995

b. 2016

Source: Calculations based on Organisation for Economic Co-operation and Development (OECD) Trade in Value Added (TiVA) data.

FIGURE 9.3   **China's foreign direct investment and outward direct investment, 2005–18**

Source: State Administration of Foreign Exchange (SAFE) data.

the potential to lead to further ODI opportunities. Also, China remains an attractive destination for foreign investments due to its large domestic market. Foreign enterprises such as BASF, BMW, Siemens, and Tesla have recently announced new or expanded investments in China.

China has progressed significantly on its "economic fitness," which measures the export capabilities of an economy (figure 9.4). Economic fitness is a measure of the complexity-weighted diversification of a country's exports (Cristelli et al. 2017; Tacchella et al. 2012). An economy is more complex if more varied and useful knowledge and capabilities are embedded in it and are reflected in its exports. China's economic fitness far exceeds that of countries

FIGURE 9.4   **"Fitness analysis" of the diversity and complexity of China's exports**

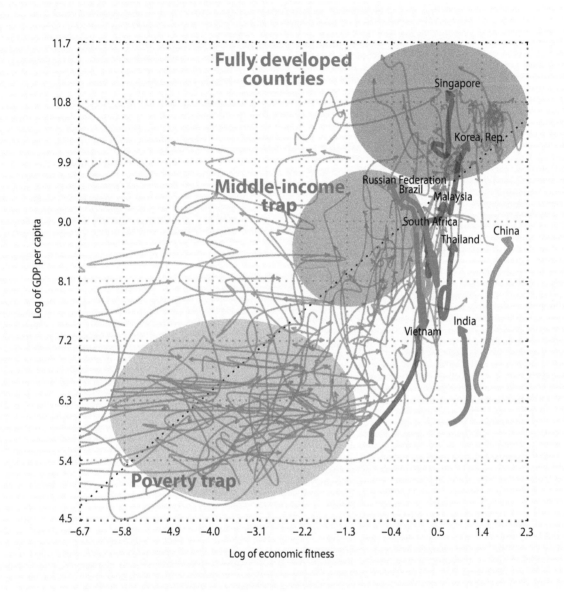

Source: International Finance Corporation analysis.

with a similar gross domestic product (GDP) per capita and is now comparable to that of some high-income countries. Its fitness is approaching the global frontier, due to the complexity of the goods and services it produces competitively and the wide range of sectors that it exports.[1] A complementary analysis of economic complexity, which measures the diversity of a country's exports (the number of products in a country's export basket) and their ubiquity (the number of countries that export a given

product), also indicates that China's manufacturing production became substantially more complex from 1995 to 2014.[2]

China has a relatively high level of capability for providing "complex" goods for export—beyond what would be expected for its stage of development. Part of this fitness reflects manufacturing exports by foreign-invested enterprises based in China and the large share of foreign intermediate inputs in its exports. Given that China's exporting capabilities surpass its level of development,

FIGURE 9.5 **Revealed comparative advantage in gross exports and value-added exports in China, 2000–14**

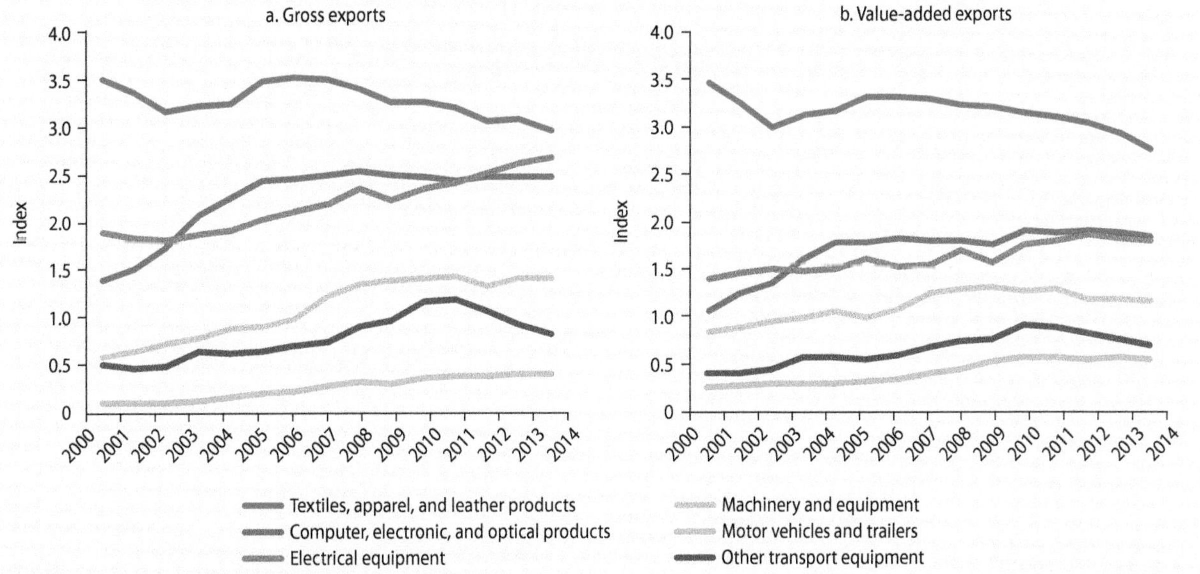

Source: Calculations based on World Input-Output Database (WIOD) data.

it also indicates that significant potential remains for the diffusion of technology and manufacturing know-how within China's economy, from the exporting to the nonexporting sectors. China's expected fitness trajectory shows that it is on a path to achieving fully developed status. It also indicates rising competitiveness in transport equipment, computer manufacturing, and plastics—all relatively complex industries—and additional opportunities for research and development (R&D)–intensive exports, particularly in ICT and robotics.

China has continued to expand its high-technology exports and domestic value added in exports. The share of high-technology manufactures in exports increased from nearly zero in 1980 to around 30 percent in 2017.[3] The export performance of computers, electronics, optical equipment, and electrical machinery particularly stands out. Export competitiveness can be measured using revealed comparative advantage (RCA).[4] China's RCA of gross exports of technology-intensive goods—such as computer and electronic products, electrical equipment, and machinery equipment—have increased significantly (figure 9.5, panel a). However, if RCA

is measured based on domestic value added in exports (value-added RCA), using the methodology proposed by the World Trade Organization (WTO) and the Organisation for Economic Co-operation and Development (OECD), then the competitiveness of China's high-technology exports has improved to a lesser degree (figure 9.5, panel b).

In parallel with the expansion of high-technology exports, China has managed to retain the competitiveness of its lower-technology and more labor-intensive exports, such as textiles and garments. The share of low-technology exports has declined, but low-technology exports still account for roughly one-third of exports, and their RCA remains relatively high, but declining (figure 9.5).

China's integration in GVCs has been a key driver of its export growth and has provided important opportunities for accessing advanced technology. China's level of participation in GVCs was analyzed by estimating its domestic value added (DVA) in exports using the World Input-Output Database (WIOD).[5] The analysis indicated that China's DVA in exports was very low in the early 2000s but has been rising steadily. By contrast, the DVAs of many major exporting countries have held

FIGURE 9.6   **Domestic value added (DVA) in exports in selected economies, 2000–15**

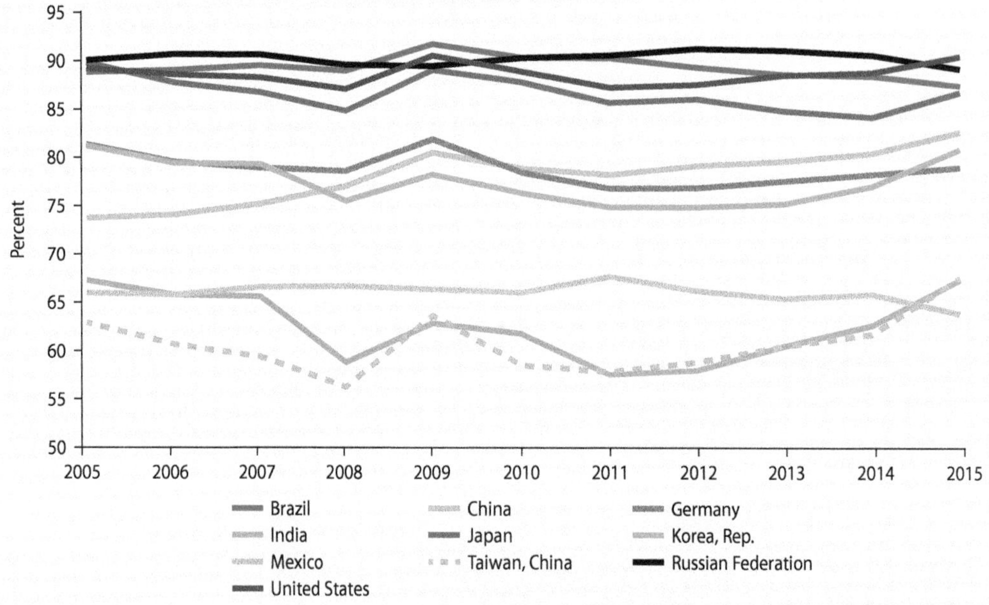

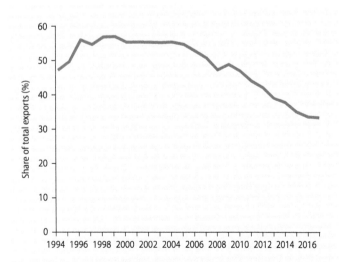

Source: Calculations based on World Input-Output Database (WIOD).

steady or have been declining. China's DVA is now higher than those of several major exporting economies (figure 9.6).[6]

China's higher DVA was achieved through improvements in its base of domestic suppliers, which grew in response to the country's trade and investment liberalization and its deeper engagement in GVCs (Kee and Tang 2016). During 2000–17, China's rising DVA reflected a shift away from the assembly and processing trade, the share of which remains relatively high but has been declining steadily from almost 60 percent to about 30 percent (figure 9.7). The DVA of technology-intensive exports is significantly lower than the DVA of labor-intensive exports, reflecting higher shares of the assembly and processing trade. For example, the DVA of exports of computers, electronic audiovisual equipment, and electronic instruments has been about 40 percent, significantly lower than the average DVA.

China's international competitiveness and integration with the global economy were achieved through policy and institutional reforms. China has been reforming its foreign investment regime and progressively expanding market access. Its accession to the WTO, and various regional or bilateral free trade agreements, provided the necessary institutional commitment to lock in and accelerate China's domestic reforms and advance its economic globalization and participation in the rule-based international

FIGURE 9.7   **Exports of processed products as a share of total goods exported from China, 1994–2017**

Source: General Administration of Customs data.

economic system. A major part of the reforms has been the active promotion of FDI, which has facilitated China's participation in global trade and integration into GVCs. As a result, foreign-invested enterprises still account for nearly half of China's imports and exports (2018). FDI, as well as ODI, have also been powerful channels for technological upgrading and learning global best practices.

China's integration into the global economy has resulted in significant global benefits. It has been the largest contributor to global growth since the global financial crisis, and it will need to continue to play a major role in jointly responding, with other countries, to global crises and ensuring an open global investment and trade system. The government has stated that it aims to "promote a fair, transparent, convenient, open, and international investment environment, through investment liberalization, investment facilitation, investment promotion, investment protection, optimizing the layout of regional opening up, and improving innovation in state-level development zones." (International Office of the State Council 2018.)

To achieve this goal, in 2018 the government issued for the first time a national foreign investment negative list, which identifies prohibited and restricted industries for foreign investment. This important reform enhances the transparency and clarity of government restrictions on foreign investments and provides a mechanism to continue to reduce the number of restrictive measures. The negative list reduces restrictions across several important sectors, including energy, natural resources, infrastructure, transportation, trade and logistics, professional services, financial services, and the automotive industry. The government also announced plans to eventually fully open all manufacturing sectors to FDI, with some sectors requiring a transitional period. While China had committed in its WTO accession to open 100 services sectors, the Ministry of Commerce has indicated that the country has opened 120 sectors for foreign investments.[7] The government has indicated that it would open its services sectors further, including the telecommunications and financial sectors.

China has also used special economic zones extensively to promote foreign investments and pilot institutional reforms to liberalize foreign investment regimes. China has used various forms of special economic zones, including free trade zones, export processing zones, industrial parks, and high-technology parks. China started with four special economic zones in the 1980s in coastal areas, and then gradually rolled out special economic zones throughout the country. There are now more than 500 national special economic zones and many more local special economic zones.[8] Since the initial free trade zone in Shanghai in 2013, China now has 12 free trade zones that have been used to experiment with the adoption of international trade and investment rules, more streamlined administrative and business registration procedures, and an improved business environment. In particular, free trade zones were used to pilot pre-establishment national treatment and the foreign investment negative list. The number of restrictive measures in the foreign investment negative list for free trade zones was gradually reduced from 190 in the original version to 45 in 2018. The piloting in the free trade zones subsequently led to the national rollout of reforms, including the introduction of a national foreign investment negative list and pre-establishment national treatment of foreign investments in 2018.

Major challenges and opportunities

International trade tensions

Recent downward risks to the global economy, and international trade tensions, have posed significant challenges to China's economic prospects and potential to benefit from economic globalization. Trade tensions and increased protectionist measures and sentiments have adversely affected market and investor confidence and amplified the uncertainty of the external environment for China's open development.

Europe and the United States have been pressuring China to open up its markets further and to liberalize its foreign investment regime. The United States has conducted investigations of China's alleged unfair trade policies and applied significantly higher tariffs on China's imports. In recent years, more than 40 percent of cases reviewed by the U.S. Committee on Foreign Investment in the United States (CFIUS), an interagency committee that reviews foreign investments with national security implications, have involved Chinese companies, and CFIUS has blocked Chinese acquisition of key technologies such as semiconductors. In the European Union (EU), the significant increase in Chinese investments has raised concerns about the transfer of key technologies and has led to the introduction of an EU-wide foreign investment screening mechanism. Some individual member states are strengthening their legal powers to investigate foreign acquisitions.

Some foreign investors have raised concerns that they are "forced" to transfer technology to gain market access in China. The Government of China has indicated that it has never introduced policies or practices that forced foreign-invested enterprises to transfer technology (Information Office, State Council 2018). It has stated that technology transfers have been voluntary contractual transactions agreed to between foreign and domestic enterprises to maximize their mutual interests.

Across a wide range of countries, it has been shown that technology transfer requirements—often in the form of joint ventures—can hinder the transfer of the latest technologies to host economies, as foreign firms often supply older technologies to their joint venture partners in developing countries. Hence the government's announcement in 2018 to loosen joint venture requirements for regular and electric vehicles is expected to encourage the introduction of the latest technologies in China and to promote market competition.

Export quality and value added

Given China's already high share of global trade, it will need to shift its focus from improving the quantity to improving the quality of its exports and from exports based on assembly manufacturing to more value-added and innovative manufacturing and services. China has been converging rapidly to the global quality frontier for manufacturing, but the gap with high-income economies remains large (figure 9.8). Therefore, significant potential remains for improving the quality of its exports. Across countries, faster growth in quality has been associated with more rapid growth in output. Substantial differences across countries and regions in the pace of quality upgrading suggest that policies have a significant impact. Both institutional quality and human capital are significantly associated with quality upgrading. Evidence suggests that quality upgrading is best encouraged through a conducive domestic environment, rather than through sector-specific policies, and diversification is important to create new upgrading opportunities (Henn, Papageorgiou, and Spatafora 2013).

ICT goods have played a significant role in China's export success. China's comparative advantage has been the manufacturing part of the value chain. However, significant shares of the higher, value-added parts of the value chain that involve greater innovation are taking place outside of China. These parts include the upstream parts of the value chain—such as R&D, design, and key high-value inputs—and the downstream parts—such as branding, marketing, and sales—which are more consumer facing. Earlier "teardown" studies of the iPhone and similar products indicated that the value added in China was negligible, consisting mainly of final assembly from imported high-value components. For the Apple iPhone, it was estimated that China's domestic value added was only US$6.54, about 1 percent of the retail price of a US$600 iPhone 4 (Linden, Dedrick, and Kraemer 2009). More recent analysis indicates that the situation has been slow to change (Sturgeon and Thum 2017). However, domestic brands now account for the largest share of the domestic mobile phone market, indicating that China is now capturing a large share of the value added of downstream activities.

Trade facilitation and logistics

GVCs have put a premium on reducing trade-related costs. Trade costs resulting from poor transportation, low efficiency in customs

FIGURE 9.8   **Quality of export manufacturing in major economies, 1980–2014**

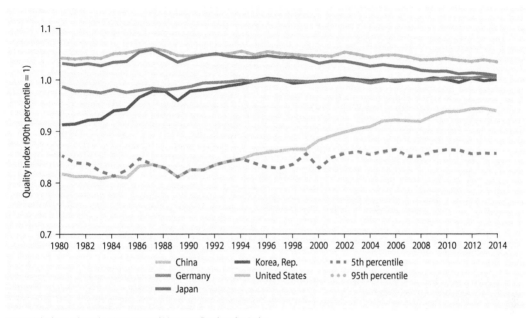

Source: Calculations based on International Monetary Fund quality index.

clearance, and cumbersome administrative procedures can hinder a country's ability to integrate into the global economy, particularly in industries that require spare parts and components to cross borders multiple times. While integration in GVCs and improved customs clearance procedures have enhanced China's trade facilitation, gaps remain relative to international best performers. As its labor costs rise, and China diversifies toward higher-value manufacturing and services, inefficiencies in logistics can hinder its international competitiveness.

Trade facilitation can be challenging for China, given its large size and multiple entry points by land, sea, and air. The volume and complexity of China's trade can place a great burden on its trade facilitation and logistics systems. China has prioritized improving customs clearance, through its Nationwide Customs Clearance Integration Regime, and has emphasized mutual exchange of information, mutual recognition of regulations, and mutual assistance in law enforcement in port administration.

China's performance in trade facilitation has been improving, particularly with regard to transport infrastructure, but there remains significant room for improvement, and overall

compliance costs of trade procedures remain high (World Economic Forum and Global Alliance for Trade Facilitation 2016). In the World Bank's Doing Business indicators, China's "trading across borders" indicator improved significantly, from 97 in 2017 to 65 in 2018. The World Economic Forum and the Global Alliance for Trade Facilitation jointly publish the *Global Enabling Trade Report*, which assesses the enabling trade index of 136 countries, based on market access, border administration, transport and digital infrastructure, transport services, and the business operating environment. According to the latest report for 2016, China ranked 61 in the world, compared to 63 in 2014. China compares significantly better than the East Asia average on transport infrastructure, ranking 12. China is comparable to East Asian countries in key elements of "soft" infrastructure, concerning border administration, operating environment, and ICT, but lags in market access.

The World Bank, working with international academic institutions, produces the Logistics Performance Index (LPI), which assesses a country's performance in trade logistics. The LPI assesses a country's relevant infrastructure, quality of logistics

FIGURE 9.9   Logistics Performance Index (2018) and logistics costs (2016) in selected countries

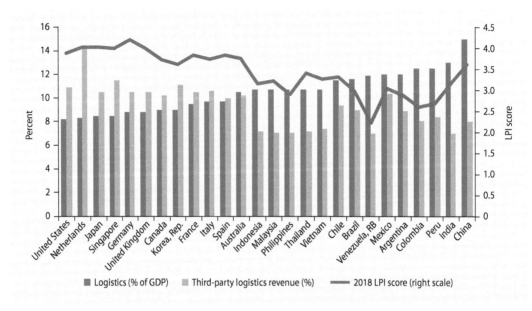

■ Logistics (% of GDP)   ▦ Third-party logistics revenue (%)   ━ 2018 LPI score (right scale)

Source: Calculations based on data from the Logistics Performance Index (LPI), South Africa Logistics Barometer (for logistics costs), and Armstrong Logistics (for third-party logistics revenue).

services, timeliness of shipping, tracking, and tracing performance, ease of arranging competitively priced international shipments, and efficiency of customs clearance. China has the most efficient customs clearance among low- and middle-income regions, better than the global average and far above countries at similar levels of development. Its LPI score is comparable to that of many OECD countries, although lower than the best-performing ones (figure 9.9).

At 15 percent of GDP, China's logistics costs have fallen dramatically, but they remain significantly higher than costs in OECD countries and many middle-income countries. Individual components of logistics—such as transport, warehousing, and management costs—are lower in China than in high-income countries. The high overall logistics costs appear to reflect inefficiencies in logistics chains, which concern goods when they are moved and stored multiple times. Such high costs could be reduced through holistic and multimodal networks, and focused investments in logistics hubs, intelligent transport systems, and better links between transport networks and selected industries.

As manufacturing relocates farther inland in China, the gaps in domestic hinterland logistics will become more critical, and more

specialized logistics services will be required. China will also require more specialized logistics services as it expands into high-value manufacturing to allow manufacturing firms to focus on their core business and to outsource logistics services. However, third-party logistics, which are outsourced contract logistics, are less developed in China than in other comparable countries (figure 9.9).

FDI and ODI

China's FDI and ODI still have room to grow. The total stock of both FDI and ODI as a share of GDP remains relatively small compared with the stock in other countries and significantly smaller than the OECD average (figure 9.10). Although China is one of the largest recipients of FDI by volume, FDI inflows made up less than 2 percent of its GDP in 2018, relatively low compared with FDI inflows in neighboring countries. China is a relative newcomer as an outbound investor, and hence its stock of ODI (as a percentage of GDP) is particularly low compared with that of OECD countries. China's ODI has been increasing, and the composition of its ODI is evolving. In recent years, a larger share of China's overseas investments has been directed to developed countries to

FIGURE 9.10 **Stock of foreign direct investment and outward direct investment in selected countries, 2018**

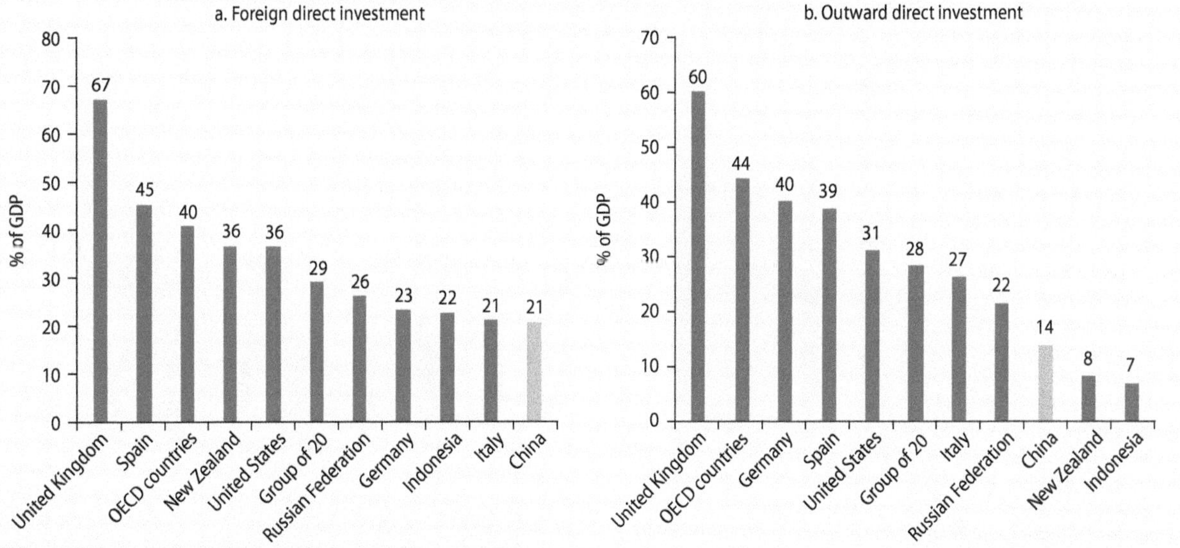

a. Foreign direct investment

b. Outward direct investment

Source: Organisation for Economic Co-operation and Development (OECD) data.
Note: Data for Brazil, the Republic of Korea, and South Africa are for 2016.

access their markets and industries, and a smaller share has been directed to developing countries and to access natural resources.

China's attractiveness as an export base now has greater competition. China's labor costs have been rising, weakening its traditional source of comparative advantage. Average monthly manufacturing wages in China were US$720 in 2016, considerably higher than in Vietnam (US$250) and in Malaysia (US$594).[9] FDI inflows into traditional industries such as textiles have been declining, and some foreign enterprises have transferred their production capacities or built new factories in neighboring countries, for exporting purposes. According to a 2019 survey of U.S. companies by the American Chamber of Commerce in China, only 42 percent regard China as one of the top three global investment destinations, compared with nearly 80 percent in 2009.

To attract FDI, China has been reforming its foreign investment regime and progressively expanding market access for foreign investments. As a result, the OECD's FDI regulatory restrictiveness index for China fell from 0.627 in 1997 to 0.449 in 2006 and to 0.25 in 2018—on a scale from 0 (open to foreign investments) to 1 (closed to

foreign investments) (figure 9.11). But despite the improvements, China still has the sixth most restrictive economy for FDI out of 64 OECD and non-OECD economies assessed by OECD in 2018.

Policy recommendations

Global trade and investments can continue to be an important source of growth for China. Facing new challenges and a new global environment, China will have to continue to improve its international competitiveness and raise the quality and innovativeness of its exports. It will need to continue to pursue policy and institutional reforms to open up its economy further and integrate with the global economy. These actions would provide critical new drivers of growth for China's economy by promoting market competition, access to global frontier technologies, collaboration with globally leading firms, and integration into and upgrading within GVCs.

China could continue to encourage pilot programs and pioneering regions to test new policy and institutional reforms. The resulting successes could be replicated and disseminated more quickly. Special economic zones and other platforms to open up the

FIGURE 9.11   Foreign direct investment (FDI) restrictiveness index, 2018

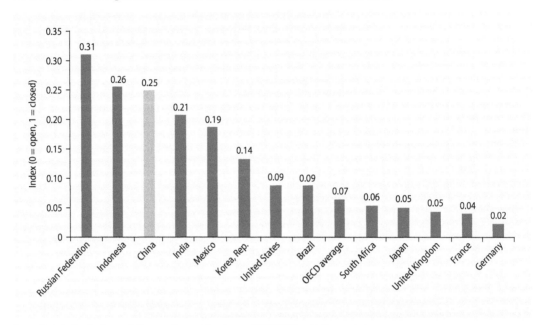

Source: Organisation for Economic Co-operation and Development (OECD) FDI restrictiveness index.

economy could continue to be used to experiment with new administrative systems, regulatory models, and international trade and investment rules to promote new industries that can compete globally. China could also explore new trade and business models, such as e-commerce platforms. It could further promote trade in services.

As the world's largest merchandise trader and second-largest economy, China's actions and policy choices will inevitably have significant implications for the global economy and global trade and investment relations. China's continued global economic integration would remain an important source of global economic growth and contribute to the expansion of global trade and investments. China could play a leading role in promoting global trade and investments, and cooperation on global issues, such as on climate change. In particular, China could ensure that the BRI achieves "win-win cooperation that promotes shared development and prosperity."

Supporting the global economy

China's commitment to building a "community of shared destiny" and safeguarding an open global economy will be important for the global community. China can be an active supporter of global cooperation by advancing economic globalization, safeguarding the multilateral system, and opposing trade and investment protectionism. The government has stated that it seeks to avoid international trade tensions, and that there is no winner in a trade war. China can continue to carry out reforms to support the global economy and the expansion of global trade and investments in the following ways.

One, China could further liberalize imports of intermediate goods and services inputs by continuing to reduce tariffs and quantitative restrictions on intermediate parts, components, and services, to maintain its manufacturing competitiveness. China recently announced that it would unilaterally cut import tariffs on vehicles and auto parts, on 1,500 taxable items of other industrial goods, and on more than 1,400 taxable items of daily consumer goods.

Two, China could pursue "deep" preferential trade agreements to stimulate GVC-related trade and FDI flows—given that FDI is, on average, higher for countries that have signed such agreements. China could further endeavor to expand deeper investment and trade agreements with wider coverage, to promote market access and cross-border investments, and to reduce nontariff barriers, strengthen investment rights and obligations, and create a level playing field for all market participants. Modern trade agreements contain newer provisions on a wide array of nontariff measures at and behind the border. China's preferential trade agreements up to 2014 tended to have less coverage of such matters, including competition policy, intellectual property regulations, public procurement, investor rights, and movements of capital. However, its more recent free trade agreements signed with Australia and the Republic of Korea have included greater coverage of behind-the-border issues and rules. Foreign trade agreements cover a sizable share of China's trade and investments, and hence they are important channels for strengthening international commerce. According to the Ministry of Commerce, in 2017 free trade agreement partners accounted for 25 percent, 51 percent, and 67 percent of China's foreign trade in goods, services, and two-way investments, respectively.[10]

Three, China could seek to advance negotiations on the Bilateral Investment Treaty (BIT) with the EU and restart BIT negotiations with the United States, which have stalled as a result of trade tensions. A breakthrough will require reaching an agreement on mutually beneficial investment relations. Much like the WTO accession, which helped to drive market-opening reforms starting in the 2000s, BIT with the European Union and the United States could drive reforms toward further integration with the global economy and greater market liberalization. It could also help to deescalate existing tensions and build investor confidence. However, reaching an agreement with high-income countries on preferential trade or bilateral investment treaties will require reforms and compromises by all sides. Concerns raised by each side have included FDI policies as well as state-owned enterprise and competition-related policies.

Four, China could continue to engage in global cooperation and coordination on economic governance and the macroeconomy to jointly respond to global challenges, improve global trade and investment rules, and promote reforms of global economic governance systems. China has engaged in international coordination to tackle global financial risks, including through the Group of 20 and related forums, and promoted reforms of the international financial and monetary systems, including implementation of Basel III and ongoing regulatory reforms of securities markets and shadow banking through the Financial Stability Board. China's support for the Asian Infrastructure Investment Bank and the New Development Bank provides further opportunities for international coordination and collaboration.

China also could provide global leadership on tackling global threats, such as climate change, and implementing global agreements, such as the WTO's Trade Facilitation Agreement (TFA). The TFA contains provisions to expedite the movement of goods across borders and to improve cooperation on trade facilitation and customs compliance. WTO estimates show that full implementation of the TFA could reduce trade costs by an average of 14.3 percent and boost global trade by up to US$1 trillion per year, with the biggest gains in the poorest countries. China has stated that it supports reforms of the WTO that reflect the needs of both developing and developed countries.

Five, China could take more actions to ensure that BRI provides mutually beneficial results for all countries involved. BRI provides an opportunity to improve relevant policy and regulations that would complement the hard infrastructure investments, including through the adoption of international standards and rules on trade, investment, and environmental requirements. China could help to adopt a more multilateral approach to BRI by introducing institutional mechanisms to coordinate investments, financing, and relevant policies and regulations; to resolve disputes and manage risks; and to make BRI investments more environmentally, socially, and fiscally sustainable.

Promoting foreign investments

Promoting foreign investments will remain a key priority for China's future growth. The government recently issued several policy documents outlining further measures to open up markets and promote foreign investments.[11] Now it needs to translate these policy statements into real improvements in access. Promoting foreign investments, particularly knowledge-intensive investments, requires complementary reforms to improve intellectual property rights, strengthen business climates, and build the local human capital and R&D capabilities of firms. Those reforms are discussed in other chapters of this report. Priority policy and institutional reforms specific to China's foreign investment regime include the following.

One, China could continue to review and streamline the national FDI negative list for industries that restrict or prohibit FDI. Recent policy documents have outlined the government's intention to open up critical sectors in advanced manufacturing and financial and business services to foreign investments. Removing those sectors from the negative list would help to lock in the reforms and address the concerns of foreign investors. The further opening up of the services sector would benefit manufacturing significantly because added value in industries is increasingly drawn from services linkages. Large potential remains for the "servicification" of manufacturing in China because the share of services' value-added in manufacturing remains comparatively low.

Two, China could further improve the transparency, consistency, and predictability of regulations and policies for foreign investors. For the new Foreign Investment Law (FIL), which will come into effect on January 1, 2020, China plans to issue a series of laws and regulations to smooth its implementation. This is an opportunity to strengthen the regulatory framework concerning the rights and interests of foreign investors by clearly specifying and streamlining the regulations, administrative reviews, and licensing procedures associated with the FIL. These laws and regulations could aim to ensure the fair and equitable treatment of foreign investors and to establish an investor dispute settlement mechanism that would promote coordination and complementarity between the dispute prevention (grievance management) and dispute settlement provisions.

Implementation and enforcement of regulations would need to be nondiscretionary and predictable to help ensure a level playing field and fair competition between domestic and foreign-invested enterprises. The formulation of these laws and regulations would benefit from extensive consultations with both foreign and domestic investors.

Three, China could introduce a transparent monitoring and grievance-handling mechanism for technology transfers to assure foreign investors and encourage the introduction of advanced foreign technologies in China. The FIL explicitly prohibits "forced" technology transfers through administrative measures. The government has indicated that it would prepare specific regulations and guidance for the implementation and enforcement of the law, which would need to cover the enforcement of the prohibition of "forced" technology transfers.

Four, China could strengthen communication and consultations with foreign firms to identify investors' concerns and minimize their misunderstanding of government policies and regulations. The government and related public agencies could carry out regular and systematic dialogues with major foreign investor associations, such as Japan, the United States, and European chambers of commerce. It could publish all FDI-related regulations online in English and improve the mechanisms for foreign investors to address trade- and investment-related grievances. In this regard, the government announced that it will establish an interministerial centralized system to receive and address the complaints of foreign investors. The government could also systematically expand opportunities for foreign firms to participate in regulatory consultations and standards setting.

Five, China could improve its ODI management system and strengthen its support for its overseas investors. China could promote a more systematic and efficient ODI management system by consolidating and streamlining administrative rules and regulations, and by improving the coordination of ODI-related authorities. China could expand and improve the quality of extension services for enterprises engaging in ODI to support risk monitoring of overseas markets and improve firms' understanding of environmental and social safeguards and the international rules and laws of host countries.

Six, China could expand programs to promote linkages between foreign-invested and local firms and to upgrade the capacity of local suppliers. Programs could identify multinational firms with local sourcing needs and match them with local firms that meet required standards for quality, cost, and delivery. Open, online supplier databases or platforms of screened local firms could be developed. The programs also could provide local firms with technical assistance and access to finance. Successful programs in other countries have benefited from close involvement of multinational firms in program design and implementation.

Seven, China could expand programs to attract global talent. A deep pool of global talent is essential if China is to gain a new international competitive edge. China could further streamline the working visa system and reduce administrative requirements for the entry and exit of foreign workers and professionals. It could improve the overall working and living environment for foreigners by expanding supportive programs and services, such as for children's education.

Eight, China could reduce its logistics costs by addressing inefficiencies in logistics chains through more holistic and multimodal networks, focused investments in logistics hubs and intelligent transport systems, and better links between transport networks and selected industries. As it expands into high-value manufacturing, China also could promote more specialized logistics services to allow manufacturing firms to outsource logistics services and focus on manufacturing.

Notes

1. Given that the assessment of economic complexity is based on export data, China's assessment may also reflect its relatively large share of foreign inputs, parts, and components.
2. Atlas of Economic Complexity of the Center for International Development at Harvard University.
3. NBS and China Statistical Yearbook on science and technology.
4. The RCA uses trade flows to determine whether a country exports more, or less, than its "expected share" of a given product, with an RCA greater than 1 signifying that the country has a revealed comparative advantage in a given product.
5. See www.wiod.org. Although not shown, the analysis was also carried out using the OECD's Trade in Value Added (TiVA) data, which also showed rising DVA for China.
6. Trends in DVA and comparisons of DVA with other countries should be interpreted with care because they can be influenced by many factors, such as export composition and degree of export diversification. By integrating further into GVCs, a country's share of DVA can actually decline, and this would not necessarily indicate lower export performance.
7. Wang Fuwen, Vice Minister of Commerce and Deputy Representative of International Trade Negotiations, delivered this keynote speech, "Promoting the Formation of a New Pattern of Comprehensive Openness," on March 25, 2018, at the Annual Meeting of the China Development High-Level Forum in Beijing.
8. See http://www.cadz.org.cn.
9. The wage estimate is the average for urban, nonprivate wages. The data sources are the National Bureau of Statistics and CEIC Data for China and International Labour Organization for the other countries.
10. See http://tradeinservices.mofcom.gov.cn/article/yanjiu/hangyezk/201810/70868.html.
11. "Notice of the State Council on Several Measures to Expand Opening and Actively Use Foreign Investment" (January 12, 2017), "Notice of the State Council on Several Measures to Promote Foreign Investment Growth" (August 8, 2017), and "Notice of the State Council on Several Measures for Actively and Effectively Using Foreign Capital to Promote High-quality Economic Development" (June 10, 2018).

Bibliography

American Chamber of Commerce in China 2017. "China's China Business Climate Survey Report." https://www.amchamchina.org/policy-advocacy/business-climate-survey/.

Amiti, M., and J. Konings. 2007. "Trade Liberalization, Intermediate Inputs, and Productivity:

Evidence from Indonesia." *American Economic Review* 97(5): 1611–638.

Brandt, L., J. Van Biesebroeck, L. Wang, and Y. Zhang. 2017. "WTO Accession and Performance of Chinese Manufacturing Firms." *American Economic Review* 107(9): 2784–820.

China Ministry of Commerce, General Administration of Customs, National Bureau of Statistics, State Administration of Foreign Exchange. 2014. "Global Value Chain and China's Trade in Value Added," Research paper (in Chinese). http://images.mofcom.gov.cn/www/201412/20141223154610238.pdf.

Constantinescu, Cristina, Aaditya Mattoo, and Michele Ruta. 2016. "Does the global trade slowdown matter?" *Journal of Policy Modeling* (Elsevier) 38(4): 711–22.

Cristelli, M., A. Tacchella, M. Cader, K. Roster, and L. Pietronero. 2017. "On the Predictability of Growth." Policy Research Working Paper 8117, World Bank, Washington, DC.

Espita, A., Mera L. Gomez, N. Rocha, and G. Varela. 2018. "China: Going Global and Gaining from It." Background paper for this report, World Bank, Washington, DC.

Henn, Christian, Chris Papageorgiou, and Nikola Spatafora. 2013. "Export Quality in Developing Countries." IMF Working Paper WP/13/108, International Monetary Fund, Washington, DC.

International Office of the China State Council. 2018. "White Paper: The Facts and China's Position on China-US Trade Friction." September.

Kee, H. L., and H. Tang. 2016. "Domestic Value Added in Exports: Theory and Firm Evidence from China." *American Economic Review* 106(6): 1402–36.

Koopman, R., Z. Wang, and S. J. Wei. 2014. "Tracing Value-Added and Double Counting in Gross Exports." *American Economic Review* 104(2): 459–94.

Linden, Greg, Jason Dedrick, and Kenneth. L. Kraemer. 2009. "Who Profits from Innovation in Global Value Chains? A Study of the iPod and Notebook PCs." *Industrial and Corporate Change* 19 (1): 81–116.

Sturgeon, Tim, and Eric Thum. 2017. "Case Studies of China's Automotive and ICT Hardware Sectors." Background paper for this report, World Bank, Washington, DC.

Tacchella, A., M. Cristelli, G. Caldarelli, A. Gabrielli, and L. Pietronero. 2012. "A New Metrics for Countries' Fitness and Products' Complexity." *Nature: Scientific Reports* 2 (723). https://www.nature.com/articles/srep00723.

UNCTAD (United Nations Conference on Trade and Development). 2017. *World Investment Report 2017: Investment and the Digital Economy*. Geneva: UNCTAD.

World Bank, IMF (International Monetary Fund), and WTO (World Trade Organization). 2018. "Reinvigorating Trade and Inclusive Growth." World Bank, Washington, DC. http://documents.worldbank.org/curated/en/874541538071614937/pdf/130272-WP-PUBLIC-Disclosed-9-30-2018.pdf.

World Economic Forum, and Global Alliance for Trade Facilitation. 2016. *Global Enabling Trade Report 2016*. Geneva: World Economic Forum and Global Alliance for Trade Facilitation.

Ye, M., B. Meng, and S. J. Wei. 2015. "Measuring Smile Curves in Global Value Chains." IDE Discussion Paper no. 530.

10

Governing the Next Transformation

Over the past 40 years, China has undergone three phases of economic governance reforms: market-*seeking* reforms, roughly from 1978 to 1993; market-*building* reforms, from 1993 to around 2003; and market-*enhancing* reforms, from about 2003 on (figure 10.1) (Hofman 2018). In the first phase of market-seeking reforms, there was a genuine search for the right economic institutions for China. Driven by politics, experiments, and decentralized initiatives, China was searching for ways to allow more market reforms in its system. Informed by reforms in Eastern Europe under communism, China's reforms concentrated largely on microeconomics, to some extent neglecting macroeconomics, as the highly volatile growth in the 1980s bears witness.

The second phase of market-building reforms saw increasing room for the market. Private investment in the economy expanded from less than 2 percent in 1992 to some 15 percent by 2003. The decisions of the 3rd Plenum of the 14th Communist Party Congress in 1993 laid out a comprehensive plan to build institutions for a market-driven economy—including a modern tax system, enterprise reforms, and a financial system that separated policy banks from commercial banks. The start of serious state-owned enterprise (SOE) reforms in the mid-1990s allowed commercial banks to become commercial, and housing and (urban) social security reforms followed. Entry into the World Trade Organization (WTO) in 2001 served as a lever for the domestic reforms and ensured much greater competition in the goods market. The State Commission for Economic Reform was abolished in 1998, and a more streamlined institution (called the State Council Office for Economic Reform) was created, which was subsequently merged with the State Development Planning Commission in 2003 to form the National Development and Reform Commission.

The third and current phase is characterized by market-enhancing or -augmenting reforms. Under the current phase, the previous expansion of markets is now being complemented by a reemergence of industrial policies. The publication of the Medium-Term Strategy for Science and Technology was a major milestone to start the third phase, through which China prioritized the strengthening of its national innovation system and the development of key technologies. The promotion of industrial upgrading and innovation has been a major objective

FIGURE 10.1   **Reforms and GDP growth in China, 1978–2014**

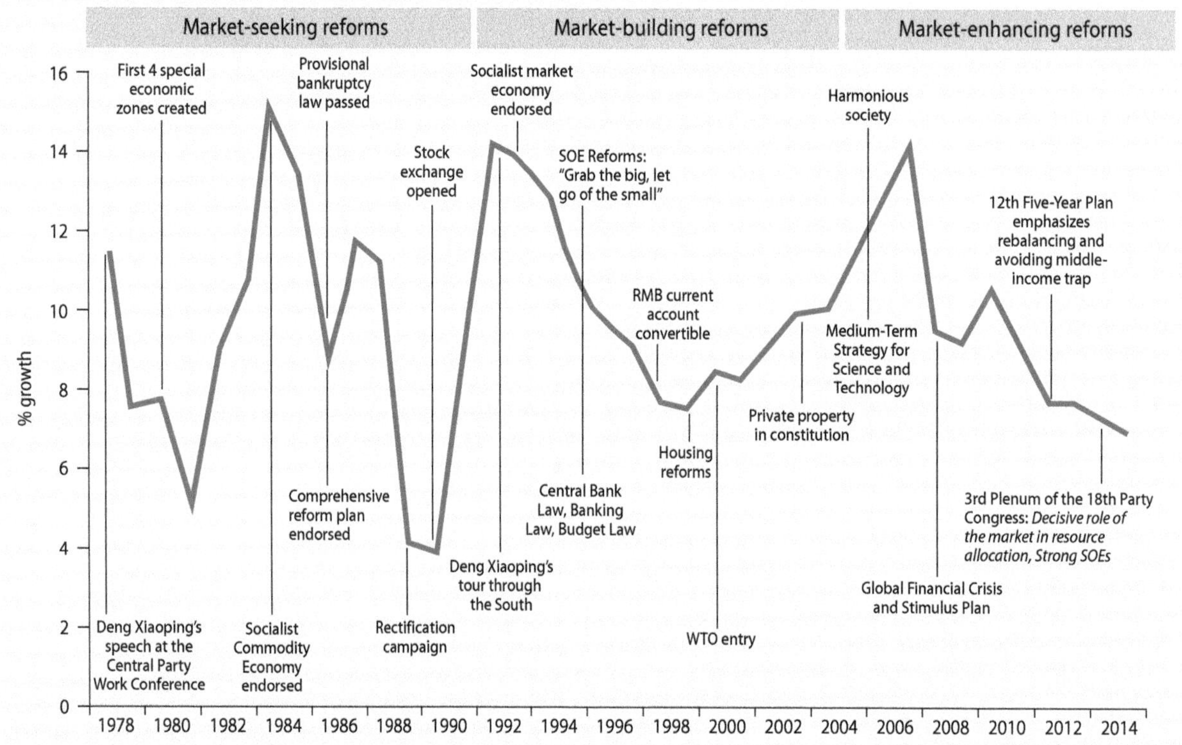

Source: Hofman 2018.
Note: SOE = state-owned enterprise. RMB = renminbi. WTO = World Trade Organization.

of the current phase, through the 5th Plenum of the 17th Party Congress (on productivity and innovation), the 13th Five-Year Plan, and the Manufacturing 2025 Strategy (2015). The 3rd Plenum of the 18th Party Congress in 2014 outlined a comprehensive set of reforms. It emphasized that the country would maintain a "basic economic system," with public ownership dominant in the economy but coexisting with private ownership, and that the market would play a "decisive role" in the allocation of production factors, while the government would play its role in an "improved and better" way.

General Secretary Xi Jinping's report to the 19th Party Congress in October 2017 also called for the "decisive role" of the market in the allocation of resources, an "improved and better" role for the government and for public ownership, and a major emphasis on industrial upgrading and science, technology, and innovation to achieve the goals of the "first phase of the New Era (2020–35),"

namely, socialist modernization. In this current phase of reform, China seeks a distinct economic governance and institutional system, with markets and the state playing complementary roles, state and private ownership coexisting, and industrial policies guiding and competition policies regulating the market. To manage the reforms, several central leading commissions have been created at the highest level of the state apparatus, notably the Central Commission for Comprehensively Deepening Reform and the Central Commission for Comprehensively Advancing Rule-of-Law Governance, both headed by President Xi Jinping.

Toward a new state-market relationship

Unlocking the new drivers of growth will require finding the right balance between the state and market and refining governance institutions to enable the market to play a decisive role in the economy. As economies become more complex and per capita incomes rise, the role of the state typically evolves from direct market interventions to more market-supportive and market-augmenting functions. In China, the central government seeks a balanced coexistence between the state and market, using industrial policies to promote industrial upgrading and to develop new markets. Local governments are at the forefront of implementing these policies in support of local enterprises.

China's decentralized governance, with local governments playing a prominent role in supporting economic development, was well suited to promoting catch-up growth. It combined high-powered career and fiscal incentives for local leaders to promote local growth, allowing them some discretion in policy implementation. Today, however, these incentives threaten the transition to more sustainable and innovation-led growth because they encourage protection for local firms (undermining creative destruction), uneven regulatory enforcement, and overinvestment in infrastructure (threatening fiscal sustainability)—all at the cost of lowering productivity. Managing the transformation from a market-interventionist role of the state toward a market-supporting and market-augmenting role thus requires adjusting the incentives set by the underlying governance institutions. It also requires rigorous cost-benefit analysis of sectoral industrial and regulatory policies.

As countries develop and transition to more complex and innovation-driven economies, they increasingly focus on promoting stable market expectations and the rule of law. The Government of China made the rule of law and the protection of property rights a priority in its reform agenda. However, at times, contradictory policy signals from central agencies, along with overlapping responsibilities and uneven enforcement of regulations, have created an uncertain investment environment and an unbalanced playing field.

China can draw lessons from high-income economies that have transitioned to a more rule-based, predictable system of market regulations. Reforms would facilitate the country's transition to innovation-led growth by providing the market certainty that firms need to invest for the long term. China's economy is transitioning to the global technology frontier, so the investment cycle will become longer and less certain. Providing more stable market expectations and more effective incentive mechanisms will thus become increasingly important. China compares relatively well with Organisation for Economic Co-operation and Development (OECD) countries on many measures of government capacity but falls short on evenhanded regulatory enforcement. Information transparency, which is critical for developing a knowledge economy, also falls relatively short.

Strengthening regulatory governance

China requires more efficient regulatory governance, in line with its plans to liberalize markets by further reducing entry barriers and transitioning from an ex ante to an ex post economic regulatory regime. Efficient governance requires improving the predictability, clarity, and fair enforcement of regulations to support a more open and competitive market and to reduce arbitrary government interventions.

An experimental approach to policy making has been vital to China's past growth trajectory—with many central policies providing only broad guidance, allowing for local contextualization and innovation. As China's economy matures and the stock of regulation grows, the downsides of this model have become more apparent. Unclear and contradictory policy signals from multiple central agencies have created an uncertain investment environment, and too much local discretion in enforcing regulations has enabled local protectionism.

Therefore, the government could consider adopting a system of regulatory governance based less on discretion and more on rules. The essence of a modern regulatory system consists of autonomous or semiautonomous regulatory bodies that are delegated by specific laws to exercise their mandate in a rules-based way that is fair, transparent, professional, responsive, accountable, and consistent. This would help to address market distortions in China resulting from regulatory failures caused by government entities wielding too much discretionary power through administrative decrees that are not authorized by laws. China could recalibrate its policy-making process by adopting and implementing more widely the regulatory principles and practices recommended by international organizations and forums, such as the Asia-Pacific Economic Cooperation–OECD Integrated Checklist on Regulatory Reform.

To design more effective and consistent policies, China could integrate evidence-based regulatory impact assessments with its experimental approach to policy making. The State Council has long advocated cost-benefit analysis, which is equivalent to regulatory impact assessment, for legislation and regulations related to the economy, but this now needs to be carried out in practice.[1] Used in about 50 countries, regulatory impact assessments could help China systematically assess the effects of proposed or existing regulations, especially on productivity. China could also incorporate monitoring and evaluation indicators in the policy making process.

To streamline the multiplicity of business policies and regulations, and to reduce the administrative burden, the government could simplify the stock of regulations and institutionalize retrospective reviews of regulations.[2] International experiences provide useful precedents, such as the Netherlands-inspired standard cost model to measure administrative burdens or "stock-flow linkage rules," as has been adopted in Germany, the United Kingdom, and the United States. Setting up regulatory oversight bodies close to the center of government could improve the quality and consistency of regulation. Such oversight bodies could strengthen coordination and help to address the inconsistent regulatory interpretations between central and local governments and across ministerial departments.

To achieve more effective and fairer enforcement and compliance with regulations, China could strengthen the vertical reporting lines of local enforcement agencies, such as environmental protection bureaus, thus reducing local government discretion. This option could be considered especially for those regulatory fields that can impede growth, such as environmental protection,

labor law compliance, occupational safety, and the judiciary.[3] However, China's own experience indicates that this approach can lead to coordination problems with other local agencies, which is a major downside.

To achieve more consistent enforcement within a decentralized model, the central government could also enhance horizontal coordination between enforcement agencies, perhaps using institutional solutions such as the European Union (EU) Bureau of European Regulators of Electronic Communications. Stronger consultation and coordination between the central and local levels in the policy-making process would help to reduce uneven enforcement. The central government could set basic standards, while allowing for local discretion in improving these standards, akin to the EU's "minimum harmonization" rules. It also would need to strengthen the quality of independent data on regulatory compliance to enable better central monitoring of subnational enforcement.

The principle of a strong and independent disciplinary commission has already been accepted in China, and such reforms could be broadened to encompass regulatory reform. China could initiate reforms by first creating relatively independent regulatory hierarchies in specific sectors, such as an independent environmental regulatory system. The regulatory environment could be improved through greater separation between regulators and service operators. Such separation would first require a clear mandate empowering regulators to conduct a regulatory overview in their sectors, which would help to insulate them from stakeholder interference. Such insulation is particularly important in sectors with a large share of state-owned enterprises (SOEs), which can influence regulators' decisions. To assess the potential economic effects of regulatory policies, the capacity of regulators will also need to be strengthened.

China could improve public communication of the interpretation of regulations and regulatory decisions, particularly authorizations and licensing decisions, and strengthen the process for reviewing decisions. China was an early adopter of public consultations, through websites, regarding draft legislations and regulations. This effort could be leveraged further to enhance public communication and improve public access to public information.

China could make consultations more effective by engaging stakeholders earlier, by making it transparent about how the consultations are reflected in regulations, and by encouraging greater voluntary compliance. China could make compliance data more widely available to the public and encourage and enable research institutions, the general public, and nongovernmental organizations to collect and disseminate such data. This effort could include wider use of whistleblowing websites (and the corresponding whistleblower protections), use of public opinion research through citizen and firm surveys, enhanced reporting to local people's congresses on compliance, and strengthening of the judiciary in disciplining administrative enforcement. Accelerating *hukou* reforms could enable labor to move to the cities with the highest quality of life and thus fuel competition between cities for sound enforcement of, say, environmental or food safety regulations.

Aligning the government's incentives with the needs of the new economy

To transform state-market relations, China needs to improve the alignment of state actors' incentives with long-term, productivity-led growth. Improved alignment requires China to modernize its civil service (cadre) management system to encourage local leaders to support market competition and long-term sustainable growth. In the past, promotions based on short-term economic outcomes effectively incentivized leading cadres to promote catch-up growth. These incentives have, however, also encouraged cadre behavior that is increasingly harmful as China moves to productivity-led growth—in particular, overinvestment in physical capital, protection of ineffective local firms, and lack of fiscal discipline. China thus faces the challenge of reorienting local leaders to pursue a more diverse, balanced, and long-term set of objectives.

China has sought to promote long-term objectives by making promotion criteria more comprehensive by including social, environmental, and innovation outcomes in the promotion criteria of local officials. Such outcomes are key indicators of "high-quality development," as stated at the 19th Party Congress. Yet, current experience demonstrates the inherent limits of hierarchically set targets in achieving this change. Local governments are asked to achieve multiple goals, with new initiatives layered on old ones. Many of the central mandates may be unfunded and misaligned with one another; they often are vague and shifting, compelling local officials to make decisions on uncertain grounds about which actions are encouraged and which actions are viewed unfavorably. Confronted with mixed signals and competing objectives, local officials have tended to focus on short-term economic goals and have less appetite for taking risks and undertaking structural reforms and long-term investment. In this regard, China could reduce the number of targets, differentiate them regionally, and make the cadre evaluation system more transparent, understandable, and effective.

Lengthening cadres' tenure appropriately can also improve the alignment of incentives with long-run-productivity growth. The relatively short tenure of local officials incentivizes them to focus on short-term growth targets, which can undermine the execution of national policies that local officials view as slowing local growth. This tendency is evident in the uneven progress of efforts to downsize industries with overcapacity or spikes in public investment prior to promotion periods. Policy options for extending the time horizon include increasing the average length of term (for example, to the de jure five years) and expanding the use of "concurrent promotions," which are promotions that retain the current position. Future promotions could be tied to the sustainability and long-term impact of reforms, to be assessed even after officials move on to new positions. China has partially moved in this direction, by adopting lifelong accountability systems for "grave mistakes" in 2014 and envisaging them for local debt.[4]

Reforms of local government incentives could aim to reduce local discretion, possibly by strengthening vertical management in selected line ministries, departments, and agencies. China's anticorruption campaign, which was initiated in 2012, may have helped to discourage the abuse of local discretion. In addition, strengthening the "downward accountability" of local leaders could help to address information asymmetry. One option is to publish firms' survey results on the quality and fairness of the business environment, which would be part of cadre performance evaluations. Publishing results could help to shift local leaders' attention from short-term growth targets to creating a level playing field for firms. The further bolstering of transparency regulations—for information on pollution, government budgets, and other policies—could help to expose local officials to greater pressures from below.

As China's economy continues to grow and become more complex, governments at all levels will need a different set of skills for the different functions required. An assessment of the capacity constraints across levels of government would identify the major bottlenecks, which may need to be addressed through an expansion of staff and other resources. Reducing the rigidity of staffing rules and reviewing the competitiveness of public service salaries could ensure that the public service attracts well-qualified staff. Capacity building within the government could be complemented by greater and more systematic leveraging of external resources, including greater external collaboration and more flexible staffing arrangements.

Reforming intergovernmental relations and tightening fiscal discipline

China's intergovernmental fiscal relations have supported rapid economic growth and infrastructure investments in the past decades. A highly decentralized expenditure system, with local governments responsible for about 85 percent of total public expenditures, combined with discretion over regulatory enforcement made local governments key agents of economic development. At the same time, derivation-based tax sharing between the center and provinces,[5] put into place through the 1994 reforms, set powerful incentives for subnational governments to compete for local economic growth and revenue collection by linking local revenues with local investments in economic development and revenue collection efforts.

Even though the economy has expanded, modernized, and reached middle-income status, China's expenditure assignment system remains much the same as it was 30 years ago. Revenue-sharing arrangements are structurally similar to those put in place in the 1994 reforms, and local governments still lack the authority to impose taxes. The system provides incentives for local governments to protect their revenue base and tends to bias investment toward physical rather than human capital. It encourages competition between local governments for investments and qualified labor.

Reshaping China's intergovernmental relations to support productivity growth will require a comprehensive and politically contentious package of complementary reforms. In the medium to long terms, China could move from derivation-based tax sharing to a needs-based formula to help encourage the shift from capital to social service expenditures. Rather than distribute intergovernmental transfers to provinces according to the origin of collections (as in the current system), the new system would distribute revenues according to a transparent needs-based formula, with the objective of closing the financing gap between the resources available to different subnational governments and the costs of providing some basic level of services. A needs-based formula would lessen the incentive for subnational governments to compete for tax bases.[6] Such a formula could encourage subnational governments to compete more based on the quality of public services and to focus on creating a good business environment rather than on intervening directly in markets. It also would help remove fiscal incentives that favor economic development expenditures over social service expenditures.

The Ministry of Finance has outlined the core principles for reforming intergovernmental fiscal relations (Kun 2018). The central government has already started the reforms to demarcate the assignment of expenditure responsibilities across central and local governments, starting with specific sectors, such as the health sector. It has defined the assignment of expenditure responsibilities for social services in education, employment, and pension provisions. The reforms will be extended to other social services, such as environmental protection and public safety, which are often larger and more complex. To ensure that revenue assignment is adequately matched with expenditure responsibilities, intergovernmental transfers would need to be increased, and the revenue-sharing system between central and local governments reformed—taking into account China's unique institutional arrangements. The core principles outlined by the Ministry of Finance indicate that the long-term resident population (not the household registration population) would be the basis for progressive equalization of per capita social service outlays across localities.

This announcement may indicate that the government is ready to proceed with the longstanding intergovernmental fiscal reform agenda, but building momentum and acceptance for the reforms will be a major task. The government will need to mitigate the risk of revenue losses, alter the distribution of revenue across provinces, and undertake major complementary fiscal reforms. Designing the new system of fiscal transfers and monitoring its impact will therefore require a significant research effort. The government might consider delegating the Central Finance and Economic Commission to coordinate the design and implementation of the system, and to review the system's success every five years and make recommendations for adjusting the system for fiscal transfers.

As one element of the reformed system, China could adopt a vertical sharing pool, including all central government taxes other than those levied on international trade and natural resources. Entitlements of subnational governments could be stated as a fixed proportion of this pool, rather than as different sharing rates for each tax. Their size would be fixed by the central government. Unconditional grants and shared taxes could be folded into one pool, with conditional grants staying separate. This approach would help to reduce unproductive interjurisdictional competition for private investment.

Reforms of the central-provincial transfer system may need to be matched by reforms of the transfers to subprovincial governments. Provincial governments now have wide discretion to decide how much they will transfer to lower-tier local governments and how they will make the transfers. Local governments are financed by these transfers and by land-lease revenues. Fiscal disparities among local governments within provinces are larger than those between provinces, suggesting wide variations in the quality of services.

The central government could continue to maintain this approach, recognizing that the difference between provinces is large and that there is value in letting provinces decide how to distribute funds to lower-tier local governments. Or it could consider whether provincial governments should be directed to adopt a formula for distributions among third-tier governments and whether this formula should be uniform across all of China. Such a regulation would complete the separation between where the tax revenue is raised and where the intergovernmental transfer revenue is distributed. It would need to clarify how "loser" provinces would make up the lost revenues and whether they would pass some of the expenditure responsibilities on to prefecture and county governments.

The central government should aim for revenue yields for each province to be at least held constant at prereform levels by allowing subnational governments to impose local taxes. Local taxing powers could encourage competition for investors and labor based on the comparative advantage of the city. The government could also be allowed to impose an annual property tax, which has already been approved in principle. Such a property tax has significant revenue potential for Chinese urban governments and could provide incentives for better land-use decisions. In the longer term, China could consider other options for local revenue mobilization in line with enhancing local government revenue, setting tax rates, and improving allocative efficiency. As in many OECD countries, local governments could be allowed to "piggy-back" on central government tax bases by selecting an additional local "urban service tax" rate.[7] Alternatively, the central government could impose special rates for each city, avoiding the issue of dividing legislative powers. China could also consider allowing subnational governments to raise user charges and other nontax revenues. Increased local taxation powers should be accompanied by stronger local accountability systems.

Expenditure responsibilities across levels of government also need to be continually reviewed, clarified, and adjusted. Those in the higher levels of government have substantial discretion in assigning responsibilities to those in the lower levels, contributing to the relative lack of clarity. This lack of clarity weakens subnational governments' accountability for service delivery and can entail unfunded mandates or duplicate delivery efforts. In addition, China can reap significant efficiency gains and improve the balance of responsibility between central and local governments by reassigning some responsibilities to higher levels of government. Restructuring expenditure assignments will require tracking what level of government does what and with what leeway, whether economies of scale are being captured, and whether externalities and distributional concerns are being handled. This huge task will take serious study and time, but it demands a policy review that is long overdue.

In parallel, it will be essential for China to harden subnational governments' budget constraints and to draw clear boundaries between the state and market at the local level. Unclear boundaries have enabled fiscal subsidies and tax exemptions for local firms and overinvestments in infrastructure. The 2014 budget reform aimed to address such concerns and sought to contain fiscal subsidies and tax preferences for local enterprises by bringing all public investment–related off-budget debt of subnational governments onto the local government's budget and requiring comprehensive financial reporting. But significant challenges remain with managing off-budget financing, public-private partnerships (PPPs), special purpose vehicles, and other off-budget investment funds.

What will be most critical is for the central government to provide clear and consistent signals to subnational authorities on the overriding importance of implementing the new 2014 budget reforms, slowing down public investments, and ensuring the sustainability of local finances. A road map for deepening budget reform could include the adoption of capital budgeting, more comprehensive and transparent financial reporting, and careful management of contingent liability risks associated with PPPs and other off-budget vehicles.

To ensure sustainable management of public investments, the central government could set aggregate growth envelopes for provincial governments' public investment spending. Provinces could do the same for subprovincial governments. Subnational governments could support these efforts with rolling out three-year integrated investment financing plans that identify all proposed public investments and their sources of finance, including on- and off-budget sources. Hunan Province and Chongqing Municipality have already piloted such plans. Priorities at the national or provincial level for public investments in excess of what can be financed sustainably at the local level would then become the explicit financial responsibility of the higher level of government. Such investment ceilings could then complement borrowing constraints (quotas for government bond issuance), though they may be difficult to fully enforce. Over time, as capacity is built for local debt-sustainability analysis, the process of setting the overall investment financing ceiling could be more decentralized. To encourage public sector capital budgeting in the longer term, China could use a set of key indicators to benchmark subnational governments' practices and their compliance with budget constraints.

China could adopt a comprehensive and transparent government financial reporting system to provide the basis for assessing the financial sustainability and performance of subnational governments.[8] This would provide greater information on public service units, SOEs, and the government's financial interactions with them. Implementing the system will be a complex and long-term project. It will first involve deciding which public entities—in particular, which public service units and SOEs—to include and how to classify them, distinguishing SOEs that produce for the market from those that do not. Second, it will require examining whether the entities included in the public sector can be justified on the grounds of economic efficiency or social equity. The iterative use of these two steps will lead to an incremental clarification and adjustment of the boundary between the state and the market.

Reforms of local government fiscal management will need to extend to PPPs, which increasingly are being used for infrastructure projects in China. At the end of 2018, the estimated total cost of China's PPP pipeline projects exceeded RMB 17.6 trillion (US$2.5 trillion) (Ministry of Finance PPP Center). The expansion of PPPs has raised concerns regarding local debt, as local governments heavily use PPPs for off-budget financing. The central government recently issued a series of regulations to close regulatory loopholes in PPPs. It would be useful to reflect on lessons from past regulations and to establish a comprehensive PPP policy and regulatory framework that incentivizes the right behaviors.

PPPs have been encouraged in China to promote greater private sector participation in the development of public infrastructure. It was envisaged that the private sector will introduce greater efficiency and innovation in infrastructure development, construction, operation, and maintenance. However, the current legal and regulatory environment creates many uncertainties that dissuade private sector participation. At its core, a PPP is a long-term contractual relationship between public and private partners. In China, frequent policy and regulatory changes and concerns about the legal protection of long-term contractual rights have tended to dissuade private participation. In the past two years, SOEs have won 75 percent of financially closed PPP projects, dominating a market initially envisaged for greater private participation. To encourage more private participation, particularly from international investors, China will need to have policies and regulations that ensure a level playing field and enforce long-term contractual obligations.

The PPP model for delivering infrastructure is relatively complex. It often requires the local government to have in-house expertise, with highly specialized technical, financial, and legal skills. Because such expertise is expensive to recruit and maintain, many local governments choose to rely on consultants to help with PPPs. However, both local governments and the industry of PPP advisory services are in the early stage of development in China. Many lack the experience, knowledge, and rigor required in PPP project development, such as value-for-money analysis, feasibility studies, structuring of PPPs to ensure appropriate risk allocation, and the use of legal documents to ensure long-term contractual obligations. As a result, many PPP projects expose local governments to contingent risks and challenges in ensuring performance and enforcing contracts.

The World Bank's *Benchmarking PPP Procurement Report 2017* assesses China's PPP procurement practices as falling short of those in high-income economies, especially in preparing PPPs, managing contracts, and terminating PPPs—areas that clearly would benefit from reform and capacity building (World Bank 2016). To strengthen PPP performance, China could consider establishing a project development facility to fund up-front project preparation activities. Like Ireland, China also could consider setting up a national center of excellence staffed with PPP specialists who can support PPP projects nationwide. As China's PPP program evolves, periodic reviews of PPP projects are needed to ensure that policies and practices improve through learning by doing.

Improving public sector transparency and accountability

China lags behind other upper-middle-income and OECD countries in the reliability and transparency of economic data. Open data support greater participation and sharing of ideas, which are critical to building a research- and innovation-oriented culture. Accessibility of data typically improves with income, and there is a wide "openness disparity" between high- and low-income countries. Based on international assessments of data openness—by Open Data Barometer and Open Knowledge International—China fares worse than the average for upper-middle-income countries.

The Government of China has been making efforts to consolidate and integrate government data. It could further improve public access to government data, including consolidated government budget data, subject to the required measures to protect individual privacy and public security. China can become a global leader by setting new international standards in data collection, dissemination, and access to public data. It could consider developing an access-to-information policy for the public sector.

The government could make the latest household surveys, industrial enterprise surveys, and economic censuses more widely available to the public, and improve labor market and education assessment data. Improving the quality, coverage, and availability of such data, within and outside government, would help increase the accountability and transparency of government policy making. It would support a culture of evidence-based policy making and nurture research in both the public and private sectors.

Improved data can help provide a more complete picture of the structure of the corporate and financial sectors. Because of the absence of a clear demarcation between private and public sectors, public data alone can convey an incomplete or misleading sense of market development and dynamics. Therefore, public data can be augmented by gathering new data from a variety of sources.

Notes

1. The Implementation Outline for Promoting Administration following Rule-of-Law at All Fronts, 2004.
2. For example, firms in the logistics sector deal with 12 departments in the central government, in addition to their 30 corresponding agencies at the local level. Each of the 12 departments has regulatory and administrative responsibility for one or more issues and its own codes and standards.
3. For example, creation of the State Administration for Work Safety in 2001 has led to marked improvements in work safety.
4. The 2014 Communist Party of China (CPC) Central Committee's Decision Concerning Several Major Issues in Comprehensively Advancing Governance According to Law moves partially in this direction by calling for the establishment of "lifelong responsibility investigation and responsibility tracing mechanisms for major policy decisions." In July 2016, the Central Commission for Discipline Inspection released Accountability Regulations that called for implementing lifelong accountability for serious violations, regardless of whether a cadre has moved on. These leaders are responsible for any subsequent "leadership failures" caused by negligence or poor work performance.
5. The derivation-based approach allocates a shared national tax among provinces according to collections of that tax within the geographic boundaries of the respective province. Revenue sharing between provinces and subprovincial governments is discretionary.
6. Many formula grants include a provision to penalize a recipient government that falls below a prescribed minimum level of tax effort.
7. Piggybacking is already used in China, with the urban construction and maintenance tax and the education surtax, but the central government sets the additional rate.
8. Since 2014, China has implemented reform to establish a government financial reporting system; on December 12, 2014, a "circular" was issued by the State Council on the Approving and Forwarding the Reform Program of the Ministry of Finance for the accrual-basis consolidated financial reporting system for the government (GuoFa 2014, No. 63).

Bibliography

Adithipyangkul, Pattarin, Ilan Alon, and Tianyu Zhang. 2011. "Executive Perks: Compensation and Corporate Performance in China." *Asia Pacific Journal of Management* 28 (2):401–25.

Bahl, Roy, Chor-Ching Goh, and Baoyun Qiao. 2014. *Reforming the Public Finance System to Fit a More Urbanizing China*. Beijing: China Financial and Economic Publishing House.

Bai, Chong-En, Chang-Tai Hsieh, and Zheng Michael Song. 2014. "Crony Capitalism with Chinese Characteristics." University of Chicago, working paper.

Chan, Hon S., and Jie Gao. 2008. "Performance Measurement in Chinese Local Governments." *Chinese Law & Government* 41 (2-3): 4–9.

China State Council. 2014. "Circular of the State Council to Approve and Disseminate the Reform Program of the Ministry of Finance for the Accrual-basis Consolidated Financial Reporting System for the Governments." Guo Fa (series) no. 63, December 12 (in Chinese).

Cordova-Novion, Cesar, and Stéphane Jacobzone. 2011. "Strengthening the Institutional Setting for Regulatory Reform: The Experience from OECD Countries," OECD Working Papers on Public Governance No. 19, OECD, Paris.

Delmon, Jeffrey. 2015. *Private Sector Investment in Infrastructure: Project Finance, PPP Projects and PPP Frameworks,* 3rd ed. Netherlands: Kluwer Law International.

Dollar, David, and Bert Hofman. 2008. "Intergovernmental Fiscal Reforms, Expenditure Assignment, and Governance." In *Public Finance in China: Reform and Growth for a Harmonious Society,* edited by Shuilin Wang and Jiwei Lou, pp 39–51. Washington, DC: World Bank.

Edin, Maria. 2003. "State Capacity and Local Agent Control in China: CCP Cadre Management from a Township Perspective." *China Quarterly* 173: 35–52.

Heilmann, Sebastian. 2008. "Policy Experimentation in China's Economic Rise." *Studies in Comparative International Development* 43 (1): 1–26. doi: 10.1007/s12116-007-9014-4.

Hofman, Bert. 2018. "Reflections on Forty Years of China's Reforms." Speech at Fudan University's Fanhai School of International Finance, Shanghai, January. http://pubdocs.worldbank.org/en/934911517472447837/Reflections-on-40-years-of-reforms-final.pdf.

Jin, Hehui, Yingyi Qian, and Barry R. Weingast. 2005. "Regional Decentralization and Fiscal Incentives: Federalism, Chinese Style." *Journal of Public Economics* 89 (9–10): 1719–742. doi: http://dx.doi.org/10.1016/j.jpubeco.2004.11.008.

Kun, Liu. 2018. Speech by Minister of Finance, Liu Kun, March.

Landry, Pierre F, Xiaobo Lü, and Haiyan Duan. 2017. "Does Performance Matter? Evaluating Political Selection Along the Chinese Administrative Ladder." Comparative Political Studies.

Leutert, Wendy. 2018. "The Political Mobility of China's Central State-Owned Enterprise Leaders." *China Quarterly* pp 1–21. doi: 10.1017/S0305741017001412.

Li, Hongbin, and Li-An Zhou. 2005. "Political Turnover and Economic Performance: The Incentive Role of Personnel Control in China." *Journal of Public Economics* 89 (9): 1743–762.

Li, Xiaoyun, Sanjeev Ahluwalia, and Dong Qiang. 2013. *Lessons in Public Sector Reform from China.* Washington, DC: World Bank.

Liu, Lili, Juan Pradelli, and Min Zhao. 2015. "International Experience on Subnational Financial Reporting for Managing Fiscal Risks" Informal, World Bank, Washington, DC.

Liu, Yongzheng, Jorge Martinez-Vazquez, and Baoyun Qiao. 2014. "Falling Short: Intergovernmental Transfers in China." *Public Finance and Management* 14 (4): 374.

———. 2015. "Frozen in Time: The Much Needed Reform of Expenditure Assignments in China." *Public Finance and Management* 15 (4): 297.

Martinez-Vazquez, Jorge, and Baoyun Qiao. 2011. "Assessing the Assignment Of Expenditure Responsibilities." In *China's Local Public Finance in Transition,* 21-40. Cambridge: Lincoln Institute of Land Policy.

Ong, Lynette H. 2012. "Fiscal Federalism and Soft Budget Constraints: The Case of China." *International Political Science Review* 33 (4): 455–74. doi: 10.1177/0192512111414447.

Persson, Petra, and Ekaterina Zhuravskaya. 2016. "The Limits of Career Concerns in Federalism: Evidence from China." *Journal of the European Economic Association* 14 (2): 338–74.

Teets, Jessica C., and William Hurst. 2014. *Local Governance Innovation in China: Experimentation, Diffusion, and Defiance.* London and New York: Routledge.

Van der Kamp, Denise, Peter Lorentzen, and Daniel Mattingly. 2017. "Racing to the Bottom or to the Top? Decentralization, Revenue Pressures, and Governance Reform in China." *World Development* 95:164–76.

Van Rooij, Benjamin, Qiaoqiao Zhu, Li Na, Wang Qiliang, and Zhang Xuehua. 2015. "Pollution Enforcement in China: Understanding National and Regional Variation." In *The Routledge Handbook of China's Environmental Policies,* edited by Eva Sternfeld and Arthur Mol. London: Routledge.

Wang, Xian-bin, Xianxiang Xu, and Jingxiang Zhou. 2010. "Political Incentive and Investment Growth-Evidence from Chinese Provincial Officials." *China Industrial Economics* 12: 003.

Wiener, Jonathan B, and Alberto Alemanno. 2010. "Comparing Regulatory Oversight

Bodies across the Atlantic: The Office of Information and Regulatory Affairs in The US and the Impact Assessment Board in the EU." In *Comparative Administrative Law*, edited by Susan Rose-Ackerman and Peter Lindseth, 309–55. Cheltenham and Northampton: Edward Elgar.

Wong, Christine, and Min Zhao. Forthcoming. *Using the Budget Reporting Framework to Redraw the Boundary between State and Market: A Two-Step Approach.* Washington, DC: The World Bank.

World Bank. 2016. *Benchmarking PPP Procurement 2017.* Washington, DC: World Bank.

World Bank, and DRC (Development Research Center of the State Council). 2014. *Urban China: Toward Efficient, Inclusive, and Sustainable Urbanization.* Washington, DC: World Bank.

World Bank, and Investment Climate Advisory Services. 2016. *Better Regulation for Growth: Regulatory Governance in Developing Countries.* Washington, DC: World Bank.

Wu, Jing, Yongheng Deng, Jun Huang, Randall Morck, and Bernard Yeung. 2013. *Incentives and Outcomes: China's Environmental Policy.* Cambridge, MA: National Bureau of Economic Research.

Xu, Chenggang. 2011. "The Fundamental Institutions of China's Reforms and Development." *Journal of Economic Literature* 49 (4): 1076–151.